PENGUIN BOOKS

HITLER'S ENGLISH

Francis Selwyn has worked in journalism and publishing. He is the author of the Sergeant Verity series of novels, described by *Screen Stories* in the USA as 'a masterpiece of suspense'. His other books include *Rotten to the Core: The Life and Death of Neville Heath* (1988) and *Nothing But Revenge: The Case of Bentley and Craig* (Penguin 1991).

FRANCIS SELWYN

HITLER'S ENGLISHMAN

THE CRIME OF 'LORD HAW-HAW'

PENGUIN BOOKS

PENGUIN BOOKS

Published by the Penguin Group
Penguin Books Ltd, 27 Wrights Lane, London W8 5TZ, England
Penguin Books USA Inc., 375 Hudson Street, New York, New York 10014, USA
Penguin Books Australia Ltd, Ringwood, Victoria, Australia
Penguin Books Canada Ltd, 10 Alcorn Avenue, Toronto, Ontario, Canada M4V 3B2
Penguin Books (NZ) Ltd, 182–190 Wairau Road, Auckland 10, New Zealand

Penguin Books Ltd, Registered Offices: Harmondsworth, Middlesex, England

First published by Routledge & Kegan Paul Ltd 1987
Published in Penguin Books 1993
1 3 5 7 9 10 8 6 4 2

Copyright © Francis Selwyn, 1987
All rights reserved

Printed in England by Clays Ltd, St Ives plc

Except in the United States of America, this book is sold subject
to the condition that it shall not, by way of trade or otherwise, be lent,
re-sold, hired out, or otherwise circulated without the publisher's
prior consent in any form of binding or cover other than that in
which it is published and without a similar condition including this
condition being imposed on the subsequent purchaser

For Paula and Frank

To die for Faction is a common evil,
But to be hanged for Nonsense is the Devil.

–John Dryden,
The Second Part of Absalom and Achitophel: A Poem

CONTENTS

	PREFACE	ix
Part One	**THE SORCERER'S APPRENTICE**	**1**
	CHAPTER 1	3
	CHAPTER 2	13
	CHAPTER 3	22
	CHAPTER 4	32
	CHAPTER 5	45
	CHAPTER 6	61
Part Two	**BERLIN**	**79**
	CHAPTER 7	81
	CHAPTER 8	95
	CHAPTER 9	108
	CHAPTER 10	122
	CHAPTER 11	136
	CHAPTER 12	150
Part Three	**RETRIBUTION**	**165**
	CHAPTER 13	167
	CHAPTER 14	174
	CHAPTER 15	183
	CHAPTER 16	202
	CHAPTER 17	212
	SELECT BIBLIOGRAPHY	225

PREFACE

It would be hard to whitewash William Joyce. He was an unsuccessful bully and thug who bore upon him the marks of failure in battle. His bullying over the airways from Berlin was a calamitous misjudgment. But he was not merely a joke, being so seared by hatred and fanaticism that it was sometimes hard to distinguish in his bitterness if he belonged properly with the extreme right or the extreme left.

A modern reader might flinch from a good deal of Joyce's pre-war street-corner rhetoric on the subject of race and religion. But his story suggests that far and away the best thing was to let him show himself for what he was. He wished for arrest and martyrdom, as the Special Branch reports show, but he wished in vain until the war transformed him into Lord Haw-Haw.

It has yet to be shown that the policy of the 1980s, the imposition of humane race relations by laws and officials, betters the 1930s. Idealists in office are proverbially dangerous, apt to do more damage by enthusiasm than their enemies by calculation. Laws and officials, the fanatic's promoters, were the only agents who might have raised Joyce from his Pimlico street-corner obscurity before 1938.

He hoped in vain for persecution. It was the war, the radio, and Germany that made his voice more famous in England than any man except the leaders of nations. Afterwards he was tried and hanged. His broadcasts had made him look a fool, but he died well however ignoble his life. The gallows gave him a final moment of personal heroism. Stern justice of the people had required his death, or so the people were told. But afterwards there was an uneasy feeling that the law had somehow been altered to fit his case.

Judicial vengeance had, as so often, missed its mark. His death

Preface

achieved more for William Joyce's influence than his life had ever done. There are even those, half a century later, who acknowledge Lord Haw-Haw as a martyr.

Part One

THE SORCERER'S APPRENTICE

And each dweller, panic-stricken,
Felt his heart with terror sicken
Hearing the tempestuous cry
Of the triumph of anarchy.
          P. B. Shelley, *The Mask of Anarchy*

CHAPTER 1

The new year of 1946 began with a bitter chill across England. Ponds were frozen over in the London parks and a thin but icy fog concealed the raw branches of the winter trees. The air was not much cleaner than Dickens had known it, reducing the sun on such days to a pale disc seen faintly through the lamplit gloom at lunchtime.

There was much that might have been better concealed, not least the ugliness of wartime necessity that had yet to be cleared away. Static water-tanks had grown rusted and foul. Abandoned air-raid shelters became improvised and treacherous playgrounds for the children of the blitz. The white-painted kerbstones and the ARP symbols on the street walls bore witness to the city's recent ordeal by fire.

Just after half-past eight on the morning of 3 January a small group of men and women entered the porch of Our Lady of the Seven Dolours in the Fulham Road. There were less than a dozen of them, as they went under the collegiate arch of the street-entrance and down the glass-roofed passageway leading to the church itself. At that date, before its modernisation, Our Lady of the Seven Dolours was still the sumptuous gothic-rococo creation of the fashionable Victorian architect J. S. Hanson. Its tall arcading and tiled floors led the eye to a magnificent altar of great width and height, the Caen stone decorated by alabaster and marble.

At a quarter to nine precisely, Father Johnson entered the church and began to celebrate Mass before the little group of kneeling worshippers. The rest of the long church remained empty and, from the Fulham Road, the liturgy was accompanied by a dull murmur of rush-hour traffic edging in slow procession towards the West End and the City. Against this background, the ceremony moved towards the prayers which commemorate the dead.

The Sorcerer's Apprentice

Far off, at St Ignatius Loyola College in County Galway, a similar commemoration had been timed to start at the same moment and also to end at ten minutes past nine. There was a third, timed with equal precision, at the parish church of Crowthorne in Berkshire.

As Father Johnson approached the altar, the man for whose soul he prayed was writing a letter, not more than a couple of miles away. Or, rather, he was finishing a letter to his wife.

'I salute you, Freja, as your lover for ever! Sieg Heil! Sieg Heil! Sieg Heil!

He signed it and added a subscription.

'Beim lestzten Appel, Volkssturmmann der Bataillon-Wilhelmplatz.'

But the time was long past for the final roll-call of his battalion of the People's Militia, recruited to defend Berlin's Wilhelmplatz district against the advance of the Red Army. Moreover, this member of the unit had not been permitted to fire a single shot in the flame and slaughter of the city's last days.

When the prayers for his soul were already being said, he took another sheet of paper and began to write again. This time the message was addressed to his friend John Macnab, who was among those kneeling before the altar of Our Lady of the Seven Dolours. 'We shall regret nothing that has happened now.' As he wrote the words, he knew quite well that his grave had been dug for him the day before, once a reprieve had been refused. It lay open and waiting a stone's throw away. By lunchtime he would be lying in the darkness and the corrosive quicklime.

On his side of the Thames, by the parkland and shrubberies of Wandsworth Common, a crowd of about three hundred people had gathered. They were standing expectantly by the main gate of Wandsworth prison, a building which gave the impression of an Italian Renaissance fortress whose square towers and long cell blocks had been reconstructed in grimy industrial brick. A tall chimney above the heating plant and workshops made it look rather like a factory under guard.

The crowd was quiet and orderly. Some had been waiting for more than an hour, arriving while it was still dark and the little

The Sorcerer's Apprentice

windows of the cells were still lit. Others had paused on their way to work. There were women with shopping baskets and men in working clothes, the *Evening Standard* reported a few hours later, as well as a number of boys and girls. Some of the children had been brought by their parents, as if for a special outing or a treat. Schoolchildren were no less fascinated than their elders by the horrors of this ritual death. A yellow van from Movietone News was parked near the gates so that the camera on its roof might film the anti-climax of the drama. To prevent protests and disturbances, the Home Office had ordered several detachments of police to stand by. Feelings were thought to be strong, on either side, about the sentence that was now to be carried out. But the onlookers remained quiet and the extra police stayed inconspicuously in the background.

Among the crowd there were heroes of the late war and some who might not have been heroes then but were prepared to be so now. Sapper O. J. Phillips had walked 'all the way from Tooting', accompanied by a massive bulldog. He had come, he told the *Daily Mirror* reporter, to be there 'in case the Fascists cause trouble'. Two other men had travelled from Glasgow in order to be close by when the great event happened.

There was no trouble. On the pediment of the main entrance, the gold hands of the blue-painted clock moved towards the hour. One man in the crowd removed his hat and stood to attention, head bowed in prayer. Others shuffled and stamped their feet as the cold from the frosted pavement penetrated the thin soles of their shoes. There were a few men and women dressed in black, who waited as silent witnesses to the obscenity of capital punishment. No one took much notice of them. This, after all, was no ordinary case of murder and they could scarcely have picked a worse example to further their cause.

Rebecca West, representing the polite world of letters at this proletarian scene of retribution, was being told by an elderly man how he had come back from viewing his grandchildren's bodies at the public mortuary and heard the voice of the condemned criminal mocking him over the radio. This bereaved pensioner was glad to be in at the present death.

The Sorcerer's Apprentice

As the hands of the clock touched nine, a small group of middle-aged men wearing sports-jackets and flannels under their winter coats stepped behind a row of bushes as if to relieve themselves. Instead, they were seen to raise their right arms in the 'Heil Hitler!' salute of the National Socialist movement. Mr Phillips and his bulldog prudently decided that such a salute did not amount to 'trouble'.

As the crowd waited outside, the macabre ritual in the prison itself approached its consummation. At its centre was a man of less than average height with thinning hair and a somewhat barrel-chested build. He was stockily good-looking and had a manner that combined cleverness and nervous amiability. He was also vain enough of his appearance to have worried about putting on weight as the days dwindled before they hanged him. His eyes were bright and his face betrayed a frustrated energy. On its right-hand side a long scar ran from just behind the ear to the corner of his mouth.

As he waited for the executioner, he was dressed in the blue suit that he had worn on his last public appearance. An official leak to the press described him as looking shabby and insignificant. But those who had made the arrangements for his last moments were not surprised to find him self-possessed and resigned to his fate. He was predictably unrepentant and, however threadbare his only suit, he was invincibly clad in the righteousness of his cause.

There was not far to walk, the formal procession to the gallows being by then a thing of the past. A cupboard in the cell was moved aside to reveal the rope and the trap only a few feet away beyond an open door. As he walked forward with his escorts, his knees trembled suddenly. He looked down at them and smiled. Some men and women who heard this felt a final satisfaction in knowing that he was a coward in the end. As it happened, he had been shot through both legs a few months before. The wound plagued an injured nerve for the last time as he took the few steps to the trap-door under the beam.

The officials who were entrusted with the task of putting him to death behaved with as much humanity as possible. He never saw the rope that would hang him for the noose was concealed in the hem of the white hood that the hangman drew over his head with the usual gentle suggestion that Albert Pierrepoint reserved for these occasions. 'I think we'd better have this on, you know.' The quiet north-country voice spoke the last words the criminal was ever to hear. In an instant the rope was uncoiled from the beam and clipped to the hidden shape in the canvas hood.

Within a few seconds he was dead. The pinioned hands of the condemned man went suddenly white as the noose and the drop snapped his spinal column. All the same, the result was somewhat less decorous than the usual 'clean' execution, for scars like the one which marked his face split open upon such a death. Thanks to cosmetic ingenuity, the damage had been repaired sufficiently for the coroner's jury to view the corpse when the inquest was held in the prison later that morning. This final glimpse of England's greatest war criminal would be an anecdote to leave to their descendants, like a family heirloom.

Outside the prison, the minutes after the stroke of nine brought an inevitable sense of anti-climax. Then, at eight minutes past the hour, a uniformed officer came out and opened the glass case on the wooden door. Within this he pinned the official announcement that sentence of death had been carried out. The Movietone cameraman zoomed in to get a close-up of the notice being fixed in place, a glimpse for the screens of a thousand Odeons and Regals from Aberdeen to Penzance. The crowd pressed round for a better view. Then they began to drift away, the women to the little shopping parades of Wandsworth, the men to their work, and the children to play, for the school term had not yet begun.

While they dispersed, the services at Crowthorne, County Galway and Our Lady of the Seven Dolours came to an end. They concluded with prayers for the repose of the soul of the dead man, who had been alive and in good health less than half an hour before. The mourners came out into the frost and mist of the January morning as the last traffic-jams of the rush-hour began to clear.

At 1 p.m. the BBC Home Service reported the execution at Wandsworth and the last public message of the man who had been hanged.

'In death, as in this life, I defy the Jews who caused this last war, and I defy the power of darkness which they represent.

'I warn the British people against the crushing imperialism of the Soviet Union.

'May Britain be great once again and in the hour of the greatest danger in the west may the standard of the Hakenkreuz [Swastika] be raised from the dust, crowned with the historic words 'Ihr habt doch gesiegt.' [You have conquered nevertheless.]

'I am proud to die for my ideals; and I am sorry for the sons of Britain who have died without knowing why.'

So passed William Joyce. As 'Lord Haw-Haw' he had been one of the most famous names of the Second World War. His voice was better known than that of almost any other public figure apart from Churchill and the characters of Tommy Handley's ITMA. He did not quite say, 'Jairmany calling! Jairmany calling!' but this parody was not far from the mark.

More to the point, in the days of reckoning which followed allied victory, William Joyce was the nearest thing to a major war criminal that the British possessed. Of millions of men and women, only a handful had turned traitor. In all but a few cases their treason had been petty, enlisting in the German ranks after being taken prisoner or something of that sort. William Joyce had been convicted of treason on the grand scale. He died without remorse, writing his last 'Sieg Heil!' not twenty minutes before the hangman entered the condemned cell.

Broadcasters and newspapermen alike were almost unanimous in their representation of the people's view on Lord Haw-Haw's fate. They quoted the old woman who announced outside the Old Bailey that 'he got what he deserved'. Or they elevated the morbidity of the prison-gate crowd to the patriotism of ordinary men and women who 'travelled miles to be outside the prison when justice was done'. When it was heard that he had been shot in the legs at the time of his arrest, the reporters assured their readers that the general view of the British people was, 'A pity they didn't aim a bit higher.' There was a sense of resentment in the press reports when, as *The Times* revealed, the ratepayers of London had to pay the costs of Lord Haw-Haw's legal defence, he having no money of his own in England – or, indeed, anywhere else.

As for the newspapers' verdict on his conduct, that was never in doubt. The public were urged to think of him as a man whose 'gibes and sneers in Nazi propaganda broadcasts against Britain during the war disgusted the British people.' He was 'Lord Haw-Haw of Hamburg, in the darkest days of the war when Britain fought on alone against the might of the Fascist dictators.' He was the man who 'gloated at Britain's reverses, who dreamed and boasted of riding triumphant as "Dictator of Britain".'

During the course of the war it had been the privilege of Fleet Street and, to an even greater extent, the BBC to proclaim what it was that ordinary men and women felt about certain issues. Whether or not the people actually held these views was another matter. The duty of broadcasting and journalism in the world struggle became not to reflect the truth but to choose what should be true, in the interest of public policy.

So the nation was intended to believe, as Joyce went to his death, that it felt a grim but laudable satisfaction at seeing 'justice done.' There was universal disgust at his work for the enemy.

At least the BBC knew, privately, that this was not necessarily so. Its own research had shown that at a random check in 1940 just over a quarter of its audience had listened to 'Lord Haw-Haw' on the previous day. Two-thirds of the BBC's audience did so from time to time and a quarter of these were regular listeners. More might have tuned in to hear him but their radio sets were not powerful enough to pick up the German stations broadcasting in English. Nor was this listening a matter of self-induced disgust. The listeners tuned in to the German wavelengths because they found Joyce amusing unintentionally or for his anecdotes, or else because they wished to hear both sides of the argument, or even because they did not trust their own authorities to tell them the whole truth. They gave these as reasons under the anonymity of a questionnaire.

A nation fighting for its life was unlikely to permit the publication of such findings. Much better to assure the people that there was a widespread and healthy revulsion for the activities of the English-speaking traitors in Berlin. Such findings also raised a question of self-esteem on the part of the BBC and its allies. With a quarter of the audience tuned in to Radio Hamburg, the reputation of the British press and broadcasting for fairness and accuracy was bound to seem less than established. The BBC's own survey of public opinion also indicated that such listeners proved to be more broad-minded and imaginative than their masters thought likely. Who, after all, would not prefer to hear both sides of the argument rather than one?

If the people were more independent in their judgments than the BBC and the press chose to represent them, they were probably also less vindictive. After Joyce was convicted at the Old Bailey in September 1945, he was driven away to Wormwood Scrubs under armed escort. A second police car followed close behind in case the first should break down. Official prudence was not dictated by any fear that a rescue might be staged by middle-aged Fascists in sports jackets somewhere along the Bayswater Road. It was thought, on the contrary, that if the first car should break down – and if the people knew whom it contained – there would be a spontaneous outburst of healthy anger. Lord Haw-Haw would be snatched from the clutches of his armed bodyguard, dragged to the nearest convenient tree in Kensington Gardens, and strung up without ceremony.

As a matter of fact, there was another sentiment which had begun to spread rather more widely than 'He got what he deserved' or 'I'd do it with my own hands, if they'd let me.' To most people, Lord Haw-Haw had been an amusement, a crank, or an inconvenience. To only a few had he been the devil who gloated over their private grief. But now a feeling grew that, though vengeance had been accomplished by his trial and execution, justice had neither been done nor its cause served.

Again, people were quick to distinguish between the fact that William Joyce might be a man of unpleasant and hysterical views, the supporter of a tyrannical regime, and the suspicion that the British authorities might in some way have rigged his trial. Perhaps it had been a matter of legal or political expediency. How could the government simply let him go – and what would happen to him if they did? Once he was captured, it was necessary that he should be hanged. His trial appeared to some people to be merely a means to that end. How, for example, can a man be a British citizen when he is born in a foreign country of foreign parents and has never been naturalised? And how can he commit treason against the King of England in a foreign country, if he is not English? To that commonsense objection, the government and its lawyers had tried to make a convincing response.

Within a few months of his execution a comment in the Notable British Trials volume which dealt with his case put this misgiving into perspective. Forty years later it rings true. The journalists' satisfaction at retribution on a man who sneered at Britain in her finest hour now sounds like delusive and individual rant. The trial volume states the consequence of Lord Haw-Haw's case plainly:

> If one treats the sensation-mongers who stand outside a prison during an execution with the contempt they deserve, it is, I think, fair to say that the conviction and execution of Joyce have caused more disquiet than satisfaction in the minds of the public.

That was probably the most accurate summary of public reflection upon the final chapter in William Joyce's story, which began at 1377 Herkimer Street, Brooklyn, and ended on the gallows at Wandsworth almost forty years later.

Through that narrative run two threads of irony whose pattern was not fully evident until its conclusion. For all the wartime jibes and contempt which he directed from Berlin at 'Mr Bloody Churchill' and his followers, he was hanged. And yet in these, he made himself so ridiculous as to become an entertainment. It was the verbal savagery of his pre-war outbursts in the streets of Shoreditch and Pimlico that made him a public danger for the only time in his life. But for such vituperation and the violence it provoked the law could not punish him, though it tried to do so on a number of occasions. On 3 September 1939 he still had no criminal record, though his name occurred with some frequency in the secret reports of the Special Branch and MI5.

The second irony of his fate was lethal. It decreed that William Joyce should be condemned to die as a man owing allegiance to George VI. He had claimed that status falsely but, with its own fastidious sense of irony, the law dismissed the truth and accepted his lie. For that he was put to death and there was, in one respect, a rough justice about it. Whatever the legal position, Lord Haw-Haw had seemed to his wartime listeners the perfect incarnation of Hitler's Englishman.

CHAPTER 2

The details of William Joyce's birth were to be a matter of life and death to him during the autumn of 1945.

He was born on 24 April 1906 at 1377 Herkimer Street, Brooklyn, New York City. It was a substantial house standing at the corner of a tree-lined street in an Irish neighbourhood of the city. His father, Michael Joyce, had then been a United States citizen for twelve years. Michael Joyce was born in County Mayo in 1868 and emigrated to New York when he was twenty. At that time he was like many young men of energy and ambition who saw little prospect of self-advancement in Ireland. Moreover, he was a natural conservative who felt out of sympathy with Irish nationalism, a cause which he thought likely to triumph in the end.

In the Court of Common Pleas of Hudson County, New Jersey, on 22 July 1892, the young Michael Joyce filed his declaration of intent to become a United States citizen. In October 1894 this was accomplished. The father of the future Lord Haw-Haw was required to 'renounce forever all allegiance and fidelity to any and every foreign prince, potentate, state and sovereignty whatever, and particularly to the Queen of the United Kingdom of Great Britain and Ireland, whose subject he has heretofore been.' Until the British parliament passed the Naturalisation Act in 1870, the Queen's subjects had been unable to renounce their citizenship. But emigration to the United States had made this restriction anachronistic and so the Liberal government altered the law.

By English law, Michael Joyce lost his British nationality as completely as though he had never possessed it. He was to regret this in the future, even to the extent of denying on occasion that he had ever become a naturalised American. He insisted that he and his family were 'all British' and he was seen by his younger son

Quentin, in about 1935, burning the documents of his American citizenship. While living in London in 1927 or 1928 he warned that younger son not to mention his father's American nationality outside the house. 'He told me in a general way that he was American. He told me not to talk about the matter outside as it might not be to his interests if the facts were made generally known.'

By 1904, Michael Joyce had obtained a United States passport. He returned to England for a visit and met Gertrude Emily Brooke, of Shaw, in Lancashire. 'Queenie', as she was called in the family, was a doctor's daughter who saw in Michael Joyce an eligible husband and the promise of a self-made man. He was then in his middle thirties, about ten years her senior, and doing well in a small way as a building contractor in New York and New Jersey. They became engaged in England and next year Miss Brooke set out for New York chaperoned by her brother Edgar, a solicitor. She married Michael Joyce on 2 May 1905 at All Saints Catholic Church, on the corner of Madison Avenue and East 129th Street. He was a Catholic and she a Protestant. William Brooke Joyce, to give the child his full name, was their first-born.

By no interpretation of the law – English or American – was William Joyce born anything but a United States citizen. There could not even be a question of dual nationality. By English law, it was the father's nationality which passed to the child and Michael Joyce had renounced his British citizenship long before. Gertrude Joyce lost her nationality upon her American marriage. William Joyce owed no conceivable allegiance to the British crown from the facts of his birth.

Michael Joyce was not one of New York's Irish immigrants who stayed and made good in his adopted country. He remained just long enough to save a substantial sum by the standards of Irish wealth and then came home with his newly acquired capital. It was in 1909, when the child was three, that the family returned permanently. They settled in County Mayo, as United States citizens with United States passports. For twelve years, until the Anglo-Irish Treaty of 1921, they lived first in County Mayo and then in Rutledge Terrace, Salthill, about a mile from the centre of

Galway. From the time he left New York, Michael Joyce regarded his United States citizenship as a moral and political incubus. As a natural Anglo-Irish conservative he regretted that he had ever renounced his British nationality. But there was no doubt in law that he had done so – and that he had done so for ever.

Michael Joyce was an entrepreneur rather than a builder by trade, though his son elevated this to 'architect' when applying for a German military passport in 1941. At other times, William Joyce referred more vaguely to his father as being of independent means. Despite this allusion to financial gentility, the truth was that Michael Joyce's income derived from rented property, and from being general manager of the horse trams in Galway. As a former building contractor, he had an eye for a sound investment in bricks and mortar. One by one the modest properties of which he was landlord in County Mayo and Galway began to show a satisfactory return.

During 1917, while visiting England to prove a family will, Michael and Gertrude were required to register under the Aliens Restriction Order. Gertrude Joyce, described in the files of the Lancashire police as an American subject, applied for an alien's identity book. Though serial numbers were issued to the Joyces, the identity books were not, since the family protested that it intended to leave the country for the United States in a few more days. There is no indication that the Joyces had any such intention at all.

Gertrude Joyce, at least, found it hard to accept that she was a foreigner in the town where she had been born and she had lived until she was over twenty-five years old. If the law thought she could be so, then the law must be an ass. So the family overstayed its permitted time and then left, not for the United States but for Galway, without notifying the authorities. The Chief Constable of Lancashire wrote with some irritation to the County Inspector at Galway, explaining this. In return, he got a letter assuring him that Michael Joyce was 'one of the most respectable, law-abiding and loyal men in the locality, and one who has been consistently an advocate of the "pro-Allied" cause since the beginning of the war.' The County Inspector suggested to the Inspector General of the Royal Irish Constabulary, at Dublin Castle, that 'there seems some doubt whether these people are aliens at all.' Michael Joyce was actually the landlord of the Galway constabulary and thus beyond reproach. But he was not the landlord of Dublin Castle. The Inspector General's office took a severely legalistic view of the incident. It ordered the Galway County Inspector to caution Mrs Joyce for the offence she had committed against the Aliens Restriction Order. In due course Sergeant Bernard Reilly arrived apologetically from Salthill police station to deliver the reprimand.

When the family had settled in Ireland again, William Joyce was sent first to a convent school and later to the College of St Ignatius Loyola in Galway, to be educated by the Jesuits. The parents and four children – three boys and a girl – lived in an air of smug bourgeois prosperity and Catholic pedagogy, not unlike the cameos of their more famous namesake, James Joyce, in the earlier chapters of *A Portrait of the Artist as a Young Man*.

Two incidents from William Joyce's time at the College of St Ignatius Loyola were to foreshadow his public personality in adult life. In the first of these, his penchant for physical combat resulted in his nose being broken during a fist-fight with another boy. He made no complaint of this honourable wound and, because he kept quiet about the injury, his nose was never properly set. The result of this slight deformity was to leave him with a rather nasal drawl. Even without exploiting it himself, he was apt to give the impression of that 'aristocratic' radio sneer which became the audible signature of Lord Haw-Haw. The microphone was likely to exaggerate the idiosyncrasies of a voice, so that he appeared to say 'Jairmany' rather 'Germany' and 'Jeeoos' rather than 'Jews'.

The second incident precipitated his departure from the Catholic church at the age of fourteen. His mother had remained a Protestant after her marriage. William inquired of his Jesuit teachers what this would mean for her eventual salvation. He was informed that salvation was impossible outside the church. In the view of that church, as he understood it, his mother would be damned.

It was not an appealing view of the hereafter. How could a loving son bask in the radiance of divine joy, indifferent to the knowledge that his mother had been cast out? William Joyce took the only action consistent with self-respect and humanity. He expressed his admiration for the educational efficiency of the Jesuits and politely renounced his allegiance to their church. Love and honour alike required him to choose the outcast. However questionable the theology on both sides, he passed his first test of personal ideology with a spirited display of the right instincts.

At the same time, the incident showed his liability to argue from passion and personal animus to philosophical or political generality. His propaganda was often at its most effective in personal abuse, and at its weakest when he tried to expound a political theory. In the case of his mother's salvation, his method showed an adolescent nobility. But the same process might equally well lead from private grievance to public fanaticism of the darkest kind.

Before his education was completed, the situation in Ireland degenerated into sporadic rebellion. In politics, the Joyces of Rutledge Terrace, Galway, became markedly more loyalist as the Irish rebellion gathered strength. They were, after all, members of a class who had a considerable stake in property and land. If war and destruction were to break loose, the small landlords with property easily burnt would be among the first to suffer. Michael Joyce was known as landlord to the Royal Irish Constabulary in the town. Not surprisingly, when the Sinn Fein insurrection began, he was marked as an enemy to the patriotic struggle and his premises were treated accordingly. Some of his buildings were burnt down and the house in Rutledge Terrace was set on fire.

Arson in Galway turned easily to murder. William Joyce, the schoolboy of fourteen, discovered a dead neighbour, shot through the head by the rebels for his membership of the Royal Irish Constabulary. He also witnessed the gunning down by the police of a cornered Sinn Feiner. Even in these circumstances, his reactions betrayed a sinister ambivalence. Like his parents, he was on the side of law and order, stability and discipline. 'I was brought up as an extreme Conservative with strong Imperialistic ideas,' he told his interrogators in 1945. Not for one moment did he doubt the validity of those ideas. But there was also an exhilaration in the atmosphere of conspiracy and violence which characterised the last years of his childhood. He grew up in a world of feud and betrayal, the hedgerow ambush on the country road, the British officers or agents in their rooms, given two minutes to say their prayers and then 'plugged' through the sheets and blankets of the beds in which they lay.

His attitude to Irish politics, however, was more complex than his schoolboy heroics. Though his first political sympathies were with the Union and the right-wing of the Conservative party, William Joyce subsequently held English misgovernment to blame for the loss of Ireland. By yielding to the seduction of 'international finance' instead of following the stern duty of imperial economy, weak and corrupt administrations in London had created Irish poverty and resentment. Writing in Berlin in 1940, he put the matter in a nutshell:

> If one sixth of the money invested and lost outside the Empire, in South America alone, for example, had been given to Ireland, there might have continued that cooperation between her and England which provided British history with Burke, Goldsmith, Wellington, Boyle, Roberts, French, Beatty and Carson. As though, however, by an inevitable destiny, International Finance wound its coils through the heart of England, and its venom was carried throughout the bloodstream to the whole Colonial and Imperial system.

The spectre of Ireland drifting beyond control by the power of law prompted the Lloyd George government to authorise the raising and despatch of the 'Black and Tans' to reinforce the Royal Irish Constabulary. In the summer of 1920, when these reinforcements arrived, William Joyce was still only fourteen. However, by his own account he had then been accepted as a volunteer in an unofficial military role. 'I served with the irregular forces of the Crown in an Intelligence capacity, against the Irish guerillas. In command of a squad of sub-agents I was subordinate to the late Captain P. W. Keating, 2nd R.U.R.'

One may doubt whether this was ever more than a schoolboy game. Rebecca West refers to a photograph of him taken at this time in army uniform as a private of the Worcestershire Regiment. But Joyce's abortive service in the regiment dated from the following year, when he had left Ireland for good and when the Anglo-Irish Treaty was in force.

What reality lay behind this piece of youthful bombast – written when Joyce was still only sixteen – proved no more than a little amateur gathering of information by a schoolboy in association with other schoolboys. But civil strife and political violence, the quick and easy expedients of the gun and the bomb, already had for him a romantic and almost Byronic aura. The shadow of the gunman fell upon the boy whose chief study was poetry and the world of the imagination. For most of his life, he quoted Dryden and Swift, Browning and Tennyson without effort. But he also kept a revolver to hand in the drawer of his desk.

However little he may have done in fact, it was enough to blacken his reputation in future among the nationalists. One of his interrogators added a gloss to the story almost forty years later. 'It is certainly true that in Western Ireland today you will hear those who say that in his teens William Joyce was a traitor who betrayed his own people to the Black and Tans.'

For the time being, his ambitions and proclivities were overtaken by a single political event. In 1921 Lloyd George came suddenly and dramatically to an accommodation with Sinn Fein. An Irish Free State was established by the Anglo-Irish Treaty of that year.

So far as the Galway schoolboy was concerned, he was not much preoccupied in future by the Sinn Fein enemy who had driven him out. His passions and hatreds had other sources, fastening more readily on the fatuous and feeble administrators, the 'old gang' by whom England and her dependent territories were governed. All the same, the Joyce family was in the first of many groups to endure the consequences of allegiance to an ousted imperial power. As the frontiers of empire contracted over the next half-century, the dispossessed loyalists were either to leave home and livelihood for the safety of the mother country or else endeavour to seek pardon and accommodation with their new masters. Perhaps the nearest parallel since 1945 is that of the *pieds noirs*, loyalist French settlers in Algeria who returned embittered and extreme in their politics to France after De Gaulle's settlement of the civil war with the Arab FLN. Like the Anglo-Irish, they had lived long in that country and had built its prosperity, only to see themselves betrayed by the politics of moderation and compromise. In the public life of the former colonial power they found it gratifying to urge hatred of the alien race and of political liberalism alike. His Irish experience provided William Joyce with such a mechanism of political hatred rather than the immediate object of it.

In the circumstances of 1921, Michael Joyce would have been ill-advised to seek reconciliation with the new order in Ireland. He was too easily identified with the English cause and the conservatism of the small landlords. He had seen himself as a man with everything to lose, opposed by the Sinn Feiners who had nothing to lose. Worst of all, he was readily confused with another Michael Joyce who denounced a priest to the Black and Tans. The priest had been summarily done to death. So, when the ink on the treaty was scarcely dry, the family left Ireland for good and made its future in England.

Michael Joyce had not suffered financial ruin by his second emigration. But he was now in his fifties and, despite his son's boast, there was no means by which he could be financially independent for the rest of his life. Eventually, he settled in East Dulwich and opened a small grocer's shop. His intelligent, aggressive, ambitious son seemed to welcome the change. He preferred to follow his own political destiny free from the provincial constraints of western Ireland.

His was the philosophy of the ambitious, the productive, the creative, which he saw as undermined by society's capitulation to the idle, the parasitical, the degenerate. Within this simple framework of social resentment it was soon possible for him to nurture an obsessive anti-Semitism, which seems at first to have no specific origin in his emotional experience.

The first role in which he cast himself, by hindsight, was that of a young irregular soldier back from 'intelligence work' in the Irish insurrection. He was not quite sixteen but he had long acted like a boy impatient of childhood. In Galway itself, the scenes and actions of the past few years had brought him to early maturity as a willing recruit for the politics of the street fight. But he was a street fighter who could also hold the attention of a pavement crowd by his eloquence. He was the soapbox orator who could quote Virgil or Shakespeare to give dignity to a bitter grudge. To those who encountered him at this time, he seemed to grow more thick-set and muscular, endowed already with a public presence. Whether there was any political party that could comfortably find room for him was a difficult question. He was neither an easy nor a tolerant companion. He had lost whatever little respect he might have had for the old guard of English political life. But that could have been predicted. Even at sixteen it was clear to some of those who observed him, as it was to William Joyce himself, that his were the qualities of a leader rather than a follower.

CHAPTER 3

The two objects which guided William Joyce's development in his later teens were self-improvement and military discipline. In the hierarchy of contemporary morals they appeared wholly commendable. If they illuminated corresponding flaws in him, these were his indiscriminate intellectual enthusiasms and a certain tight-lipped intolerance. But his contemporaries were impressed by a literate and articulate sixteen-year-old, his political views formed and matured in the Irish conflict. His manner was somewhat sharp and self-assured, not yet fanatical, and though his evenness of temper might be doubted, he was on the whole good company.

In appearance he was certainly not the insignificant figure whom his enemies later described. Though no more than five feet and seven inches in height, he was strongly built, with the air of one who has just emerged from the gymnasium or the boxing booth. Indeed, he was to train as a featherweight boxer during his year as a student at Battersea Polytechnic. He was also a good swimmer, diver and horseman, as well as a fencer. His head was a little large for his body, the features firmly set, the blue eyes bright and animated by a sardonic sense of the ridiculous.

As soon as the family had settled in England, he presented himself at Worcester barracks, falsified his age, and joined the army. At the end of four months it was discovered that he was only just sixteen. The army sent him home again. However, his appearance had been that of an eighteen-year-old, which makes nonsense for a second time of the press claims that Lord Haw-Haw was as puny in appearance as he had been in his human sympathies.

Despite his energy and ability, it was unlikely in 1922 that this son of the dispossessed would be accepted at Oxford or Cambridge. He had neither the background nor the inclination for life in those institutions whose products he so roundly despised. He was nature's outsider and proud of it, as his writing and broadcasts indicate. In any case, at that moment his father's circumstances would probably not allow for the added burden of a son's university education. As it happened he was well able to look after himself in such matters. Other young men of his type passed their matriculation exam at schools for which their parents paid the fees. William Joyce did the same, without such assistance, and entered his name for Battersea Polytechnic, where he proposed to study for the intermediate examination of the London University BSc degree.

Whatever scientific ambition he may have had was not matched by his ability. But the time spent at Battersea developed his skill and enthusiasm for combative sport. The Victorian philosophy of 'playing the game' and sport as good for the character was already dead. Though it is now unfashionable to dwell on such matters, there is in sport an insistence upon physical supremacy and the partisanship of an élite, strength through enjoyment and the worship of the hero, the bond of uniform and nationalism, lying uneasily parallel to the appeal of those same traits in popular Fascism. The relationship is rather like that of pornography to sexual aggression, cathartic or stimulant according to one's prejudices. The skills of boxing, fencing and riding made of Joyce what one observer called 'a thug of the first order'. Coming from Norman Baillie-Stewart, an even more experienced Fascist than he, it must have sounded like praise indeed.

Joyce's time at Battersea brought him no closer to getting a degree or to having the money to pay for a conventional education. But London offered a solution not available elsewhere and particularly appealing to a young man of his temperament. The university had one college, Birkbeck, which awarded degrees to evening students so that they might work at their jobs during the day. Ramsay MacDonald, soon to be the first Labour prime minister, was one of its graduates. The college had been founded in 1823 by George Birkbeck as a 'Mechanics' Institute', enshrining those virtues of self-improvement and industry which corresponded with the best qualities in the character of William Joyce. It was housed in old and dilapidated buildings between Holborn and the Strand.

At Birkbeck, Joyce passed the intermediate examination for his BA and then read English language and literature for the second part of his degree. His tutor, Marjorie Daunt, and others who taught him remembered him years later as an intelligent if somewhat odd member of their classes. He had a retentive memory and an unspoilt enthusiasm for English poetry.

There came a day when he arrived for a lecture in army uniform and carrying a rifle. Joyce explained that it had always been his intention to apply for a commission in the army once he had got his degree. It had not occurred to him that he might seem rather out of place in his present dress. Surely the uniform of an officer cadet was something to be proud of? He was asked politely not to bring the rifle to lectures in future – or at least to leave it with the umbrellas in a corner of the room. The nervous enthusiasm of his expression was such that Miss Daunt afterwards confessed that she thought he was about to use the gun on her. But whatever the irregularity of carrying an army rifle about, he was certainly entitled to wear the uniform. He had applied to and been accepted by the Officer Training Corps of the university.

The means by which he had got this cadetship proved the first strand in a complicated web that snared him at his trial for treason. He had been born in America of American parents. Yet no one could have been more English in sympathy than Joyce as an undergraduate. He applied to join the OTC as a trainee infantry officer in the autumn of 1922, a year before the date when he proposed to begin undergraduate studies. 'It is my intention, if possible, to study with a view to being nominated, by the University, for a Commission in the Regular Army.' He listed his experience as a fourteen-year-old 'irregular' in Ireland and his knowledge of the 'rudiments of Musketry, Bayonet Fighting and Squad Drill' which he had acquired during his four months of under-age service at Worcester.

The crux of the letter which he wrote to the secretary of the OTC on 9 August 1922 was the matter of his nationality. 'I must now mention a point which I hope will not give rise to difficulties.

I was born in America, but of British parents.' This was not accurate. 'I left America, when two years of age, have not returned since, and do not propose to return.' Joyce added that he had been informed at Galway, 'where I was stationed', that he possessed the same rights and privileges as if 'of natural British birth'.

A good deal of the letter was fantasy on the part of its sixteen-year-old author and it ended with a great flourish of romantic rhetoric. He offered testimonials as to his loyalty to the crown. He vowed to sever all connections with the United States, 'against which, as against all other nations, I am prepared to draw the sword in British interests.' He described himself as 'a young man of pure British descent, some of whose forefathers have held high positions in the British army. I have always been desirous of devoting what little capability and energy I may possess to the country which I love most dearly.' Pedigree was important to him. In a few years more, he was to decide that it was German blood which ran most compellingly in his veins.

On 23 October, the adjutant of the OTC dictated a letter to the young man's father. If Michael Joyce had not become a naturalised citizen of the United States during his residence there, then his son would have inherited British nationality from his father. 'It appears, however, that he is in doubt as to whether he is a "British subject of pure European descent". From what he tells me I think he comes within this definition, as he says you were never naturalised as an American. Perhaps therefore you would confirm this point.' Michael Joyce replied obliquely, 'We are all British and not American citizens.' He could hardly have forgotten that five years earlier the authorities had required him to register under the Aliens Restriction Order. He himself had been an American citizen for twenty-eight years when he replied otherwise to the adjutant's inquiry.

No one could doubt that William Joyce behaved like a young man who was English and proud of it. It was later to be alleged that he deliberately falsified his nationality, claiming to be English when he was not. It is at least possible that he did not know otherwise and that his father was responsible for this fiction, assuring his son that he truly was the child of British parents, though American-born. There is no doubt that Michael Joyce wished it could be so.

As an undergraduate William Joyce joined with enthusiasm in literary and political life. He wrote for the college magazine, played Kestrel in the college production of Ben Jonson's *The Alchemist*, and was president of the Conservative Society. There were those who found him an oddity and some who were repelled by his right-wing and reactionary views. The puritan military ethic remained his inspiration, as when he attacked the decadence of modern culture – dismissing Bernard Shaw as an impious reptile and Noel Coward as 'sickly, putrid, maggot-eaten' – in a pastiche of Augustan satire:

> In days when martial valour was appraised,
> They loved a duel or a standard raised;
> But now Hypocrisy and Humane Cant
> Transform the honest soldier's blows to rant.

Like most Birkbeck students, he was obliged to support himself by working at a job of some kind. Joyce became a part-time tutor at a crammer's, while still participating in the social life of his peers. Perhaps such a range of activities seemed to endanger his chances of getting a degree but those who thought so had underestimated the strength of his neurotic energy. In 1927 he took first-class honours in his final examination.

Those who knew him only as a fellow undergraduate would have been still more surprised by his degree result had they known the extent of his other activities. Though he was a college Conservative of a patriotic and nationalist kind, he had shown at first no sign of the bitter and obsessive anti-Semitism that became the hallmark of his speaking and writing. Outside the college as well as within it, he worked for the Conservative party, attending meetings and electioneering.

In 1923, at the age of seventeen, he also joined the oddly-named British Fascisti Ltd. The founding of the Italian Fascist movement by Mussolini in 1919, the first election of its members to the Italian parliament two years later and the street violence for which it was known, were primarily intended as a response to the new threat of

'Bolshevism'. The Soviet Union, through its dupes and sympathisers, was exporting revolution by violence. Therefore the defenders of the old order must meet the threat by organising themselves to a similar end. Liberalism could never sustain the challenge. Force must be countered by force.

When Joyce joined the British Fascisti in December 1923, it had been in existence for seven months. It was founded in imitation of Mussolini by the improbable figure of Miss Rotha Lintorn-Orman, a young woman who was the daughter of a major, the granddaughter of a field-marshal, and whose clothes seemed to emphasise her more masculine qualities. The entire organisation, with its membership of eccentric senior officers and local groups of para-military ladies on the look-out for the Red Menace, seems like nothing so much as raw material for a comic novel of post-war manners.

But the British Fascisti were in earnest, though doomed to extinction in a few years with the creation of Oswald Mosley's New Party. Their limited aim was to support the efforts of the law against Communism and to take on the job themselves where those efforts were inadequate. More specifically, they were to support the Conservative party as being the most likely to turn back the revolutionary tide.

In October 1924 the Labour-led coalition of Ramsay MacDonald was defeated in a House of Commons vote over the proposal to prosecute *Workers' Weekly* and an election campaign began. The debate was inflamed by rumours of Bolshevik backing for the Labour party and the publication of the so-called Zinoviev Letter, in which the Communist International instructed its British members to infiltrate the Labour party and the trades unions. By the time that the letter was revealed as a forgery and Conservative Central Office had been implicated, the damage was done. The Tories were returned with a Commons majority of two to one.

On the evening of 22 October, a week before polling day, Joyce went to Lambeth Baths hall where a meeting was being held by Jack Lazarus, the Conservative-supported candidate for Lambeth North. He was fighting in difficult territory and was to come bottom of the poll, beaten by Labour as well as by the Liberals who won the seat. But the antagonism of his opponents was the more bitter for the way in which the left felt that it was being robbed of victory in the country by the propaganda stunt of the Zinoviev letter. Indeed, it had been a violent election campaign by post-war standards and the columns of papers like *The Times* were filled day after day by reports of 'Labour rowdyism'. The British Fascisti had therefore sent 'I Squad' of its army to keep order. It was under the command of the eighteen-year-old undergraduate, William Joyce.

He stationed his Fascists in the building before the meeting, so that the candidate on his platform should be protected from the crowd. Warning was given that the 'Reds' were planning a violent demonstration to disrupt the proceedings. It seems doubtful that much planning was necessary. A Conservative candidate in such circumstances was likely to provoke hostilities very easily.

Before long the disruptions began and the meeting became a scene of struggle and abuse. Within the confines of the hall escape was difficult and the individual fights spread to a general *mêlée*. Joyce, hardened by the playground combats and the punishments of St Ignatius Loyola, trained in the gymnasium of Battersea Polytechnic, led his squad of Fascisti in an attempt to impose order. He was wearing a coat and a thick woollen scarf, to which he later claimed he owed his life.

His own version of what happened next never varied. In the confusion, someone jumped him from behind, a man he later identified as 'a Jewish Communist'. Something struck his face, though he did not at first realise what it was. The man who jumped him had gone and the crowd about him was drawing back in horror. He felt blood on his face but still did not realise the full extent of the wound. Someone handed him a 'filthy handkerchief' to staunch the flow. Others cleared a way through the crowd and he was helped outside to Lambeth Infirmary.

The name of his assailant was never discovered but Joyce was adamant in repeating that he was a 'Jewish Communist.' There is every indication that he believed it to be true, whether it was or not. Nor did he doubt that the assault was attempted murder. He always insisted that 'an attempt was made to cut my throat but the razor slashed a quarter of an inch too high. There is something to be said for having a well-fed appearance.' Despite the laconic aside, the assailant had inflicted upon William Joyce at eighteen a most savage wound. For the rest of his life he bore a thin but livid scar on the right-hand side of his face. It ran from just behind the lobe of the ear to the very corner of his mouth.

The press version of the events at Lambeth Baths was that the meeting had been rowdy. 'A steward had his head cut through being struck, it is believed, with a spanner,' the *Times* correspondent wrote, 'The chairman read the Public Meetings Act 1908 in the presence of a large number of police.' This reading of the Riot Act in its modern version ended the disturbances and the meeting was resumed.

Joyce was given to describing such events so that he should seem the hero – even the wounded hero – of a hair-breadth escape. He had been a secret agent for the British in Galway. His throat had nearly been cut by a Jewish Communist in Lambeth, as he struggled nobly and outnumbered against the forces of international Bolshevism. But there was another version of the Lambeth story told within the British Union of Fascists, to which he later belonged.

The incident had not occurred during the election meeting, however rowdy that may have been. It was a darker and meaner crime than even Joyce's account suggested. He had been walking away alone after the meeting. He was caught in the dark street by left-wing ruffians – those whom he would have called Jewish Communists. They overpowered him and, while the rest held him down on the pavement, one of them put the razor in the corner of Joyce's mouth and slit his cheek backwards beyond the ear.

If this were true, the incident acquired a still darker and more ignoble quality. To a man of Joyce's stamp it added a degree of humiliation and defeat, in that the wound was not sustained in the course of open battle but as a captive of what he soon called his 'sub-human' enemy. The recurrent memory of that humiliation and agony might well account for his near-hysterical loathing. When, not long before his execution, he passed comment on the mass-murder of the Nazi camps, it was only to point out that there were problems in supply and control during the last days of the

Third Reich. No country, he argued, would have given priority to such criminals as the camps no doubt contained. To measure the intensity of his hatred, it is only necessary to add that he wrote these words when it was public knowledge that women and children by the thousands were among the population of those camps. In him there was no remorse to weaken the crusade of Fascist self-righteousness. If he countenanced a philosophy of sadism, it was the more dangerous in that its stimulus was closely allied to puritan susceptibilities.

At such a level Joyce exemplifies the simple yet shrewd analysis of the Facist leader made by W.H. Auden in his poem *September 1, 1939*, summing up Adolf Hitler, 'the psychopathic god', that those to whom evil is done, do evil in return. To Joyce, the assault upon him was the particular *casus belli* that determined his general view.

The injury done on that October night in Lambeth was certainly a lurid reminder of the reality of extremist campaigning. To Joyce himself, it opened the way to a broader question, just as the refusal of salvation for his mother had invalidated the doctrines of the Catholic church. Arguing once more from the personal to the universal, he concluded that those who had done such a thing to him were the enemies of all civilised society. They had not only forfeited the right to a political vote. They and their values had also forfeited the right to exist.

To accomplish this forfeiture, it was only necessary to elevate the philosophy of the street gang to a political creed by means of a little persuasive illustration. 'The Jewish organizers of the extreme Left', he wrote, 'armed their sub-human hirelings with razors to attack young fascists who dared to cry "A plague o' both your houses!" As early as 1923, a young friend of mine was killed by this scum, dying of blood-poisoning as a result of wounds in the testicles inflicted by a rusty hat-pin.'

The papers carried his own version of the Lambeth story, the brave young warrior grievously wounded in the thick of the battle against alien subversives. He bore the truth in his face and in his heart.

In October 1922 he was still a bright and energetic undergraduate with enthusiams for Dryden and Carlyle. Political fanaticism at eighteen is rarely durable. But at Lambeth Infirmary a week or so later they removed the bandages from his face. He had been marked for life. Moreover, the thin weal of the scar along his cheek was of a kind to tell its own story. It did not suggest a wound of honour or an injury sustained for political conviction. In the world of the 1920s, it was the mark of the racecourse or the dog-track. In appearance, even with the flattening of the broken nose, William Joyce had been a personable young man until that October night. Now he looked like a gangster.

CHAPTER 4

'Winston Churchill – remembered by all those who lost their relations and friends in the holocaust of the Dardanelles, so assiduously organised by this imitation strategist.... Butcher-in-Chief to His Majesty the King.... His personal habits are such that his chief following consists of unpaid tradesmen.... Constantly in the wilderness, despising the odds and sods who share his exile.... Willing to serve under any flag in order to improve fortune and minister to self-admiration!'

'Lloyd George – Liberal animal in a Tory skin.'

'The Liberal party – formed out of the scum and dregs of all that was left in the worst elements of the Whig menagerie.'

'Ramsay MacDonald – The Loon from Lossiemouth – Bright Hope of Socialism installed as head of a Tory government amidst the ape-like grins of the City Financiers.'

'Hore-Belisha – his melon-like physiognomy expanded in a horrible Moroccan Jewish grin...Thought better by Jewry itself to withdraw him from the public gaze. Chamberlain was tired of being told that his War Minister was an Oriental pedlar of furniture.'

William Joyce's political rhetoric – the oratory of the street-corner and the municipal baths – came pat as a flick-knife to the hand. He employed it with the subtlety of a knuckle-duster. Nor, in the end, did he spare the leader of the Conservative party to which he first attached himself, Stanley Baldwin, 'the steel merchant metamorphosed into a squire by casual experiments in pig breeding....

Baldwin's swinish physiognomy on every hoarding with some such legend as "Safety First!" or "Trust Me!" inscribed beneath it.'

Here was a young man who could undeniably hold his own at a pavement meeting as well as in the more impressive surroundings of an election hustings. However deplorable the level of his abuse, he became master of the insult that stuck to its target and was remembered. True, he had not yet stood in the dock at assizes and petty sessions charged with physical assault, riotous assembly, and offences against the Public Order Act. But that time would come. At eighteen his apprenticeship in rhetorical violence and grievous bodily harm had only just begun.

To begin with, after the attack on him at the Lambeth Baths hall, his view of himself changed in a literal sense.

Each time that Joyce looked in his shaving-mirror and whenever he caught the reflection of his face, the livid and disfiguring streak reminded him of what he had become. From that time, his anti-Semitism grew so shrill and scurrilous that its virulence still makes one wince. Ironically, it was so bitter that it made him a liability to the early Fascist movement, from whose main body he was later to break away. But having identified his natural enemies and spoiling for a fight, his resolve was not to be undermined by the moderation of others.

Fate had branded him on that October night as a gangster and a street-fighter. Now he was prepared to live up to the role. But he would be the alley-fighter who could argue over modern philosophy and quote the poets of the Augustan age. There was still room on his desk for Dryden and Pope beside his knuckle-duster. Because he was literate and articulate, he showed a bitter contempt for the self-appointed intellectuals of the inter-war years. He scorned them as a man of action must despise all faint-hearts. 'Fascism', he said, 'is not a creed for the smug mice who choose to emerge from under Bloomsbury tea-cosies to have a nibble at it.'

His attachment to the literature and ideas of the past served only to fuel his fanaticism on these occasions. Perhaps only William Joyce could have taken for his text, as he once did, Edmund Burke's axiom, 'In politics magnanimity is often the truest wisdom' – and promptly used it to show the necessity for the extinction of

Jewry. He was a debater, if not an intellectual. But when he argued over the great issues of human belief, he still did so in the tone which he reserved for the politics of the pavement and the public baths, the voice pitched somewhere between a sneer and a snarl. Not even the race which had pioneered Fascism and fostered Christianity was safe from that.

'I can imagine no greater handicap upon any universal creed than that the Son of God should come upon earth as a Jew and His Church be left to the tender mercies of the Wops.'

For the time being, however, he did not discard his academic first-class honours and it remains one of the oddities of his life that the first published work of the future Nazi propagandist was a scholarly contribution to the *Review of English Studies* in 1928: 'A Note on the Mid Back Slack Unrounded Vowel [a] in the English of Today.' He began working for a master's degree, studying the language of medieval petitions in the Public Record Office. It came to nothing because, he later alleged, his work was stolen and used by the Jewish tutor supervising his studies. The work was not stolen nor, as a matter of fact, was his tutor Jewish. But the outburst served to confirm the extent of his alienation from reality.

His middle twenties were, to Joyce, his wasted years. They were marked by projects that came to nothing and avenues of commitment that proved to be culs-de-sac. He left the British Fascisti Ltd in 1925, seeing no way forward through their policies. For two years he was a member of the Conservative party, on the grounds that its members were 'upholders of Anglo-Saxon tradition and supremacy'. He spoke at its election meetings and worked actively on its behalf, or rather on behalf of his own views which he sought to spread through the party.

At the same time he was turned down by both the Civil Service and the Foreign Office. With his academic background, he would probably have done well in the written examinations but he was never invited to take them. The selection board interviewed him and rejected his application without further ado. Even on first acquaintance, it was clear that he was not 'the right type'.

It was one of the rare instances when Joyce managed to excuse his failure without blaming it on Jewish influence. To those who knew no better, he told a story of having first taken the examinations and done brilliantly. Only then did the selection board turn him down. He was not rich enough, they informed him. Such posts as this were intended for the sons of the well-heeled or at least the well-connected. There was no place for a young man of humbler origins who had shown what he could do by his own energy and determination. The 'old gang', as they soon became in Fascist terminology, held the strings of patronage. They recognised Joyce, quite rightly, as alien to their outlook and methods.

The rebuff did much to undermine his enthusiasm for the Conservative party. All the resentments which were latent in him now fused in an outright rejection of the system which had brought the country to its present state. Commander Leonard Burt, who was to be the recipient of Joyce's confessions many years later, noted this sense of grievance which characterised him as a young man:

> To begin with, he felt he had a right to be bitter. His father had never received compensation from the British Government – *his* government – for the destruction of his property by those cursed Sinn Feiners. He himself was acknowledged to be a brilliant, witty fellow. Yet, for some reason, he was treated as an outcast. Nobody recognised him at his true value. He was good enough to work like a black for the Tories, but would they offer him a seat? Would they, hell!

Joyce put the matter quite unselfconsciously to Burt. 'People would talk to me,' he said of this period in his life. 'It would come out I'd got a first at London University. They wouldn't believe me. I could see them disbelieving me.'

On the other hand, none of them ever doubted his ability to give as good as he got when the street-fighting began. If they hesitated, he could show them his revolver and his stick to convince them that he was in earnest. But for his present rejection he blamed the old men of the Conservative party who controlled the professions and the means of political advancement. These were the weak, the grasping, and the dishonest, who had betrayed the nation to the agents of international finance. No less than the Jews, they became the natural targets of his invective.

'You don't understand,' he said impatiently to Burt, describing the impossibility of dealing with such turncoats, 'they were determined that people like me should never come into our own. They were the murderers of the heroes of the true blood.'

It was hard to see what other political opening there might be for him. By the end of the 1920s Miss Lintorn-Orman's brand of Fascism had not caught on and the Bolshevik revolution in England, which it had been formed to combat, had ceased to be an event worth waiting for.

Joyce had personalised the razor-slash as the work of a Jewish Communist. Now he laid about him in his denunciations of England's political leaders and institutions. The public schools, the Stock Exchange, and the so-called democracy of parliamentary procedure became objects of his attack in a manner that might have warmed the heart of a good Communist. With the formation of a National government in 1931 a dictatorship by mediocrity was established, in Joyce's view, though 'the government decided to pay the leader of the opposition two thousand pounds a year for pretending to obstruct the conduct of its business.' His membership of the Conservative party was to prove of short duration and he left it for good just before the government of 1931 was formed.

Politics did not, of course, bring him an income. He qualified as a teacher, a Licentiate of the College of Preceptors, and worked as a crammer at the Victoria Tutorial College. Later, he registered as a PhD student at King's College, London, studying philosophy and psychology under Professor Aveling. In his tutorial work, mainly the preparation of students for institutional examinations, he was remembered as an energetic teacher, generous with his time and sometimes sharing with his pupils an enthusiasm for the only recreation his life permitted – chess.

During his early years in London he lived south of the river. His parents had settled in East Dulwich at the time of his registration for Battersea Polytechnic, Michael Joyce having by then cut his losses in building or 'architecture' and opened his grocer's shop in this prosperous middle-class suburb. Soon afterwards William

Joyce found rooms of his own in Longbeach Road, among the grey urban wastes of Clapham.

In 1927, a month before he took his final degree exams, he had married Hazel Kathleen Barr, a chemist's assistant and the daughter of a dentist. Joyce later described himself, when applying for his German military passport, as a believer in God but not a member of any church. It was consistent with such an answer that the couple were married at Chelsea Registry Office on 30 April. The bride was an attractive and lively young woman who under normal circumstances would have made a sympathetic wife for an energetic and ambitious young man. But a short experience of married life showed that she and Joyce were temperamentally unsuited to one another, if only by virtue of his moods and outbursts of temper. After eight years, young Mrs Joyce left her husband for another partner, taking with her their two daughters, upon whom William Joyce resigned all claim.

There was a yet greater strain upon the marriage, as there must be when one of the couple discovers and surrenders to the appeal of an all-prevailing fanaticism. It might have been a religious conversion, in which the partner did not share. In the case of Joyce, it was the advent of Sir Oswald Mosley.

Politics apart, Mosley and Joyce had little enough in common, nor did they greatly like one another personally. Mosley was capable of being urbane, relaxed, and downright frivolous. Women found him charming and attractive, though not in the most conventional way. Ellen Wilkinson called him 'The Sheikh.... not the nice kind man who rescues the girl at the point of torture but the one who hisses, "At last... we meet!"' Mosley also lived in a private world where there was leisure and a sense of fun. Joyce was rarely anything but intense, impatient, sardonic. He inhabited a narrow world of self-dedication, as surely as the Jesuits who had taught him. In his presence, fun shrivelled and died. Mosley in his autobiography made only one reference to Joyce, his sometime Chief of Propaganda, as a deserter and as one who was 'intensely vain; a quite common foible in very small men.'

But this personal unpleasantness lay some years in the future. When the British Union of Fascists held its Brighton rally in 1934,

The Sorcerer's Apprentice

Joyce proclaimed Mosley before the mass of spectators as 'the greatest Englishman I have ever known'. On another occasion he went to the extreme of adulation, describing Mosley as the greatest man God had ever created. It must have seemed a pardonable exaggeration in the political rhetoric of a young man who had joined the British Fascisti Ltd on 6 December 1923 and had seen the brave hopes of the movement degenerate into a crackpot collection of factions and rivalry by the 1930s. International Bolshevism had little to fear from a counter-revolution led by Miss Lintorn-Orman and her friends.

Though Mosley was represented to future generations as if he had been no more than a gutter politician and demagogue, the truth was that he had first attracted sympathy – if not support – from many political figures who were subsequently to disown him. John Strachey and Harold Nicolson, Aneurin Bevan and Randolph Churchill were among them. So was the future President Roosevelt. Above all, to Joyce, Mosley was the epitome of uncorrupted Conservative values, the upholder of Anglo-Saxon tradition and supremacy whose heart was, none the less, with the common people. His was an ancient family, the first Oswald Mosley dating from the time of the Tudors. When the latest holder of the name married the daughter of Lord Curzon – former Viceroy of India and Foreign Secretary – in 1920, it was a royal occasion with King George V and Queen Mary among the guests.

But the young Conservative member, whom Beatrice Webb thought the most brilliant man in the House of Commons, crossed the floor to sit as an independent in protest against the use of torture to interrogate Sinn Fein prisoners in 1920. He subsequently fought and held his parliamentary seat against his former party. Those who denounced him as a political maverick were not surprised when, in 1924, he joined the Labour party. His career as a Labour politician brought him membership of the party's National Executive in 1927, beating Herbert Morrison in the constituency section. After the Labour victory of 1929, Ramsay MacDonald considered him for the post of Foreign Secretary. In the end he was given office as Chancellor of the Duchy of Lancaster. No one doubted that Mosley would be a contender for the future leadership of the Labour party.

Unfortunately for the government, it became clear that Mosley meant what he said about the scandal of mass unemployment and the greater scandal of Labour's failure to do anything about it. By submitting to the cabinet the so-called Mosley Memorandum of 1930, he brought matters to a head. His proposals were not adopted. Mosley resigned among the general sympathy of the press. There was widespread contempt for the 'old gang' of whatever party. Harold Macmillan was by no means alone at that time in looking forward to a government of Mosley and the younger men who would do something for the country at last. On 15 February 1930, Harold Nicolson described a dinner party at Oliver Stanley's house with Mosley, Robert Boothby and Walter Elliot among the guests. The discussion centred on 'whether it would be well to have a Fascist coup.'

To embody this revolt of the young against the old, Mosley founded his New Party, encouraged by the triumph of his appearance at the Labour Party Conference in 1930, after his resignation from office. In 1931, the New Party launched its magazine *Action* with Harold Nicolson as editor and a general manager, Hamlyn, who was Jewish. Mosley's brand of Fascism was certainly to become anti-Semitic after 1934 but anti-Semitism was not a condition of its early development. The New Party had been funded in January 1931 by a gift of £50,000 from the motor manufacturer William Morris, later Lord Nuffield, and encouraged by defections from the Labour party, including six members of the House of Commons.

Twenty-four members of the New Party, including Mosley himself, stood for parliament in the general election of 1931. Some of the rallies were violent, if only because of the resentment which Labour supporters felt at the splitting of the anti-Conservative vote. To keep order, Mosley's supporters organised the so-called Biff Boys. Their leader denied that these middle-class hearties were the equivalent of Hitler's thugs. 'We shall rely on the good old English fist,' he said reassuringly.

But the 1931 election was a disaster for the New Party. Mosley at Stoke-on-Trent and Sellick Davies at Merthyr polled just over

10,000 votes each, though neither was close to winning the seat. Only four of the others managed to get more than 1,000 votes. The party's total vote was just half that given to the Communists in a similar number of boroughs. The consequence of this was to intensify the party's contempt for parliamentary democracy and spur it towards overt Fascism. After the defection of members like John Strachey and Harold Nicolson, Mosley's movement relaunched itself as the British Union of Fascists on 1 October 1932. It might seem an extra-parliamentary oddity in English political life, but it had money and a good many supporters. There was enough of both to provide an organisation and there would be paid officials. Inspired by the example of Mussolini's achievements and the promise of Adolf Hitler, the BUF would be a potent influence upon British political life.

The appeal of Mosley's campaign in its new form drew Joyce to it. So long as it had appeared to be an alternative force to the Labour party, he kept clear. But as the BUF acquired a Chelsea headquarters where activists lived as soldiers in barracks, and a Blackshirt uniform was issued to remove the distinction of class and wealth, there emerged a political ideal to which he could give his complete loyalty.

He made his reputation as a speaker almost at once. No one who heard him could doubt the strength of his commitment. By the autumn of 1933, he was deputising for Mosley as chief speaker at the largest rallies of the BUF, where the audiences numbered several thousand. At Streatham and Liverpool in November he made his mark, observed by the Fascist apologist A. K. Chesterton (cousin of G. K. Chesterton) who recorded in his own life of Mosley that it was William Joyce who was the 'brilliant writer, speaker, and exponent of policy... addressed hundreds of meetings, always at his best, always revealing the iron spirit of Fascism in his refusal to be intimidated by violent opposition.'

John Beckett, formerly an ILP member of the House of Commons, was won for Fascism after hearing one of Joyce's first addresses to a rally in 1933 at Paddington Baths. 'Within ten minutes of this 28-year-old youngster taking the platform, I knew that here was one of the dozen finest orators in the country.

The Sorcerer's Apprentice

Snowden's close reasoning and unerring instinct for words were allied with Maxton's humour and Churchill's daring. That great audience assembled to hear a speaker quite unknown in the political world and the enthusiasm created was an eye-opener to me, and would have been to most of the Westminster hacks with whom I had previously associated public influence.'

It has to be said that many of the BUF's 'orators' would not be hard to improve upon. There was, for example, their great parliamentary hope at Whitechapel, Teddy 'Kid' Lewis, a professional boxer. He was almost illiterate and could make only one speech, which he had painstakingly learnt by heart. Unfortunately, his hecklers also learn it. Each time that he got up to speak at a meeting, they would chant the lines in unison with him – even correcting his lapses of memory – until the predicted riot broke out. Despite Fascist claims that the working class of the East End was with them, Lewis could muster only 154 votes at the general election.

Joyce's services to the cause were recognised by a paid appointment as West London Area Administrative Officer of the BUF, which enabled him to leave the Victoria Tutorial College and abandon his PhD thesis at King's. In 1934, he was promoted to become the movement's Director of Propaganda. His salary of £300 a year was adequate to his needs but the greater reward was in being a full-time Fascist at last.

In his light-coloured trench-coat which resembled Adolf Hitler's, feet braced astride and hands thrust into the pockets, he appeared the emblem of Fascist militancy. His platform photographs show him sometimes in a Blackshirt uniform like an army battledress, sometimes in a black suit buttoned tightly across his broad chest and a high-necked pullover, microphone clutched in his right hand, and left pushed into his jacket pocket. He was never hesitant or nervous, even before the largest and noisiest crowds. The exhilaration of applause and heckling acted upon him like a shot of adrenalin.

In 1933 it was suggested that Mosley should visit the new German leader, Adolf Hitler, and discuss with him the future of Fascism in Britain. He had already been to see Mussolini in the previous year and had been advised to call his New Party 'Fascist' but to play down its military organisation. If the Hitler visit were to go ahead, Mosley would take one or two of his colleagues with him. He no longer had men like Harold Nicolson who had accompanied him to Rome, but it seemed likely that the new deputation to Germany might include William Joyce.

Joyce would need a passport, and that with the minimum of delay. On 4 July 1933 he made out an application to the Passport Office. That application still exists, accompanied by a head-and-shoulders photograph of Joyce, smartly-suited and with hair plastered down. In the course of filling in the form, he included a significant falsehood. He declared that he was 'a British subject by birth', born at Rutledge Terrace, Galway, a house which his family did not inhabit until some years after William Joyce had been brought back from New York. He still described himself as a private tutor and the purpose of his journey abroad as 'holiday touring'. At that time it was not necessary to produce a birth certificate in support of the application. It was enough to have the declaration endorsed by a public official. Joyce persuaded the accountant of the National Bank in Grosvenor Gardens, Belgravia, to endorse the truth of his statements. They had known one another for five years and the accountant, Mr Costello, had not the least reason to think that Joyce was born elsewhere than Galway.

No doubt Joyce felt a certain satisfaction in this small triumph over the petty snobbery of British civil servants, who considered that only the word of a professional gentleman could be relied upon. A bank accountant was to be believed but not his clients or his clerks. In retrospect, however, Joyce did himself fatal damage by the falsehood which he employed. For once, the phrase of melodrama rang with truth. He had effectively signed his own death-warrant by describing himself as a British subject. Although the lie itself could not alter his nationality, it would be argued that he was now, for practical purposes, amenable to the laws of treason. Nor was that all. Whether or not he were a British citizen, his possession of a British passport abroad meant that he enjoyed the protection of the crown against any malice or misfortune that he might encounter. For that reason, by some arguments, he owed

The Sorcerer's Apprentice

a continuing obligation of loyalty to the sovereign after he left the shores of England.

And it was all for nothing. Mosley did not go to see Hitler until April 1935. By then he felt no need to take William Joyce with him.

Throughout 1934, Joyce remained, next to Mosley, the most powerful figure of the BUF in the popular imagination. His was the voice that ranted and sneered at the nation's internal enemies, over the boarded baths at Paddington and Lambeth, the arenas of Streatham and Liverpool. Some who heard him were impressed and a few were frightened. His own followers cheered him repeatedly as the rhetoric boomed out through the slight electronic distortion of the public address systems. The arenas hired for these meetings seemed to match the modern creed of the new popular movement. On other evenings they were the scene of boxing programmes or wrestling spectaculars where, as *Vogue* reported, young and titled women went to see blood flow in the latest thrill of erotic *chic*. There was to be no place here for the slow debates of timbered parliamentary chambers. The rhetoric of contemporary Fascism rang on tile and steel and iron-framed glass, the electronic shrillness of the microphone amplifying the sardonic zeal of the burly scar-faced orator who held it in his grip.

There came a night in Chiswick, in January 1934, when Joyce appeared in his Blackshirt 'battledress' with a military style blouse-tunic. By next day his picture was in the papers. He had set Mosley and the BUF on a new and far more dangerous course.

Someone at the Chiswick meeting had asked him a question after his speech. It was about class war and the Jews. 'I don't regard Jews as a class,' he snapped back at his questioner, 'I regard them as a privileged misfortune.'

It was mild by contrast with some of his later invective, but it marked the beginning of a year that was soon to be darkened by violence, malice and crime. Apprehension grew to alarm among the targets of his abuse. Then the fear of him that had been generated bred a will to resist. The hostile groups outside Fascist meetings increased from a few protesters to thousands of demonstrators on certain widely reported occasions.

'Hitler and Mosley, what are they for?' chanted the anti-Fascist crowds, 'Thuggery, buggery, hunger and war!'

With variations, this was the theme of the hecklers to be heard at Olympia and Earls Court, the White City and the Birmingham Bull Ring. Moreover, in the 1930s offensive weapons were openly and legally sold. The enemies of Fascism went into ironmongers' shops and bought brass knuckle-dusters. Sometimes they made weapons for themselves by bedding razor-blades in potatoes. Their enemies equipped themselves in the same fashion. And then both factions waited for the battle that must come.

CHAPTER 5

The British public, during the remaining twelve years of his life, was never quite able to make up its mind whether William Joyce was a joke or a threat. Ironically, he was to be hanged for broadcasts most of which were known at once as comically improbable in their boasts of German victory. In almost every respect, they posed less of a menace than the civil and racial violence which he advocated and assisted as Mosley's Director of Propaganda. In wartime, when the nation's peril put a ban on all mockery of its leaders, there was a refreshing schoolboy satisfaction in listening to a man who was prepared, as it were, to stick his tongue out at the Churchill cabinet and blow sounds of derision at them. It was unthinkable that the BBC should do other than support its own government. Too often, however, it did this by lecturing its listeners in the manner of a public school housemaster reproving the slackers who let the side down by their want of 'team spirit.' There was a reason, if not a justification, for the rumour that the initial letters BBC actually stood for 'Bloody Baptist Cant'.

The events of 1934 showed Joyce the propagandist in a different and more chilling role. Given time, he might have destroyed the British Union of Fascists single-handed by his cold-hearted vindictiveness. But if that movement were to succeed and in so doing carry him to power, he promised a systematic cruelty or slaughter as precise, impersonal and ineluctable as a quadratic equation. To hear the harsh and vaunting tone of this promise was frightening in itself. But to hear the storm of applause with which his BUF followers greeted it was more terrifying still. This was the William Joyce who mattered – the man who moved thousands to cheer his own version of the 'final solution' – not the political slapstick of Lord Haw-Haw for which he was put to death.

Mosley's own preoccupation among the BUF's immediate policies was the raising of a protectionist barrier so that goods which could be produced by British labour from British materials should be prohibited imports. He argued that even the procurement of raw materials from abroad should be subject to government control. Centralisation and nationalisation were to be the means to full employment. Such aspects of Fascist economics were almost an anticipation of Labour government policy in the crises which followed the Second World War. But economics were a secondary issue to Joyce. His was not a preoccupation but an obsession, the threat of Jewry and the hope offered by the new example of National Socialism. He exulted in the triumph of the new order now established in Germany and the new justice that was to be applied to his racial and cultural antagonists.

Anti-Semitism is no longer a prevalent strain in English society, as it was in the years before the war. This comes in part from a sense of shame at the memory of the Nazi concentration camps. At the same time, the post-war years have provided a larger and more easily identified target for racial animosity in the new populations of Caribbean and Asian immigrants. Even in the 1930s the anti-Semitism of literary figures like Hilaire Belloc and G. K. Chesterton co-existed uneasily with their revulsion at the racial policies of the new Germany. In British political life of the previous twenty years, latent anti-Jewish feeling had been apt to surface in response to particular events. It had been provoked, for example, by the involvement of the Attorney-General Rufus Isaacs and his brother in the Marconi scandal of 1912–13. It was also kept alive between times by such publications as *The Eye-Witness* or Leo Maxse's *National Review*, which saw German Jews in England as agents of the Kaiser before 1914 – 'Hebrew journalists at the beck and call of German diplomats.' However incompatible the roles of agents for the old order, exporters of revolutionary socialism and pillars of international capitalism, they were tailored to fit by the antipathy of such anti-Jewish hostility.

In the decade before the war, Jewish settlement in the East End led to some involvement in the London underworld on the part of the Jewish population. This was put before a wide reading public by reports of court cases and in such novels as Graham Greene's *Brighton Rock*, where Colleoni the 'rich middle-aged Jew' commands his racecourse thugs. When Pinkie is cornered he sees, as perhaps Joyce did in a Lambeth alley, 'Semitic faces ringing him all round. They grinned back at him: every man had his razor out.' Eight years earlier in Patrick Hamilton's widely-acclaimed novel *The Midnight Bell*, the young Jews of Soho were presented with little more charity except the reservation that they were 'brigands rather than crooks, and would probably end, not in jail, but business.' The association of race with crime, in the public view, was as clear in this case as in that of West Indian immigrants half a century later.

Yet even by the standards of the day, it seems extraordinary that Joyce should have thought the British people at large would respond sympathetically to his shrill and truculent celebration of the fate of Jews in the first year of Hitler's dictatorship.

In one tirade of this kind – by no means his most bitter – he denounced those English intellectuals who 'skulked in lecture rooms' during the First World War to avoid the rigours of battle, and who were unmoved by the German execution of an English heroine like Nurse Edith Cavell. Now they were heard to 'twitter with execration' at the news that the Nazi SA had seized a number of Jews in the town of Worms, thrown them into a pigsty and beaten them. Dismissing the assault as a subject of no concern, Joyce turned upon the intellectuals themselves with a promise of what was in store for them. 'When the spoilt body of capitalism is put into the straitjacket of the Fascist State, these little by-products of the political system which capitalism has made possible will of course be cleaned up too.'

These predications were delivered with a considerable force of oratory, all the more chilling for the total lack of humanity and the unreason of the argument. Despite the quality of mind which had won him his first-class honours degree and led him to a study of modern philosophical and psychological theory, he rode like a conqueror over the rules of logic and morality. Those who listened to him critically were dismayed he could not see that it was not disapproval by pacifists, intellectuals or even cowards that made the Nazi assaults an atrocity. They were no less repugnant to tens of thousands of men who had fought in the previous war, as they would have been to tens of thousands more who died in it.

Like any man who turns a grudge into a crusade, Joyce's alienation from reality grew more pitiful. He lived in a world of his own mythology peopled by an enemy of his own creation – the Jewish Communists with the razors – who had marked him for what he was. No man's soul was ever a more secure prisoner of its enemy than Joyce with his obsessive and lifelong hatred. Certainly such people existed, but the man who allowed his mind and soul to be ruled by their existence had already handed them the better part of the argument. Yet the limits of his moral perception were not to be enlarged. There was no room for argument or compromise in the matter. Those who thought him in error became the co-traitors of his personal mythology, the Bloomsbury 'mice', who would be 'cleaned up' by the truncheons and boots of the new heroes, once the Fascist revolution had been accomplished in England.

This view of the future had now acquired a greater clarity for him. Increasingly when he used the term 'Fascist' he appeared to be thinking of it more narrowly as National Socialism. Adolf Hitler, not Mussolini, was his idol. Fascism must not share the fate of Christianity in being left to what Joyce had called 'the tender mercies of the Wops'.

Even at a distance, William Joyce in 1934 is a frightening figure. People who were questioned as to why they listened to him during the war very often said they found him 'good for a laugh'. There was very little laughable about the sardonic promises of destruction and pain which echoed from the loudspeakers of Wembley and the White City, Earls Court and the Albert Hall, five years before the war began. He denounced democracy as a psychopathic expression of inferiority and compromise as an aberration that must be crushed out of existence. Most of his wartime broadcasts were to seem patently ridiculous in their claims. But the political solutions which he advocated in the 1930s were not so. They appeared to be gaining ground on the continent of Europe with a terrifying self-confidence and a nightmare rapidity.

The movement whose new star he became in 1934 soon showed

the public how greatly it had gained strength. It could afford to hire the great arenas and fill them. Its uniform was to be seen in the massed ranks who paraded in Hyde Park and at Olympia or the White City. Two or three thousand at a time turned out to salute their leaders in the military unison of the raised arm and the clenched fist. Black House, as the Chelsea headquarters in the King's Road became known, had uniformed sentries at its doors, for all the world as if the private army was ready for the great coup.

Even at the beginning of 1934 the anti-Semitism of the British Union of Fascists was not as a rule overt. For this reason, it was still possible to raise money by donations from big business. The BUF set up the January Club, a social and intellectual front whose members did not have to be Fascist and who were addressed by Joyce in his calmer tones. Those who attended the club had connections with Vickers, Handley Page and London Assurance. It was also said that money was received from Dutch Shell and Courtaulds. Joyce himself claimed that he was approached by Edward Barron whose father was proprietor of the Carreras Tobacco Company. Barron, according to Joyce, offered to contribute £100,000 to the BUF coffers on condition that the movement should not be anti-Semitic. 'Without even consulting the Leader of the organization,' wrote Joyce, 'I rejected the offer with an impolite message.'

Far more dramatic than rumours of who had offered what in terms of cash was the wholehearted support which the *Daily Mail* and Lord Rothermere gave the Fascists as 1934 began. On 8 January, Rothermere himself was the author of the paper's principal feature, 'Hurrah for the Blackshirts!' He saw them not as a party of racial obsession but as a right-wing ginger group to keep the Conservative party on the proper lines. In the BUF itself there was money for propaganda publications, including *Action, Blackshirt, Fascist Weekly* and *Fascist Quarterly*. Despite Joyce's denunciation of intellectuals, a number of them were allies of the Fascist cause in the 1930s. They included Ezra Pound and Roy Campbell among the poets, Henry Williamson and Wyndham Lewis among the novelists.

On 22 April there was a mass rally at the Albert Hall where Mosley addressed an audience of 10,000 supporters. It was a scene of Union Jacks and Fascist banners, an orchestra playing the Nazi *Horst Wessel Song*, though set to English words. Then, as the spotlights shone upon the figure of the leader, head thrown proudly back, the entire audience rose to its feet and the Albert Hall rang to a chant of 'Hail, Mosley! Mosley! Mosley!'

Mosley spoke for an hour and a half, a performance of theatrical rather than political power. In flat contradiction of his Director of Propaganda, he insisted that the Fascist movement in Britain was neither anti-Jewish nor racialist in any other way. He spoke of his belief in democracy and of the necessity that a Fascist government should come to power by constitutional means. Later, if the people endorsed the proposal by their vote, the parliamentary system might be replaced by a corporate state along the lines that Franco's Spain was subsequently to follow.

Despite the usual blazing peroration with which the speech ended, full of 'greatness and glory', it is hard to imagine that Mosley and Joyce could long be accommodated in the same political movement. For the last time, at the Albert Hall meeting, there was no trouble from hecklers or the Blackshirt bodyguard. It had been an organised demonstration of Fascist power and the authority of leadership.

In terms of political influence and popular appeal, April 1934 probably marked the zenith of Fascism in England. At the level of street violence and contempt for democratic opinion, towards which William Joyce was urging it, the BUF would get far more sensational publicity in future. But in April it still retained an image of patriotism and integrity, attracting by this the support of financiers and of the Rothermere press. The press in general might not greatly favour the movement but a good deal of its comment was still cool and non-committal. Above all, Mosley had tried to reassure the country that persecution of race or religion was against the fundamental tenets of Fascism as it had evolved in England.

None of this brought much comfort to William Joyce. On the other hand, he had learnt one lesson that was applicable to Communism, Fascism, and indeed any anti-democratic movement. What may not be achieved by argument can be brought about by provocation. Mosley might talk about the BUF's racial tolerance as long as he wished. It required only a limited number of Joyce's searing denunciations of Jewry to undo all his leader's soothing words. It was impossible to listen to Joyce without believing that he meant every word he said about the 'cleaning up' of dissenters and racial groups when the Fascists should take power. Those to whom he referred were unlikely to believe that Mosley would stand between them and their destruction.

As the spring of 1934 turned to summer their unease grew to alarm. Mosley had offered the olive branch. William Joyce presented the clenched fist in an armour of brass knuckles.

The great Fascist rally that summer was to be held at Olympia on 7 June. It marked the turning of the tide in public opinion and, more notably, the defeat of any attempt at moderation by Mosley. In effect, Joyce and National Socialism were to win the day. Perhaps Mosley did not mind as much as he pretended. As the political argument had developed, it seemed that he must fight Communism and Jewry together, sooner or later. But from this point the admiration which Joyce had expressed for the natural Conservative who upheld Anglo-Saxon tradition and supremacy gave way, in other members of the BUF, to a less critical admiration of the leaders of European Fascism.

The appearance of Mosley before an audience of 12,000 at Olympia was intended to demonstrate to newsreel cameras and radio listeners the existence of Fascism in England as a mass, popular movement. There were to be no less than 2,000 uniformed Blackshirts, marching and parading as the advance guard of revolution. For that reason alone, the Communist party saw that it must either stop Mosley now or else perhaps lose all chance of a populist vote in its own support. There must be disruption, disorder, and martyrs for the cause.

The result of this was to plant the seed of Mosley's destruction. No longer was he to be a free agent in the matter of policy. William Joyce and the Communists between them had seen to that.

Scotland Yard's Special Branch officers, who had infiltrated both the Communist and Fascist movements, reported that the

Communists were organising disruption as assiduously as the BUF was planning the details of the rally. As a matter of fact, any reader of the *Daily Worker* could have told them that. Joyce and his kind had given the Communists a ready argument for enlisting working-class Jews in an anti-Fascist crusade.

In the weeks before the meeting, the *Daily Worker* published plans for a five-column march on Olympia and even a map to show its readers how to get there. The columns were to merge in the Hammersmith Road at 6.30, an hour and a half before the rally. Here, if ever, was the chance for Jewish and non-Jewish enemies of Fascism to unite in putting a stop to the world which Joyce tauntingly promised them. In a final exhortation to defeat the Fascists, the paper added, 'The workers' counteraction will cause them to tremble. All roads lead to Olympia tonight!'

The sequel is best described in outline. In response to the appeal, about 3,000 demonstrators converged on Olympia, where a cordon of 500 police, mounted and on foot, kept the way clear for the ticket-holders. Some of these demonstrators, by their own later accounts, armed themselves with razor-blades or with knuckle-dusters bought from ironmongers. So far as the will to violence went, both sides seemed equally matched. It was true that the marchers were outnumbered but many of the men and women attending the rally had merely bought tickets for the show rather than as a gesture of commitment to Mosley. More to the point, several hundred tickets had been bought by Communists and their sympathisers.

As the cars of the *beau monde* arrived to see the spectacle of Mosley in action, their passengers discovered – as Lord Trenchard complained – that they were surrounded by a jeering crowd of protesters. There was such disruption at the entrance to Olympia that the start of the meeting had to be delayed for half an hour. At length, among music and spotlights, flags and banners, the black-clad figure of Mosley arrived with a uniformed bodyguard of more than fifty supporters. It was noticed that he limped. For some while he had suffered from phlebitis and several times in the previous months he had been unable to speak at meetings. When that happened, William Joyce deputised for him. But the thought of

Joyce's Hitlerian ranting before a crowd of 12,000 at Olympia, the newsreel cameras turning and the radio reporters listening, was enough to put phlebitis in its place. The familiar voice of Mosley, theatrical and vibrant, came over the speakers.

'This meeting, the largest outdoor meeting ever held under one roof in Britain, is the culmination of a great national campaign...'

As if at a prearranged signal a chant began high up in the gallery: 'Fascism means Murder! Down with Mosley!'

The Blackshirt stewards moved to deal with the interrupters. As they did so the spotlights, under the control of the newsreel cameras, swung round to illuminate the fracas, leaving Mosley in twilight.

'One! Two! Three! Four! What are the Fascists for? Lechery, treachery, hunger and war!'

By now the cameras were filming the fists, and the bodies struggling in the grip of those blond, uniformed young men who tried to drag them from their seats.

'Two! Three! Four! Five! We want Mosley, dead or alive!'

For an hour the uproar continued. Two of the protesters climbed up into the roof where, from the girders high overhead, they scattered anti-Fascist leaflets upon the audience.

It was impossible to continue with the meeting and difficult to tell where the next outburst might come from. There were shouts and jeers from every part of the huge auditorium. Here and there the anti-Fascists were grouped together and running fights broke out with the Blackshirts. Elsewhere, individual protesters were being held down while Mosley's guards beat them over the head and about the face. Women jeered at Blackshirts who made their way to them, only to find that they had been lured into a group of Communist sympathisers intent on vengeance.

But the protesters were outnumbered and at the end of an hour they had been thrown out, some of them after suffering enough physical damage to require a visit to the casualty department of Hammersmith hospital. The number of injuries was not recorded but three people – two Fascists and one anti-Fascist – were kept in hospital overnight.

The BUF held its rally at last but it was a bitter victory. William

Joyce, on the other hand, had won his argument. Compromise had, as he put it, been crushed out of existence. Now it was National Socialism or nothing – and the faint-hearts must fall by the way. Images of women thrown down, kicked and beaten, men held and knocked senseless by Blackshirt stewards, filled the press in the days and weeks that followed. An equal amount of injury might have happened at a football match but that was beside the point. Men like Rothermere surveyed the wreckage of Olympia and quit.

Even this defection by Rothermere was not allowed to pass without a characteristic explanation from Joyce himself:

> Actually, he admitted in private that Sir Isidore Salmon had told him that continued support of the British Union of Fascists would mean the withdrawal of all Lyons's advertisements from the *Daily Mail*, as well as any other financial inconveniences which could be arranged. Rothermere had thirty million pounds and could have stood the struggle. His directors, however, were prepared for no such sacrifice... Whatever opinions may be entertained concerning Mosley and his movement, there could be no graver stigma on the so-called freedom of expression said to prevail in Britain than that a body of Englishmen should be prevented from expressing their views by an Oriental confectioner.

Mosley, as if capitulating to the iron logic of Fascism, confronted the question of race at a final Albert Hall rally on 28 October 1934. The building was almost half empty, for the problem of excluding enemies was greater than that of filling the seats with true believers. His speech made clear that he had been brought reluctantly to much the same view as his Director of Propaganda. His opponents stood clearly identified, by their own wish. He had, he told his audience, no racial or religious animus against the Jews. He sought only to take up the challenge they had thrown down in their fight against Fascism and Britain. 'They have declared in their great folly to challenge the conquering force of the modern age. Tonight we take up that challenge. They will it: let them have it.'

But throughout the country, and on both sides of the argument, Olympia had woken the sleepers to political reality. Once and for all it put Fascism back on the street. To William Joyce that was no hardship. It was in the street that his own form of politicised gangsterism had always belonged. If, indeed, Mosley had capitulated, the instrument of his surrender was signed after the Olympia rally in June. It was announced that William Joyce had been appointed Deputy Leader of the British Union of Fascists.

Purged of its comparatively moderate and democratic elements, English Fascism came into its own. Even before the last Albert Hall rally, Joyce and Mosley had joined the street fight. It happened in the seaside town of Worthing on the night of 9 October 1934.

That the place chosen should have been a quiet seaside resort, on a dark night of cold wind blowing from the Channel and the summer season over, made the events seem more bizarre. However, Mosley was to address an audience of several hundred in the Pier Pavilion. He was accompanied by a number of Blackshirts from his Chelsea headquarters, by Joyce, and by Captain Budd who was a town and county councillor. Those who were admitted to the meeting had been vetted and no trouble was expected. On the other hand, Joyce arrived to find a large crowd outside the pavilion, some of whom had probably travelled to Worthing to make their feelings known.

The events of that night were to be described in detail from varying points of view. What was not described was the atmosphere generated by the prophetic posters with the heroic blackshirted leader depicted at the salute and the promise of 'Mosley is Coming!' as the Fascists' motorised cavalcade entered town after town. An ambulance was kept at hand.

By his own account, Joyce arrived at the pavilion, in Blackshirt uniform, about half an hour before the meeting. He found a crowd of people 'strolling about'. They began shouting 'We'll give Mosley a hot time!' and 'To hell with the Blackshirts!' As Mosley approached, the crowd surged forward and almost engulfed him among calls of 'Throw Mosley into the sea!' By the aid of his Blackshirt bodyguard, the leader reached the entrance to the pavilion, where Joyce was already telling Captain Budd that the police should have been called.

The Sorcerer's Apprentice

'I asked Budd to telephone the police in quite a peremptory way, as I considered he should have done this before.'

It was that time of year when England began to prepare for the Guy Fawkes celebrations of 5 November. Roman candles, squibs and rockets were already in the shops and the protesters had armed themselves. The first fireworks now exploded outside the pavilion. The crowd sang 'Poor old Mosley's got the wind up!' to the tune of 'John Brown's Body'.

Captain Budd got through to the police station by telephone, only to be told that the constabulary had the situation well in hand. That was certainly not true. Budd said, rather foolishly, that unless reinforcements arrived the uniformed Blackshirts would be obliged to take the law into their own hands. Rockets continued to go off outside the building. For the moment, however, those in the pavilion were in no danger and the crowded audience which waited was entirely sympathetic to the leader's case.

To a background of chanting and the explosion of fireworks outside the building Mosley got up to speak. There was considerable applause from his listeners as he advanced his familiar protectionist argument. The cure for unemployment and the nation's economic ills lay in the exclusion of all imports which could otherwise be made in Britain. He also dismissed the arguments of those who criticised the use of Blackshirt 'stewards':

'The great "crime" of the adherents of Fascism is that they have dared to defend themselves. But by that very defence they have restored free speech to areas in this country where organised Socialist and Communist opposition had prevented it before in open public meeting.'

As he developed this argument, William Joyce and the other admirers of National Socialism sat by, a curious and unconvincing array of advocates for that freedom of expression. However, the meeting was orderly. Mosley spoke for an hour and then went on to answer questions. Outside, the crowd waited for its chance. Joyce described the scene as he and Mosley tried to leave the pavilion:

When Sir Oswald appeared on the steps, the crowd surged round him and I saw him struck from the right. As far as

I could see, the blow fell on his cheek. Before Sir Oswald could do anything but lift his arm up, a man swung his arm round Sir Oswald's neck. Then I was pushed against Sir Oswald, whom I saw trying to free himself.

At once, what the *Sussex Daily News* called 'a strong bodyguard' of Blackshirts surrounded their leader and deputy leader, forcing their way through the crowd until the main party reached a café nearby. Mosley and Joyce, however, were determined to make some gesture of defiance towards the growing crowd which had booed them all the way. They reached the arcade and then, still surrounded by the bodyguard, 'came out into the road again and the party marched round the traffic lights through the dense masses.' The situation began to look ugly but Superintendent Bristow and all the available men on duty – some in plain clothes – kept things in hand. So wrote the *Sussex Daily News* next morning.

Entering the café, the Blackshirts went upstairs and showed themselves at the window, which provoked a hail of missiles from the crowd below. One Fascist who had climbed out on to the ledge prudently withdrew, and the windows were closed. But the crowd remained outside and, Joyce said, he heard the familiar chanting, 'Two! Three! Four! Five! We want Mosley, dead or alive!' It was, Joyce explained, 'a song generally used by anti-Fascists of Communist persuasion, and one which would not be used by nice Worthing people.'

The time came for the Blackshirts to leave the café. One group, including a woman, was seen by the press 'on the run' in South Street with part of the crowd at its heels. Mosley and the main group marched along Marine Parade with the object of reaching the BUF office in Warwick Street. It was here that the fighting began. Joyce described a crowd of three or four hundred blocking the way, shouting, chanting, and giving the clenched fist salute of the 'Red Front'. He was walking beside Mosley as the bystanders pressed in upon them. 'I warded off the blows that were struck at me and Sir Oswald did the same. I did not see any police officers at the time.'

Then, Joyce added, there were shouts of, 'Mosley! Let's get the bastard!' and 'Come on, lads! Let's get stuck into them!'

The Sorcerer's Apprentice

At that moment, like the cavalry to the rescue, the main body of Blackshirts arrived to extricate the beleaguered group in Warwick Street. There was 'a general mêleé and blows were struck.' The press reports confirmed this, adding that the Fascists cornered their victims in shop doorways and left them felled and bleeding. Before it was over, knuckle-dusters had been used and two of the combatants were taken to hospital. Only then, said Joyce, did the police arrive in Warwick Street.

An argument began between Joyce and Superintendent Bristow. Bernard Mullan, one of the Fascists who had come down from the Chelsea headquarters, was under arrest. Joyce was trying to arrange bail. Mullan had had an altercation with a youth who had called Mosley a 'Black Bastard'. Mullan asked him if he wasn't ashamed to use such language when ladies were present. The youth said nothing. 'Don't you understand English?' Mullan asked. 'I don't understand Italian,' the boy said, referring to the Fascists' origins. At this point blows were exchanged, Mullan claiming that he was hit first. The *Sussex Daily News* could only say that it was the boy who had the black eye when they got to the police station.

'This is a very serious incident,' Bristow said to Joyce, 'Two men have gone to the hospital.'

'It might have been a dozen so far as your conduct of the operations is concerned,' said one of Joyce's companions.

Whatever understanding there might have been between the police and the BUF ended at this remark. According to Joyce, Bristow said, 'So that's your attitude is it? I wish I'd known that sooner and I would have acted very differently. So you wish a dozen anti-Fascists had gone to the hospital, do you?'

'Don't misinterpret his statement,' said Joyce. 'There's no reason why we should wish any casualties at all.'

The streets were cleared and Mullan was bailed. But the fracas at Worthing was merely an instance of the civil disorder promised by the BUF in its new phase. Mosley, Joyce, and the leaders of the meeting at the pavilion were charged with assault and riotous assembly. When the case was heard before Worthing magistrates it ended on 15 November with the assault charges being dismissed but Mosley, Joyce, Budd and Mullan were commited to Lewes Assizes on charges of riotous assembly.

The case was heard in December 1934, though overshadowed by another in the assize calendar, the prosecution of Tony Mancini in the Brighton 'Trunk' Murder. Sir Patrick Hastings, who was briefed for the defence of Mosley and the others, had little difficulty in demolishing the prosecution case. That case was based on the premise that the crowd outside the Pier Pavilion had been good-natured, intent on 'ragging' the Fascists but not on violence. It was Mosley and his companions who had struck people in response to this. This was a half-truth, which Sir Patrick soon presented as an untruth. A good many were there for the fun, rather than any dedication to the anti-Fascist cause. But some were there in earnest support of that cause.

It was a rather jolly occasion, like a football match, one prosecution witness said. 'Perhaps if they had got at Sir Oswald it would not have been so jolly,' Sir Patrick said acidly. The café had been pelted with tomatoes and eggs but that had not been premeditated. 'Can they be bought at Worthing at 10.30 at night?' Sir Patrick asked.

The prosecution and its supporting witnesses made such a poor showing that, at the end of their evidence, Sir Patrick Hastings submitted there was no case for the defence to answer. Mr Justice Branson agreed. He directed the jury to return verdicts of not guilty, which they did. So on 18 December, Joyce, Mosley and the other two defendants left the dock among the congratulations of their supporters. The legal concept of what constituted riotous assembly had proved utterly inadequate to the complexities of modern politics.

At another level it appeared to vindicate the BUF's tactics of street campaigning, in which Joyce had always believed and to which Mosley had been drawn. Confrontation with the enemy and violence done to him when necessary were not only justified but appeared as ends in their own right. The distinction between the BUF and the Nazi SA grew finer in the months that followed.

At the same time, it was not to be supposed that William Joyce had put himself entirely on the wrong side of the law. The savagery which he showed towards his opponents was equalled only by that of the discipline that he imposed upon his supporters. Nor did this do him the least harm in his relations with the police. One officer spoke nostalgically of the manner in which Joyce had co-operated with the forces of law:

'Joyce really had his men under control and he was always fair to us. We could never come to an understanding with the Communists.... But if I went to Joyce and told him that his men were doing something that wasn't fair to the police, trying us too hard or interfering with our time off, he'd have his men right off that job in half an hour and there'd be no grumbling.'

Extraordinary though such a testimonial may now appear, it was invaluable to Joyce in the few years before the war. It was possible for the authorities to see him, at this level, as a figure of 'law and order' without a single criminal accusation that could be sustained against him. In this guise, he remained at Mosley's side during the events of 1935 and 1936, though the rapport between them was failing. Privately, Joyce ceased to refer to him as 'The Leader' and called him 'The Bleeder' instead. 'Mosley was hopeless', he told his captors in 1945. 'He was the worst leader of what should have been the best cause in the world.' To Joyce, in any case, the British Union of Fascists was to seem increasingly irrelevant in a world where the beacon of National Socialism shone brightly from Berlin.

CHAPTER 6

There was but one saviour for Europe, in Joyce's view, and he made no secret that Mosley was not the man. In 1940, Joyce recalled how he had attended a pre-war dinner of English historians, at which the 'fifth-rate' G. P. Gooch 'assured his frightened colleagues that Hitler would amount to nothing.... At this news, there was a great laugh and calm descended on the port-bibbing assembly. I ventured to express exactly the opposite opinion and was stared at as if I were a hawker of ladies' underwear who had accidentally strayed into a monastery.'

But it was not his opinions so much as their force of expression that caused his hearers to stare at him in awe on these occasions. Cecil Roberts was present to hear Joyce give an after-dinner speech at the Park Lane Hotel:

After dinner we adjourned to the ballroom in which a member of the British Fascist hierarchy was to make an address, in the unavoidable absence of Sir Oswald Mosley. I did not catch the name of the speaker, a person utterly unknown to most of us, I think. Thin, pale, intense, he had not been speaking many minutes before we were electrified by this man. I have been a connoisseur of speech-making for a quarter of a century, but never before, in any country, had I met a personality so terrifying in its dynamic force, so vituperative, so vitriolic. The words poured from him in a corrosive spate. He ridiculed our political system, he scarified our leading politicians, seizing upon their vulnerable points with a destructive analysis that left them bereft of merit or morality. We listened in a kind of frozen hypnotism to this cold, stabbing voice. There was the gleam of a Marat in his eyes, and his

eloquence took on a Satanic ring when he invoked the
rising wrath of his colleagues against the festering scum
that by cowardice and sloth had reduced the British
Empire to a moribund thing, in peril of annihilation.

When Joyce sat down, Cecil recalled, his white face was
'luminous with hate'. The chairman invited questions, but no
questions were forthcoming. Such a flood of vituperation had
paralysed the audience. 'I felt as if I had seen something unclean,'
Cecil concluded, 'so fearful in its cold frenzy that one blanched,
asphyxiated in so nauseous an atmosphere.' Moreover, the performance
at the Park Lane Hotel was Joyce in his more restrained
style, endeavouring to insinuate Fascism among the uncommitted
and the influential. His uncontrolled and vicious rhetoric before
assemblies of the faithful would have shocked the polite Park Lane
diners far more profoundly. This liberal bourgeoisie belonged to a
more genteel and sheltered society. Cecil Roberts and his kind
scarcely knew of the existence of such productions as the Deputy
Leader of the British Union of Fascists.

But Joyce had come too far in his pilgrimage to turn back. He
was to travel to the end upon the path marked out for him by
National Socialism and the saviour of Germany. Indeed, his own
influence was sufficient to persuade the BUF to change its name
early in 1936. Henceforth, it was to be the British Union of Fascists
and National Socialists. The extravagance of Joyce's abuse and his
utterances acquired a tone of *credo quia absurdum est*. It was as if the
more extreme and indefensible the moral expressions of Nazism,
the more he thrilled to its rhythms of infamy. Rumours, and later
allegations, suggested that he had used his British passport to attend
at least one of the Nuremberg rallies. His family, after his death,
denied that he had ever done so.

He remained at Mosley's side as the BUF lost the support of its
most influential followers, and as it increasingly employed its
members for the provocation of violence. Those areas of the East
End of London with large Jewish populations were the most easily
chosen targets for this. Mick Clarke and William Joyce pioneered
the soapbox oratory which led to fights and attacks, sometimes by
Fascists and sometimes by their opponents. Among the Jewish

population of these areas there was a section of the opposition which had no intention of submitting to Fascist aggression. Men like Barnet Becow and Jack Spot served gaol sentences for assault and grievous bodily harm respectively in cases where the targets were Mosley's followers.

A Special Branch report was made on Joyce by an officer who had infiltrated the BUF. In defiance of Mosley's warnings, Joyce was urging speakers to use language in attacking the Jewish community which would be strong enough to break the law. Arrests might rouse public sympathy for those who were thus apparently denied freedom of speech:

> On September 15th, William Joyce (Director of Propaganda) called together the principal Party speakers and delivered to them what amounted to a tirade against Jews and the attitude taken up by the Government on anti-Semitism. While he advised them to refrain from indulging in personal abuse of Jews... he exhorted them not to retreat in the face of Police persecution and declared that, if necessary, all Fascist speakers should be prepared to face imprisonment rather than comply with the dictum of the authorities that they were not to attack Jewry. Large scale arrests would, in his opinion, inevitably tend to intensify antagonism towards Jews.

The report added that in Mosley's absence a decision was taken to court prosecution by the delivery of a carefully prepared speech at a major rally, probably to be held on 4 October.

In the six years which followed his resignation as Chancellor of the Duchy of Lancaster, Mosley himself had passed from Labour minister to Fascist leader. In his uniform and riding-boots he now took the salute in the style of Hitler or Mussolini from an open car and inspected the detachments of his uniformed men drawn up in Hyde Park or near Tower Green. In October 1936, matters came to a head at the so-called Battle of Cable Street. He had planned a march for 4 October from the Royal Mint, through the East End, to Bethnal Green. His opponents, massed in Cable Street, were determined that he should not pass, and 6,000 police were needed to keep order and to make an attempt at clearing the way. In the end, it proved impossible to get through. The carefully-prepared speech that Joyce had in mind was never delivered. In Cable Street itself, the main battle took place between the police and the anti-Mosley faction. In the middle of such chaos, Sir Philip Game, Commissioner of Police, telephoned the Home Secretary for permission to order the cancellation of the march. Sir John Simon agreed and Mosley's squads withdrew to the Embankment, where their leader accused the government of surrendering to 'Red violence and Jewish corruption'.

It was by no means the end of violence in the East End, though the indications were that ordinary folk had grown sick of Fascists and Communists alike. An anti-Fascist march soon after the Cable Street incident was the occasion for Mosley's supporters to go on the rampage in the Mile End Road, smashing the windows of shops whose owners were Jewish and inflicting injury at random.

In a belated attempt to put a stop to such scenes, the government hurried the Public Order Bill through parliament, banning the wearing of uniforms such as the BUF had adopted. The appeal of the private army and the provocation it offered to others were eliminated as easily as that.

But 1936 brought its political excitements in other ways. There was the abdication crisis, in which Joyce and the Fascist movement supported Edward VIII and his right to marry whomsoever he chose. Joyce dismissed Baldwin and Archbishop Lang as a pair of 'hardened schemers', and taunted those who professed a religious objection to the King's marriage. 'Some stoutly affirmed that as Head of the Church of England he could not marry a divorced woman. Unless our recollection is at fault, the founder of this Church was Henry VIII, who had six wives. Of these, he executed two and divorced two in order to remarry.' Joyce's epitaph on Edward VIII recalled the King's visit to the South Wales valleys in November 1936, his dismay at the poverty and despair of mass unemployment, and his often-quoted words at the Bessemer Steel Works in Dowlais. '"Something must be done," he said, and it was done – to him.'

But the nation needed no assistance from the Fascist movement in taking sides over the King's cause. By the beginning of 1937,

Mosley and Joyce badly needed more evident public justification and legitimation of their policies. They had lost members and they had lost money by taking to the streets. No one in his senses supposed that a Fascist candidate could win a parliamentary seat. But, in the right areas, there might be a chance of victory in the municipal elections. Two candidates were put up in each of three boroughs, Bethnal Green, Limehouse, and Shoreditch, for the LCC elections of March 1937. Mosley kept aloof, as if reserving himself for better things, but Joyce stood with Jim Bailey, a furniture trader, for Shoreditch. None of the BUF candidates was elected and the Fascist vote in Shoreditch, at 14 per cent, was the lowest of all.

Joyce did not take his defeat gracefully when his turn came to speak after the result was announced. He stood, 'his expression grim... his hands to his sides.' In the manner which had stunned Cecil Roberts and the audience at the Park Lane Hotel, he denounced his opponents, shouting at them that they had turned the election into a thoroughly dirty fight. When he had done, he turned and marched away from the platform.

The Shoreditch election offered little encouragement but much worse was to follow. The election results had been announced on 6 March. Two weeks later Mosley called his principal supporters together. The party had 143 salaried staff, most of whom it could no longer afford to keep. The number would be reduced to thirty. Among those to be dismissed were William Joyce and John Beckett, Director of Publications. To say that Joyce took the news badly would be an understatement. All his personal dislike of Mosley was reanimated. Within a few weeks he had resigned from the party and become the founder of a new movement, the British National Socialist League. About sixty former members of the BUF joined him and the last phase of his career in English politics had begun. To the public at large, if not to the combatants on the right and left, it seemed that the high tide of British Fascism had come and gone. The division of the movement suggested this and the spectre of a resurgent Germany under Hitler's leadership made Fascism as alien as Bolshevism had been ten years before.

The Sorcerer's Apprentice

During the period between the Fascist ascendency of 1934 and the collapse of Mosley's hopes in March 1937, Joyce's personal life had undergone a change which seemed to be for the better.

In 1935, when his first marriage had ceased to exist in all but name, he met Margaret Cairns White. She was a pretty and vivacious brunette, who had been trained as a dancer. At twenty-two years old she was already a Fascist speaker and organiser at Manchester, though she had a full-time job as a secretary with Morton Sundour Fabrics. Her father was manager of a textile warehouse and Margaret Cairns White, her Fascist commitment apart, belonged to the aspiring middle-class of a great manufacturing city.

She and other party activists travelled to Dumfries to hear Joyce address a meeting on 7 February 1935. It was not love at first sight, but between the speaker and this member of his audience there developed a rapport that was fascination on her side and intense curiosity on his. She travelled to hear him at Kirkcudbright next evening, and to other meetings after that.

Joyce was no longer living with his first wife. He had moved into a flat, in Bramerton Street, Chelsea, with another member of the BUF, John Angus Macnab, the editor of *Fascist Quarterly* until 1937. 'A thin man with fierce blazing eyes behind thick glasses,' Rebecca West called him in 1945, 'a tiny fuzz of black hair fancifully arranged on his prematurely bald head, and wrists and ankles as straight as lead piping in their emaciation.' Temperamentally, he and Joyce had a similarity and a compatibility. Macnab had read classics at Oxford, and appreciated the range of Joyce's literary and linguistic knowledge, not least his ability to quote at will and to the point from Virgil and Homer.

Into this friendship, Margaret Cairns White made her entrance. It was at a time when Joyce had brought proceedings for divorce against his first wife, an action which ended in the dissolution of the marriage in 1936. In February of that year, Margaret came to London for a BUF meeting at the Albert Hall. It was a noisy but not a violent affair, the clashes between the Blackshirts and the Red Front outside being mainly verbal. Afterwards there was a party at a Mayfair house, to which Joyce ensured that the visitor was invited. There, in a manner that might seem offhand or peremptory, he explained that he was divorcing his wife and asked the girl to marry him.

Despite the unceremonious manner of the suggestion, she agreed that they should give the idea a try. She moved to Chelsea and waited for Joyce's divorce decree to become absolute. At last, on 13 February 1937, they were married at Kensington Registry Office. The apparent casualness of the alliance, and the stormy passages of their wartime life in Berlin, did not alter the resolve with which Margaret Joyce was to stand by her difficult husband in the most onerous and tragic phases of the eight years of life which remained to him.

A month after the wedding, he had lost the municipal election at Shoreditch and been dismissed as Director of Propaganda by Mosley. He had, it seemed, no job and no future except such as might be offered by his own National Socialist League.

The readiest means of making money was to fall back on private tutoring. In one sense it was an occupation that Joyce had never abandoned, for he had held classes in public speaking for members of the BUF. Until 1936 he had also continued to do a certain amount of coaching for the Victoria Tutorial College. After the wedding he and Margaret and Macnab moved to another flat, in Onslow Gardens, South Kensington, where the two men issued a prospectus and set themselves up as private tutors. The only specific suggestion of their pro-Nazi sympathies was in the presence of a large radiogram which filled their own rooms, and – more irritatingly – those of their neighbours, with the music of Wagner.

It was their intention to concentrate on foreign students learning the English language for professional examinations. Joyce insisted that coloured and Jewish students would not be accepted, if he had anything to do with it. Yet, as he revealed in one of his later outbursts, he did take Jewish pupils, perhaps without realising at first that they were so. His book *Twilight over England*, cites the case of a Jewish student who burst into tears when he discovered that he was only the second best and not the best in the list of those who had passed their medical exams. Why this should have been thought evidence of scurrility was known only to Joyce's peculiar logic. He did not explain nor enlarge upon the story.

Joyce was committed to providing for the two daughters of his first marriage, to whom he was a conscientious father, as well as supporting his second wife. Margaret had had a paid job with the BUF in the last few months of her membership but with Joyce's departure from the movement she had lost that as well. Now Joyce proposed to exclude from his tuition those pupils whose racial origin offended him and to take very little care about concealing his admiration of Hitler and his total commitment to National Socialism from those who came under his influence.

It was hard to see what future there could be for the embittered and ranting Nazi or his new and pretty wife, other than a steady descent into the poverty of hired rooms and unpaid bills. There was nothing to raise him from this unless world events should create the opportunity for him. But still there was his National Socialist League.

By any description, the National Socialist League sounds more like the germ of a situation-comedy than a serious political movement. When Joyce broke away from Mosley, he took with him Macnab, John Beckett the former ILP Member of Parliament, and about sixty Fascist supporters all told. But, as Mosley noted with satisfaction, these supporters were no more use to their new leader than they had been to the BUF. The numbers dwindled quickly. Before long, the entire National Socialist League consisted of about twenty people. There were no mass rallies attended by thousands of the enthusiastic or the curious. To judge from police reports, the average crowd at Joyce's street-corner speeches was not more than a dozen or twenty. It was more like a neighbourhood argument than a political address.

How, then, did the National Socialist League survive? It was not an easy matter to build the organisation upon the resources of ordinary men and women, as Joyce later revealed:

> We in the League lived National Socialism. As a small
> band, we were united in the struggle: and we were all
> poor enough to know the horrors of freedom in
> democracy. One of our members was driven mad by

> eighteen months of unemployment and starvation. We did
> what we could to help him but I am afraid it was little
> enough. I lived for months with real friends who loved
> England and could not get enough to eat from her.
> Unemployed members who had only two shillings a day
> came twelve miles by train to attend street corner
> meetings, or to undertake office duties, spent the surviving
> pennies on food, and walked home into the small hours of
> the morning in winter weather. These unknown men were
> great patriots. They all had the hope that out of their
> sacrifices a greater England would be born.

Joyce described the predicament of his followers, whose political obligations grew irreconcilable in the two remaining years of peace:

> The misery of these people was indescribable when it
> seemed to them that all their efforts would be cancelled by
> war between their country and Germany. They had family
> ties. Having been brought up as patriots, they were
> benumbed at the thought that there was to be a conflict
> between their country and all the beliefs that they held
> dear.

How, if this were a complete picture of the League's activities, did it survive at all? In the first place, there was one wealthy supporter and a long-time admirer of Joyce who had transferred his allegiance from Mosley to the new organisation. He was Alec Scrimgeour, an elderly and successful stockbroker, who lived with his sister Ethel in a fine house near Chichester. The old man was a cripple and in the last years of his life. But he and, after his death, his sister were genuinely attached to Joyce, through whom they had contributed to Mosley's organisation as a bulwark against Communism. Ethel Scrimgeour, 'a tall and handsome maiden lady given to piety and good works, whose appearance was made remarkable by an immense knot of hair twisted on the nape of her neck in the mid-Victorian way,' remained Joyce's friend to the last. She visited him when he was under sentence of death at Wandsworth and he wrote one of his last and most affectionate letters to her.

How much the National Socialist League benefited by the donations of this couple was never recorded. The Joyces and other leaders of the organisation were frequent guests at the Sussex house and at Miss Scrimgeour's cottage near Midhurst. Though no political movement could safely rely on one source of financial support, Joyce was able to issue a steering-wheel badge to members with the motto 'Steer Straight' as the emblem of the Nazi creed in England. He also put on sale a long pamphlet of his own, *National Socialism Now*, to justify his secession from Mosley and the new course he had chosen. Most important of all, there was enough money to set up an office as party headquarters at 190 Vauxhall Bridge Road.

The pamphlet appeared as a statement on behalf of an avowedly British organisation, with a preface by John Beckett introducing the author to his readers. Joyce reiterated the British character of his movement. He professed a true respect for 'the German Leader's gallant achievement against international Jewish finance and its other self – international Jewish Communism.' But there his overt support for Hitler right or wrong ended:

> I would gladly say, 'Heil Hitler!' and at once part
> company with him, realizing what a pitiable insult it is to
> such a great man to try to flatter him with an imitation
> which he has always disdained. His way is for Germany,
> ours is for Britain; let us tread our paths with mutual
> respect, which is rarely increased by borrowing.

With his well-practised sardonic glee, Joyce looked forward not only to the destruction of Jewry but denounced the 'dribbling old prelates, verminous Bloomsburgians, myopic printers' hacks, and every sort of meddlesome old woman, male and otherwise.' These had undermined the empire by their spineless pacifism and now showed their hypocrisy by demanding war against Germany. The pamphlet's twin pillars of policy were an alliance against the Soviet Union by Germany, Italy and Britain, and the abolition of parliamentary democracy in favour of a Fascist syndicalist state.

There was nothing in this which he had not advocated before. If his tone grew shriller, however, the words reached a dwindling audience. He cursed and denounced the left on the one hand and what he called the 'spoilt darlings' of fashionable society on the other. But as the months passed he was reduced to the expedient of holding his meetings in the street before small groups of the curious and the hostile. By 1938, however strongly he might protest that his was an English political creed, he was plainly identified with German Fascism. In his light-coloured trench-coat, cut as if to imitate Hitler, he became both the instigator and the magnet for casual brawling.

The pavement meetings of Hitler's English disciples resembled more accurately a noisy Pimlico pub turning out at closing time. Sardonic and chilling by turns, Joyce harangued a small and often antagonistic group of bystanders, protected himself by one or two stalwarts of the League. Stentorian and off-key, the few opponents dutifully raised their chorus. 'The workers' flag is deepest red' or 'The Internationale unites the human race'. As he struggled on, according to witnesses, there were shouts of 'Bloody well go and live in Germany, then, if you like it so much!' Presently the scuffles began. Sometimes blows were exchanged with effect, a battle from which Joyce never shrank and which he usually began. More often, when the police were in the area, the confrontation fizzled out in bad temper and verbal insults. The National Socialist League won few converts and lost most of its original members. It seems that new recruits were likely to have been the spies of political opponents or officers of the Special Branch. Only the war saved Joyce from declining into the crankiness and obscurity of those who, for instance, demanded in small newspaper advertisements and at Speakers' Corner why the bishops refused to open Joanna Southcott's box.

The will to violence was never absent. It took only one or two followers to give an impression of political might if the right means were chosen. And so, for example, a small National Socialist shop was opened in Park Street, Bristol, from which one or two members of the League sold rubber truncheons and daggers, as if arming a great revolutionary force for the day of democracy's overthrow.

Twice Joyce was prosecuted in the police courts. The first occasion was in the wake of the Czech crisis and the Munich agreement of 1938. Few people in England, outside the Fascist movements, retained any illusions about Hitler. He was the natural and inevitable enemy of their country and of its liberal democracy. On 17 November Joyce appeared on charges of assault before Paul Bennett, the magistrate of the West London Police Court. The incident arose from a street meeting of the National Socialist League, addressed by Joyce himself. When the police ordered him to end it, he complied at once, his half-dozen supporters singing the National Anthem as they invariably did at the conclusion of their gatherings. But there had been a certain amount of argument with the police and one National Socialist was arrested for obstructing the footway. Joyce went across to speak to the police officer on the man's behalf and, as he did so, was jostled by a heckler whom he disposed of with 'a tap on the head'. He used the stick which he habitually carried. The blow caused a minor cut.

When the case came to court, the magistrate evidently decided that it was impossible to say which party was to blame in a scuffle of this sort. He dismissed the charge.

On 22 May 1939, Joyce appeared at Westminster Police Court, charged this time with assault and offences against the Public Order Act. With five of his supporters he had tried to hold a street-corner meeting, heckled by a group of twenty onlookers, some of whom began to sing the 'Internationale'. As happened on almost every occasion when he tried to preach the gospel of Hitlerian Fascism, a man in the crowd suggested that if Joyce thought Nazi Germany such a wonderful place, he ought to go there instead of trying to import its political system into England. According to the prosecution evidence, Joyce then punched the heckler in the face. Joyce insisted that he had merely been trying to make his way through the group and had pushed the man in an attempt to get past. Once again the magistrate dismissed the case against him.

The principal interest of these court appearances is in the confirmation they give to the portrait of the National Socialist League in the last months of peace. In place of the 12,000 who had packed Olympia to hear Mosley, a dozen or twenty people – almost equal in number to the entire strength of the National Socialist League – gathered at street corners to heckle and jeer the embittered oratory of William Joyce in his Adolf Hitler mackintosh. It was not surprising that the police and the courts saw him not as a threat, scarcely even as a nuisance, but an eccentric example of English political freedom.

In Berlin, in 1940, Joyce looked back on these incidents and tried to explain the cause of the prosecutions for assault that had been brought against him. As usual, he could see the explanation only through the tunnel-vision of his racial obsessions:

> I had studied certain aspects of the law to some purpose. The Police Force of London was very anti-Jewish: but special measures were taken by Sir Samuel Hoare to enforce upon them the dire necessity of pampering the Israelites. Of the hundreds of meetings that I addressed, the Commissioner of Police had notes on every one. I was warned again and again by friendly police officers of some rank to slacken the pace: and I refused. All the circumstances of the last charge brought against me point to the probability that I was arrested at the urgent instance of the Home Office.

But despite the self-importance of the boast, the League no longer existed as much more than a figment of its leaders' fantasies. John Beckett, despite his gallant preface to *National Socialism Now*, resigned and joined another diminutive Fascist group. The headquarters of the League became a club where members could go for a drink and where Joyce served behind the bar. He was a prophet without honour and yet he had kept the purity of his belief unsullied. Though he continued to profess his patriotism as an Englishman and refuted the suggestion that he wanted to imitate Hitler, it was in Germany alone that his hope seemed capable of embodiment.

England had had its chance and had scorned him. There was a higher loyalty than mere nationalism. In that belief he was at one with the Communists. Better to choose National Socialism and Germany than England and liberal decadence.

To all who thought as Joyce did, the Munich crisis of 1938 had posed a problem of conscience that admitted only one solution. It is uncertain at what date Joyce knew the full details of his United

States citizenship by birth. He may have thought that his father spoke the truth in October 1922, 'We are all British, not American citizens.' But soon after his marriage to Margaret Cairns White in 1937, he told her that he was not British but American. Moreover, Quentin Joyce, his brother, had known for at least ten years that their father was American by naturalisation. It seems unlikely that William Joyce would not have known it at the same time. But like his father he took no satisfaction in the thought.

Repeating a five-year-old falsehood about his nationality, he applied for a one-year renewal of his passport on 24 September 1938 and, on this occasion, repeated what he now knew to be false – that he was British by birth. The extension was granted. He needed the means to get abroad as the nation drifted closer to war with Germany. When conscription was introduced, he could not plead a conscientious objection to war in general. At the same time, he would regard it as dishonourable to fight against Fascism in a war provoked, as he described it, by Jewry and international finance.

It was decided that the Joyces and John Macnab should leave for Dublin if war seemed imminent in September 1938. There was nothing illegal in this and, indeed, if Joyce's story of having been born in County Galway were accepted, he would merely be the returning exile. Once in Ireland, they could wait and see how the situation developed, either remaining there or finding a way to Germany in order to fight for National Socialism against Bolshevism.

Though passages were booked for Macnab and Margaret Joyce, who were to go first while Joyce settled their affairs in London, the tickets were never used. The return of Neville Chamberlain from Munich with his 'piece of paper' allowed them a respite but not a reprieve. Joyce was undismayed by the subjugation of the Czechs. To those who asked him what he thought of Hitler now, he replied, 'I think him a very fine fellow.'

By August 1939 it was clear that the respite had been all too brief. Nothing had gone well personally or politically. The income from private tutoring was falling and the Joyces were obliged to move to a basement flat near Brompton Cemetery. One or two of his friends and sympathisers began to take their departure for Germany while there was still time. One of them, Mrs Frances Eckersley, whose first husband had been German, left for Berlin. Joyce was to meet her and work with her again before she became one of the defendants in the trials of 1945. Macnab went on holiday to Berlin with a letter from Joyce to Christian Bauer, a contact whom they had made in London and who was said to be on good terms with Goebbels. Joyce wished to be assured by the Nazi Minister of Propaganda that there would be no difficulty in becoming a naturalised German subject. Macnab brought back a favourable reply from Berlin on 21 August.

On the same day the non-aggression pact between Germany and the Soviet Union was announced. Communists were later to justify this as Stalin's bid for time. Joyce accepted it as a necessary tactic by Hitler. As time grew short and the last days of peace slipped away, he began to make arrangements for his departure. Neville Chamberlain announced that the dispute between Germany and Poland over Danzig must be settled by legitimate negotiation. In the event of a German attack, Britain would stand by Poland.

First thing the next morning, 24 August, Joyce took his passport and the accompanying form to the National Bank in Belgravia, where the manager endorsed it. Once again, Joyce had declared himself to be a British citizen by birth. He went straight to the Passport Office and applied for another one-year renewal. While this was being granted, parliament was recalled in order to pass the Emergency Powers Act.

Joyce had no illusions about his fate in England once war began. Though he might seem a minor political nuisance, his name was on the list of those to be rounded up and interned. Not long before, meeting another member of the National Socialist League in the Fulham Road, Joyce revealed that the police were already watching him. The day before, while driving his car, he had been stopped and charged with some trivial traffic offence. His friend remarked that, 'All sorts of people get run in for motoring offences.' Joyce was scornful of the explanation. 'Do you call this a motoring offence? I would call it a holding offence!'

Perhaps it was. Possibly, as war drew closer, the police wanted some pretext to keep Joyce on their books. Then on the night of 24 August 1939 the phone rang in the Earls Court flat. An unnamed sympathiser informed Joyce that the Emergency Powers would become effective in two more days, on Saturday 26 August. It was possible that he would be detained and interned for the duration of the war which now seemed only hours or days away. There was hardly time to think carefully and logically of what to do. Next day, Margaret went down to Midhurst to inform Miss Scrimgeour that they proposed to leave the country. She took Joyce's revolver and buried it nearby.

Joyce called together such members as he could gather of the National Socialist League and its intellectual offshoot the Carlyle Club. He told them that as from 27 August the organisations would be dissolved. Only then did he disclose to John Macnab that he and Margaret were leaving for Germany next morning, 26 August, the day on which the powers of detention and internment would come into effect. He and Margaret went with their luggage to Victoria Station and booked single tickets to Berlin.

Though they might have been thought unwise to travel to Berlin in the worsening international crisis, they had done nothing illegal and there was no authority to stop them. The entire nation seemed caught between acceptance of war's inevitability and the hope that peace might somehow be sustained. As the Joyces waited at Victoria Station, the bookstalls were piled with that month's issue of *Vogue* magazine, urging holidaymakers to choose 'Germany – the Land of Hospitality'. The couple boarded the cross-Channel steamer at Dover for Ostend, while crowds returning in haste from the Continent streamed towards London, which was already a scene of departing evacuee children and sandbags mounting round government buildings. No one impeded or questioned the two fugitives. They crossed the Channel and landed in Belgium. There was a train waiting at the Gare Maritime of Ostend with a through carriage to Berlin, reached by a long overnight journey across the flat plains of northern Europe.

On the morning of Sunday 27 August they arrived at the Friedrichstrasse Station in the heart of the German capital. They were uninvited, unexpected, without a single close friend or any means of subsistence. They found a city where almost everything was closed on that Sunday in the warmth of late summer. Any suggestion of war seemed far removed. William L. Shirer, CBS correspondent in Berlin, noted in his diary that it was another hot weekend in a summer which had had more than its usual share of them. Most Berliners made for the network of lakes surrounding the city, the waterside promenades and the pleasure steamers, putting from their minds the threat of European conflict. While the Joyces stood, apprehensive and bewildered, under the glass of the Friedrichstrasse terminus, the citizens of their adopted country streamed out of the old imperial station at Wannsee, across the road to the low cliffs with their Italianate villas, cafés, and a view across tranquil water to the wooded shores and palaces of Potsdam.

The news in the *Berliner Zeitung* that day was of German families fleeing from persecution in Poland and German civil aircraft fired on by the Poles. At any moment, the propagandists assured their readers, there would be naked aggression by the Polish army against the territory of the Third Reich.

As it happened, there was still a week of peace to run. William and Margaret Joyce had not even now committed themselves irrevocably. They might yet change their minds and return to England, indeed they soon thought of doing so. But in a few more months, Joyce wrote his apologia and made it clear that despite their apparent freedom of choice, there was in reality only one decision that he could have taken:

For my part, the decision was easy to make. To me it was clear on the morning of August 25th that the greatest struggle in history was now doomed to take place. It might have been a very worthy course to stay in England and incessantly work for peace: but I had one traditionally acquired or inherited prejudice, which many will think foolish and which may be logically difficult to defend. England was going to war. I felt that if, for perfect reasons of conscience, I could not fight for her, I must give her up for ever. Such an argument I do not commend to anybody else, but man is guided by more than reason alone, and in this great conflict, I wanted to play a clear and definite part. In small matters, it is easy enough to be guided by conventional loyalty. In great matters, a man has the right to hold himself responsible to Higher Justice alone.

With this message already composed in his mind, William Joyce picked up the suitcases and led his wife from the echoing terminus of glass and iron. They came at last, in the warm Sunday stillness, to the broad avenues of central Berlin.

Part Two

BERLIN

Men in exile feast upon hope and fear.
> Aeschylus, *The Agamemnon*

CHAPTER 7

Joyce had remained consistent to his promise given at the time of the publication of *National Socialism Now* two years earlier. 'If war breaks out, I will fight for Hitler since such a war would be against Jewry.' But it was still not certain that war would come and, moreover, the reality of Berlin was less appealing than the romantic challenge seen from a basement flat in Earl's Court.

Not far from the Friedrichstrasse station was the Potsdamer Platz, a great conjunction of tramways, tree-lined islands, and major thoroughfares. Its famous traffic tower was surrounded by the heavy façades of department stores and grand hotels, and the pavement pitches of flowersellers. Even to this hub of metropolitan life the afternoon calm extended. Just off the square, in the quieter area of the Saarlandstrasse, the Joyces found a hotel and booked a room. The entire district now lies buried under a stretch of the Berlin wall and its field of fire, except for the name of the Potsdamer Platz immediately on the western side.

Berlin showed far less sign of preparing for war than London, except in one particular which made life a good deal more difficult for its visitors. On the day of their arrival, it was announced that food rationing would be introduced. Ration cards were to be available next day and without these it would be impossible for the Joyces to stay. Meanwhile, there was evidence that despite the calm in the capital itself, war was being prepared elsewhere. By Monday morning the streets of the city were busy with removal vans and grocery trucks which had been commandeered by the government. They were filled with troops, moving east towards the Polish frontier.

The Germans themselves, reported William Shirer, seemed glum and resentful at the prospect of war. Only 500 people assembled

Berlin

before the Chancellery on 29 August to hear Hitler's speech, most standing 'grim and silent'. The announcement of rationing had done much to depress their spirits, promising years of deprivation and misery. Too many of them had clear memories of the last war to relish another. In the Wilhelmstrasse, a procession of diplomats, including the British Ambassador, Sir Neville Henderson, came and went with their instructions.

At the beginning of the week the official announcements from the German Foreign Office took the view that war might still be avoided. Despite Poland, the common sense of European statesmen must prevail. Then, at midnight on Tuesday, Hitler announced the formation of a Ministerial Council for the Defence of the Reich, under the presidency of Hermann Goering. This was, in effect, a war cabinet. 'The sands are running fast tonight,' wrote Shirer in his diary.

Joyce met his German contact in the Ministry of Propaganda, Christian Bauer, who was optimistic over finding employment for him so long as there was no war. If war should break out, however, the Joyces would both be interned for the duration as enemy aliens. They were thunderstruck by this revelation. Not for a moment had they considered the possibility. Surely those who extended the hand of ideological comradeship to the Third Reich would not be treated in such a manner? They were soon assured of the truth. Their flight to the aid of National Socialism seemed doomed to failure and fiasco, whether in London or Berlin.

On Monday they had lunch with Mrs Eckersley at the Hotel Continentale, where she was staying. She gave them the name of a friend in the German Foreign Office, Dr Schirmer, whom they might approach. But after forty-eight hours of Berlin the Joyces had lost their nerve. On Tuesday, they decided that the most sensible course must be to return to London. That morning they went to a travel agent in the Unter den Linden to buy tickets, having only booked a single journey from London. But they had left it too late. The travel agencies were not prepared to take Reichsmarks for journeys to be made beyond the German frontier. It was a quirk of financial prudence that attended the coming of a great war. The Joyces had changed all their money into Reichsmarks and had no means of buying tickets. They had travelled to Berlin merely in order to join the queue of refugees trying to get home.

Advised by the clerk, they walked down the Unter den Linden to the British Embassy. Like others who visited the embassy that day, they found the hallway full of luggage, packed and labelled for England. No one seemed to know what the situation was or what was going on but the diplomats, at least, had prepared for the worst. An official informed Joyce that he had, in any case, come to the wrong place. Repatriation was not the concern of the embassy, they must go to the British Consulate, a little distance away on the other side of the Brandenburg Gate. They hurried there but the consulate could offer no assistance. Joyce was now informed that since his problems concerned travel outside Germany, he must first take a train as far as Cologne and go to the consulate there.

By any reasonable interpretation of the advice they were receiving, it was clear that the Joyces were trapped in Berlin. The attack on Poland was less than forty-eight hours away and no one any longer doubted that there must be war. To travel to Cologne might well be to find that the battlefront between Germany and the western Allies had already been established just beyond the city. There was certainly no guarantee that the British Consulate there would be able to offer help. Even if the couple got to the city before war began, it was unlikely that they would get out before the trains stopped running to the Channel ports.

Wednesday was the last day when Berlin retained some appearance of a great capital at peace. Unlike London, there were no evacuees and no sandbags. On Thursday, however, the telephone links to England, France and Poland were cut. The German radio announced at 9 p.m. that Hitler's proposals to the Polish government had been rejected. He had, of course, ensured this by demanding the presence of a Polish envoy to discuss them in Berlin before it would have been possible for anyone to get there.

On Thursday, the Luftwaffe gunners began putting anti-aircraft batteries in place along the main axial road running east to west through the Tiergarten, to protect the Chancellery and the Reichstag against bombardment. Earlier that morning, the German attack on Poland had begun.

To William Joyce, the news made little difference. Having tried to arrange repatriation and found it hopeless, he was resigned to whatever future faced him in Germany. He and Margaret had gone from the consulate to a bar in the Friedrichstrasse. There they drank beer and vodka, and decided to take their chance in Berlin. It seems doubtful that they could have done otherwise. They had hesitated too long and were regarded with suspicion by those British officials who might have helped them but thought, perhaps, that two people who deliberately set out for Berlin in the last week of August 1939 deserved all that they got.

The number of people whom they knew personally in Berlin could have been counted on the fingers of one hand. They had no ration cards for buying food and, in any case, their money would last only a little while. Apart from the wad of Reichsmarks that Joyce had acquired at the *bureau de change*, they had nothing at all. By living in a hired room somewhere, they might spin out their financial resources a little longer. Even before the money ran out, they would probably be interned as enemy aliens.

In all his self-justifications, Joyce talked of having come to Germany to fight for the new order against Bolshevism and Jewry. He had not intended to offer his abilities specifically as a propagandist, more probably to seek active service of some kind. But his two immediate concerns were to find a room and a job. In both quests he was luckier than he had expected. He and Margaret found lodgings near the Friedrichstrasse with a German couple who put new-found friendship before national differences. Mrs Eckersley had also given Joyce the telephone number of a German Foreign Office department which required English translators. This was freelance work, paid by the hour, and consisted mainly of translating German propaganda into English. Joyce began this at once, before war between the two countries had been declared, though after the attack on Poland was launched. Indeed, those Berliners to whom he spoke could see nothing but futility in an Anglo-German conflict over Poland. In the hours that followed the announcement of the attack, they seemed convinced that Hitler had triumphed in the east without provoking war in the west. There was nothing the English or the French could do to save Poland. Surely, then, they would not precipitate hostilities?

'During the critical 48 hours which preceded 11 a.m. on 3 September 1939,' wrote Joyce, 'not one of the people whom I met in Berlin could conceive that Britain would go to war with Germany. I told them that they were mistaken.'

By then Joyce was committed to the German cause. He had already done his first translation of one of Hitler's speeches into English. Then came Sunday 3 September and the news which, it was later argued, turned political preference into high treason:

> At twenty minutes past twelve Central European time, my landlady rushed into my room and told me 'Jetzt ist es Krieg mit England!' It's war now with England! Her husband at once came in and shook hands with my wife and myself, saying, 'Whatever happens, we remain friends.' We had known these simple people only since the previous day, they had no proof that I too was not an enemy, but their action was typical of the whole attitude of the German people.

That most German people did not want war with England was true by almost every account of neutral witnesses. Joyce and his wife went out into sunlit streets of Berlin on that Sunday afternoon to see what further news they could gather. The men and women whom they encountered showed neither hostility towards their new enemies nor enthusiasm for a great patriotic war:

> At about 3 in the afternoon, the first newspapers announcing England's declaration of war were on the streets. They were given away free. Under the bridge outside the Friedrichstrasse Station, we all scrambled for papers. There was no sign of anger or hatred: people looked at each other as if the incredible had happened.

Later that afternoon the Joyces were the guests of a descendant of Prince von Bülow, whom they had encountered in London:

> We talked of England: and my host was so inspiring in his eloquence on the subject of what England might have achieved in friendship with Germany that, as I looked out

on the twilight enshrouding the Kurfürstendamm, I could
think of nothing to say but Marlowe's famous lines:

> *Cut is the branch that might have grown full strait*
> *And burnèd is Apollo's laurel bough!*

Despite the orator and prophet of National Socialism, there
lingered in the new Germano-Fascist personality of William Joyce
the shade of the clever and nervous undergraduate, bright and
enthusiastic, to whom the scattered gems of his own literature
clung forever. He saluted as the great pioneer of National
Socialism not Friedrich Nietzsche nor Oswald Spengler, certainly
not Hitler nor Mussolini, but the embattled genius of Thomas
Carlyle. His comments on the great world conflict were studded
with quotations from Marlowe and Dryden, Milton and Tennyson.
In that respect also he was unmistakably Hitler's Englishman.

Joyce, of course, accepted the explanations of Nazi propagandists for the outbreak of hostilities. It was Poland who had initiated them by repeated acts of racial and territorial aggression. The Wehrmacht, he later wrote, had crossed the frontier in response to the occupation of the German radio station at Gleiwitz on 31 August by 'a band of Polish desperadoes.... Now it was clear that unless the German troops marched at once, not a man, woman or child of German blood within the Polish territory could hope to avoid persecution and slaughter.' The die had been cast, and all that Germany stood for – admirable as well as abominable – entered into his soul. For the first time, he claimed to be of German descent:

> Apart from my absolute belief in National Socialism and
> my conviction of Hitler's superhuman heroism, I had
> always been attracted to Germany. Perhaps the attraction
> was due to the German blood which flowed in the veins
> of some of my ancestors; it was no doubt helped by my
> veneration for the genius of men like Wagner and Goethe.
> Perchance my studies in Germanic Philology did much to
> make me aware of racial bonds that time and money have
> obscured. Whatever the reason may be, I grew up with
> that mystical attraction which has ended by my making
> Germany my permanent home.

Joyce wrote this early in 1940 and it was understandable that he should exaggerate, in retrospect, the part which German culture had played in his life. The strains of Wagner had certainly filled those rented rooms in Earl's Court or South Kensington, to the annoyance of the neighbours, though like his practical study of the German language they belonged only to the period of Hitler's influence upon him. When he sought to justify National Socialism generally – the creed of the rubber truncheon and the dagger from the little shop in Park Street – he was still apt to do so by the incongruous example of Thomas Carlyle.

So far as the timing of his escape to Germany was concerned, Joyce had hardly moved too soon. In London, the day after war was declared, two policemen arrived to question John Macnab and search his flat. Having also tried and failed to find Joyce, they asked Macnab where he was. Macnab showed them a postcard, sent to him by Joyce from Berlin a few days before. Miss Scrimgeour had received one at the same time.

Apart from a day trip to Boulogne in 1937, there is no evidence that Joyce had ever travelled abroad since his arrival in England from Ireland in 1921. In that case, he adapted to his new situation with remarkable speed. Mrs Eckersley's friend at the German Foreign Office, to whom he now offered his services as a full-time employee, passed him on to Dr Erich Hetzler, private secretary to the Nazi Foreign Minister, von Ribbentrop, whom Joyce was rather ungratefully to refer to in future as 'Ribbentripe'.

Hetzler saw in Joyce an intelligent and dedicated recruit to the Nazi cause, though it was unlikely that he could be found a job in any of the ministries. However, in the process of being passed from one office to another Joyce was making contacts who might prove of some use. They were names to be dropped. But his round of departments in the Wilhelmstrasse was cut short. Hetzler recommended him to Walter Kamm, head of English language broadcasting, as a possible announcer on the foreign service of Reichsrundfunk.

As it happened, Walter Kamm almost dismissed Joyce after the first audition. William Shirer, whose CBS broadcasts went out from the Rundfunkhaus, noted in his diary that Goebbels's Ministry of Propaganda thought the drawling nasal voice 'wholly unfit for broadcasting'. He was saved by a radio engineer who had studied in England and who happened to be monitoring the audition. He insisted that this was a voice with characteristic qualities which might be exploited to some purpose on the air. He was soon proved right, as the numbers of those listening to him in England equalled two-thirds of the audience for the BBC news. Shirer, like many others who knew Joyce, saw the irony of the situation. After a year of Joyce's performances, Shirer wrote, 'On the radio, this hard-fisted, scar-faced young Fascist rabble-rouser sounds like a decadent old English blue-blooded aristocrat of the type familiar on our stage.'

Though Joyce was soon to be one of the best-known radio voices of the entire war, there was no guarantee that his sardonic and ranting denunciations before rallies of the faithful could ever be subdued into a radio technique. Roosevelt's 'fireside' chats to the American people had already demonstrated that broadcasting as a persuasive agent worked best at a quiet and confidential level of address. By such means it could win trust and acceptance of ideas that would seldom have stood a chance when presented through public oratory. Hitler intimidated by rant and anger. Churchill inspired but also unnerved his listeners at the same time by painting the prospects of the armed struggle in darker and more dramatic tones than might seem necessary or desirable. Joyce managed to develop and moderate his style of vituperative public rhetoric. He might have been a natural broadcaster but for the quality of his scripts. He became not so much a propagandist as a radio 'character' who had been created by a darker comedy than Tommy Handley's ITMA.

On 19 September 1939, a fortnight after the declaration of war, William Joyce was formally appointed as an 'editor and speaker' for the Reichsrundfunk at Berlin-Charlottenburg – the German transmitters for Europe. He had found his place in the 'new order' with unexpected ease.

By the time that his German State Workbook was issued on 4 October, Joyce and his wife had moved from the busy Friedrichstrasse area to the semi-wooded suburban avenues of Charlottenburg. They were eventually to settle more or less permanently in a pleasant apartment in the Kastanienallee – 'Chestnut Avenue'. It was close to the main studios of Reichsrundfunk in Charlottenburg's Masurenallee. The street in which Joyce found their flat led north from the long wooded undulations of the main axial road that runs to the west from the centre of Berlin. It was near to the smart stores and little shops of Westend. There were bars where the exiles of the foreign service could gather, English and Irish among them. In the mild autumn of the phoney war, it was a prosperous and agreeable neighbourhood in which to live.

When he provided the details to be entered in his Workbook, Joyce's past career sounded as impressive as his future was promising. He had been a lecturer at Victoria Tutorial College for nine years from 1926. From 1933 until 1937 he had been Director of Propaganda and Deputy Leader of the British Union of Fascists. Best of all, from 1937 until 1939 he had been 'Leader, British National Socialist Party, London, England'. Ludicrous though the description might sound in print, for an organisation that had never numbered more than sixty followers and had rarely mustered more than twenty, it was strictly accurate and hardly to be dismissed by a regime uniquely devoted to National Socialism. To his hosts, it must have seemed a possibility, at least, that in William Joyce they had their most important catch of all the queer fish at Charlottenburg.

Perhaps the most interesting entry made by Joyce in his Workbook related to his place of birth and nationality. Despite his boasts of political eminence in England, the Leader of the British National Socialist Party had a dread of being bundled off to internment in Silesia as an undesirable alien. Therefore, he must stick to the same story and tell the same lie as when he had applied for his British passport. To alter that story would offer a discrepancy to the bureaucratic mind, making him a liar in the past and a suspect now. So, for at least the fourth time, he told the mortal untruth. He was a British citizen, born at Galway.

The web was so finely woven that he had no way forward but by continuing the deceit. Perhaps it scarcely mattered to him.

Berlin

Poland was conquered and the other fronts were quiet. It was still possible that the second great war of the century might end in a grudging peace.

Since the police visit to John Macnab on 4 September 1939, the British authorities knew that William Joyce was in Germany. Though his journey had been imprudent, it was still not in itself treasonable. Had he been interned until the end of the war in Tost or one of the other civilian camps, he would probably have faced no charges.

There was one man who soon put that out of the question. Albert Hunt was an inspector in Scotland Yard's Special Branch. In 1934 he had been detailed to keep the British Union of Fascists under surveillance. Subsequently he kept watch on Joyce's National Socialist League, even to the extent of infiltrating it as a member. Since the membership rapidly dwindled, there is a surreal possibility that the number of those planted by the police or the Communist party may have equalled or outnumbered the genuine British Nazis.

At the beginning of the war, Inspector Hunt was sent to Folkestone to vet potential spies who might enter the country across the English Channel, from neutral Belgium and Holland. On a date which he could not subsequently remember but which was before 3 October 1939, he was tuning in his radio, when he heard a familiar voice. He had no doubt that it was William Joyce. 'He has got a voice I would recognise again,' said Hunt laconically. Though the inspector made no note of the time nor the wavelength of the broadcast, he remembered its contents. Joyce was informing his listeners of a massive air strike by Luftwaffe bombers against the Kent coast. The towns and ports of Dover and Folkestone had been destroyed.

This was the broadcast which was, as a matter of legal technicality, to put the hangman's rope round Joyce's neck. Yet Hunt could not say what station the broadcast came from nor upon which date it was transmitted. As propaganda, it was a self-defeating absurdity. Not a single German bomb had fallen anywhere in the British Isles since war had been declared. The first solitary bomb fell in the Orkneys in October 1939. If Hunt's account is correct, his identification of the voice based upon years of listening to Joyce's street-corner oratory, then the blackest irony of Lord Haw-Haw's career was to die for such rubbish as this. 'To die for faction is a common evil,' said one of Joyce's most-quoted English poets, John Dryden, 'But to be hanged for nonsense is the devil.' Apart from the destruction of the Channel ports, the greatest amusement of 1939 for English listeners lay in the increasingly desperate claims of the German radio to have sunk the aircraft-carrier *Ark Royal*, the only modern carrier in the Royal Navy at the outbreak of war. She was indeed torpedoed by a German submarine, but that was two years after the claim that she had been sunk in September 1939.

For the time being, Joyce remained a prisoner of the scripts approved by Goebbels's Ministry of Propaganda. It was not likely that a man who had come to Germany only a few weeks before would be given *carte blanche* to say what he liked. He was still under the shadow of a more famous British broadcaster in Berlin, Norman Baillie-Stewart, an officer of the Seaforth Highlanders who had been court-martialled and sent to prison for five years in 1933 for selling military secrets to Germany. Baillie-Stewart had renounced his British citizenship before the war and applied for German naturalisation, a gesture which was to save his life in 1946. But though he continued to broadcast for the Nazis throughout the war, he was never to match the growth in fame of the new arrival at Charlottenburg.

Hunt was not alone in picking up the broadcasts that Joyce now made from the Reichsrundfunk studios, relayed through Hamburg, Zeesen and Bremen. But as the newsreader's voice became more familiar to listeners, so he acquired an individual reputation. The nasal tone produced by the badly-set broken nose easily became a sneer at times. It sounded to some as though he might be a languid and disdainful aristocrat. As early as 14 September 1939, Jonas Barrington in the *Daily Express* described this voice that called from Germany, though in the first instance it probably belonged to Norman Baillie-Stewart: 'He speaks English of the haw-haw, dammit-get-out-of-my-way-variety, and his strong suit is gentlemanly indignation.' On 18 September 'Lord Haw-Haw of Zeesen' was formally christened in the same newspaper, the name soon becoming exclusively attached to the tones of William Joyce. In radio music-hall, the Western Brothers introduced a new comic song on the topic of 'Lord Haw-Haw of Hamburg'.

For the time being, the newspapers and the radio listeners were content to regard the voice as belonging to a monocled ass of the Bertie Wooster type, though some felt this to be an unfair reflection on Wodehouse's hero. But whoever he was, he provided the first public anti-German joke since the war began. On 24 September, in the *Daily Mirror*, 'Cassandra' urged his readers to listen to the comic capers of the Nazi propagandist.

On the basis of his own evidence, Inspector Hunt identified the broadcasts by William Joyce before 3 October 1939. The Special Branch had known for some weeks that he was in Germany. Yet in the first autumn of the war he seemed neither a famous traitor nor an infamous war criminal. He was, and he remained for the time being, a figure of comic relief.

But while these public performances continued to the general amusement of the audience, Joyce was dedicating himself more earnestly and more narrowly to the triumph of National Socialism in the world struggle. His intellectual abilities, his ambition, his energy, put him in a class above colleagues like Baillie-Stewart or Mrs Eckersley. Alone among them, he appreciated the full potential of radio as the means to insinuate doubt and disaffection among his listeners. Though he was to fail in his exploitation of this, it was not for want of seeking to undermine national self-confidence through sardonic innuendo or weaken the will to resist by boasts of the invincible military initiative now held by the Wehrmacht. He was wise enough in his broadcasts to refrain from one tactic, the inspiration of that chill fear which some of his political ranting achieved in the 1930s. To the targets of those terrible promises, there could have been no course but resistance at any price.

Christmas 1939 brought the first recognition by his superiors of the service he had performed. After a dinner at the famous Kaiserhof Hotel, chosen because Hitler had made it his headquarters before he came to power, the Joyces went back to a party at the Reichsrundfunk building. Among the presents on the table, personally addressed to him, were boxes of cigars from Goebbels and from Goering. Within three months, the refugee from England had become the known and acknowledged assistant of two of the greatest powers in the land.

By this time Joyce had also taken the final and logical step of applying for German citizenship on behalf of his wife and himself. It was unlikely that he would have been refused, now that he had acquired such patrons and had shown the service that he might offer his adopted country. On the other hand, the process was protracted and inefficient. Norman Baillie-Stewart had suffered three years of bureaucratic delay while his application was passed from one office to another and back again. Joyce did not suppose that German nationality would protect him in the event of a Nazi defeat. It was, rather, a matter of showing the world where his loyalty lay. He had already and deliberately defaced his own British passport and Margaret's. Whatever the outcome, there was to be no going back.

As if embracing the limbo of the stateless person, Joyce called himself Wilhelm Froelich, the surname 'Joyful' being a pun upon his own. William Shirer, the CBS correspondent in Berlin, attended the Rundfunk party, finding a big Christmas tree set up in one of the offices, where 'the people were dancing and making merry with champagne... Lord Haw-Haw, the British traitor who goes here by the name of Froelich, but whose real name is William Joyce and whose voice millions of English listen to on the radio every night, and his English wife were at the party, but I avoided them.'

Shirer was later to meet Joyce under more adverse circumstances, finding him more likeable and a good deal braver than he had supposed. But for the moment his comments revealed that there was no longer the least doubt as to which of the contending voices on the Reichsrundfunk had acquired the title and character of Lord Haw-Haw. Norman Baillie-Stewart, Joyce's early rival, had been found 'too unbending' by his masters in the Ministry of Propaganda. They found him a job as a Foreign Office translator.

As the cold Berlin winter turned to early spring in 1940, the joke of Lord Haw-Haw ceased to be quite so amusing. On the other hand, even those who listened with loathing or contempt found it easier to have a real man with whom the sneering drawl could at last be identified. While the new medium of radio offered obvious advantages to the propagandist, it also enabled the listener to bring into sharp focus the object of his derision or hatred.

That sharpness of personal antagonism was also to draw the rope a little tighter round the throat of the sneering presence that filled the air in millions of English homes.

CHAPTER 8

In the first six or seven months of the war, as the English listener combed the airwaves, or tuned his set from one programme to another, he was almost certain to hear incongruous voices. The most common experience was to pick up a programme that had already begun and to discover English voices engaged in a pastiche music-hall dialogue between the comic and the straight man. There were two performers of this kind who went by the names of Schmidt and Smith. One was a shrewd well-informed German, the other a monocled ass of British stage farce:

SMITH Well now, old man, tell me about this war of yours.

SCHMIDT My dear Smith, I don't know all about it and it isn't ours.

SMITH Don't get cross. I mean, after all, Hitler started it, didn't he?

SCHMIDT Who declared war on Germany?

SMITH Well, of course, actually we did. But you see we are solemnly pledged to defend the independence of Poland. We couldn't back out, you know.

SCHMIDT I see. And if I'm not mistaken you promised to give the Poles full military support, should they become involved in a military conflict with Germany.

SMITH Yes, old chap. I'm glad to find one German who really understands.

SCHMIDT I'm sorry but I just don't understand. I want to know how many troops and how many planes you sent to the assistance of Poland before she completely collapsed. I mean, what did you actually do to save your gallant little ally?

SMITH I don't know about that. But I do know that my income tax has gone up to 7s. 6d. in the pound, and I suppose we aren't making all these sacrifices for nothing.
SCHMIDT My good old John Bull, let us stick to the point if we can. Do you know that on the second day of the war in Poland, Smigly-Rysz wanted to surrender, but the British ambassador in Warsaw told him that hundreds of your planes were on their way to help him, laying Germany in ruins *en route*?

Only at the end of the broadcast was it announced that the political comedy came from Radio Hamburg or Bremen, both of which relayed the scripts from Charlottenburg. By then the listener had been intrigued and, quite possibly, amused by the exchanges between the cosmopolitan, politically educated German and the well-fed but obtuse English bourgeois. The premise of these sketches was that the two men had been friends before the war and, meeting on neutral ground in a Swiss hotel, they now sat down to discuss the conflict and the world situation. The fact that England, not Germany, declared the war was frequently mentioned. So was the manner in which the British government first 'encouraged' the Poles to fight and then abandoned them to their fate.

These dialogues were a main feature of the output from the Reichsrundfunk at Charlottenburg between the outbreak of war and the fall of France. They were carefully wedded to the main themes of Nazi propaganda but unlike the later broadcasts they also set out in some degree to entertain the audience. Though Smith was caricatured as a fathead with more money than patriotism, the very extravagance of the portrayal made him amusing to English listeners. That Joyce had a hand in these scripts, if not as sole author, is strongly supported by the particular topics from English life that were chosen. Some of these, like his obsession with agricultural self-sufficiency, were parallelled in his book *Twilight over England*, which he wrote during the winter of 1939–40, as well as in his own radio talks.

The first dialogue, in which the outbreak of war was discussed, was broadcast on 26 October 1939. BBC audience research found that most listeners thought the contents funny and even appreciated the mockery of their own leaders, but that they were not persuaded by the clever Schmidt.

On 9 December 1939 the subject of the dialogue was rationing in Germany. Its recollection of poverty in Shoreditch – the scene of his campaign in the municipal elections of 1937 – echoes Joyce's experience of England:

SCHMIDT   As a German, I'm glad to think we have rationing at present. It prevents people like you buying everything up.
SMITH   People like me? What the blazes do you mean?
SCHMIDT   Don't be annoyed. I only meant people with plenty of money.
SMITH   Oh, did you now? Well, let me tell you, my good fellow, that I'm a damned poor man – and this new income tax is going to make things worse.
SCHMIDT   Now, my good Smith, I have been in England – down in Shoreditch, you know – and I never thought that the English poor could afford to spend months in fairly expensive Swiss hotels. As for income tax, you had better complain to those who led you into this war.

Throughout the months of these broadcasts there were recurrent themes in the dialogues. England had started the war by its declaration of hostilities against Germany. England had deserted the Poles when the fighting began. It was the ordinary people of England who were suffering deprivation, while the rich found ways to avoid sharing the burden. Smith is shown moving his money out of England to the safety of New York. Despite the success of his investments in British companies like Neverfly Aircraft, the war is costing people like him 'a pretty penny'. By the spring of 1940, he lives in fear of the emergence of a Fifth Column, 'Those Gestapo fellows who wander round foreign countries disguised as Chinamen and all that sort of thing.' When Schmidt reproves him for his indifference to social change, Smith protests that 'socialists don't behave like gentlemen'. And so far as the unemployed and the poor are concerned, he has a simple answer: 'I've got my cash and I'm going to hang on to it. I'm one of the lucky people, that's all.'

In the broadcast of 25 March 1940 the exchanges between the two characters are more heated. As Schmidt advocates the benefits of National Socialism, Smith exclaims with horror, 'You're Bolshevik!' 'And you're losing the war,' retorts the wise Schmidt quietly.

In that quiet, sardonic response as surely as in the references to Shoreditch, unemployment, the betrayal of British agriculture, the parasites of 'Stock Exchange, public schools, and all that – huntin' and fishin' type', the style of William Joyce was recognisable. The dialogues were sometimes less than half truth and sometimes more. As propaganda their greatest effect was in undermining British confidence in the ruling class and the rich, who were having a very comfortable war in the view of Schmidt.

That, at least, was something with which many English observers might have agreed. J. B. Priestley paid an unwelcome visit to Bournemouth and published his findings in *Picture Post* on 21 June 1941: 'If you have money, you have a choice of many large comfortable hotels. The shops still look opulent, and thousands of well-dressed women seemed to be flitting in and out of them.' The magazine published a set of photographs of well-stocked shop-windows with the caption: 'One of those places where they hardly know there's a war on.' Despite the general deriding of Lord Haw-Haw, he knew how to touch upon a sensitive nerve of class rivalry.

On 25 March 1940, those English listeners who heard the quiet scorn in the words 'You're losing the war' at least had cause to stop and ponder them. England might not be losing the war but, just as surely, there was no sign that she was winning it or ever would. A stalemate and virtual cease-fire on the western front had lasted for six months. No one, it seemed, wanted to fight. Were not negotiation and peace still possible?

With the coming of war, the radio became the principal source of public information upon which such thoughts turned. Moreover, the events of world news assumed an unprecedented importance in the lives of individuals. There were fears of death from the sky by bombs and poison gas, reinforced by the building of shelters and the issue of gas-masks. Such horrors would be sudden and random as the thunderbolts of the ancient gods. There were soon fears of another kind for those who had passed into captivity in Germany. The BBC was censored by the government but perhaps the lack of information might be made good by Radio Hamburg. Goebbels's Ministry of Propaganda played up to this by reading out occasional lists of prisoners-of-war and, more chillingly in Joyce's broadcasts after Dunkirk, announcing which English towns were to be destroyed next.

It was hunger for information, and perhaps reassurance, that guaranteed an audience for foreign broadcasts. But the richest chance for propaganda still lay some months in the future. For Joyce there were few events of consequence to comment upon, except England's folly in beginning the war and her betrayal of Poland. He was reduced to discussions of United States fiscal policy, which must have lost him a good many English listeners. The dialogues of Smith and Schmidt were still popular but these were lightweight by his standards of political debate. His talents were underemployed. It was in these circumstances, in the Berlin snows of January 1940, that he sat down to write his major political work.

In the event, *Twilight over England* was no more than 50,000 words long but it encapsulated all his contempt for the old capitalist order and his corrosive anti-Semitism, which had so far been excluded from the bulk of the broadcasts. Because the Soviet Union was a new-found friend of the Third Reich, overt denunciations of Communism were not welcome. So Joyce trained his vituperation on the corrupt and rotten capitalist system. In consequence, much of the narrative reads like the private obsession of an anti-Semitic Communist. The book was written in three weeks for a fee of 10,000 marks paid by the German Foreign Office. It was to be published in Berlin, in English, and the print-run was to be 100,000 copies.

Twilight over England is far more a personal revelation than either historical analysis of the past or political diagnosis of the present. The result is obsessive without being consistent. It reads like some curious attempt to write history with the sonority or sweep of

Macaulay, fused with the street orator's shrill denunciation of those whom Joyce saw as his targets. Churchill appears as the Home Secretary who gunned down the miners in 1911 and in less flattering references as 'the thing' that Mr Chamberlain 'picked up out of the political gutter to make First Lord of the Admiralty'. But *Twilight over England* also shows far more clearly than broadcasts or speeches the range and the limitations of Joyce's mind. He could assert, sometimes shrewdly and with well-chosen innuendo, but he could not argue.

Perhaps this mattered little in a style marked principally by a command of slogans. 'Britannia was once the mistress of the seas. Now she has become a lodging-housekeeper for permanent but non-paying Jewish guests.' He struggles for the succinct universal truth of the aphorism and produces nothing with the least hint of memorability. His epigrams were destined to be chalked on the walls of Pimlico or Bethnal Green rather than graven in the hearts of men.

Yet Joyce was certainly the student who knew the grandeurs of Carlyle and Macaulay as historians – 'Great philosophers like Thomas Carlyle and evil Jews like Karl Marx' sums up his view of nineteenth-century thought. Here and there, sitting at his typewriter in the Charlottenburg apartment or the Masurenallee office in the cold days of January 1940, he attempts to assume the mantle of Macaulayan authority. William Shirer recalled him at work. Two rooms away he could hear 'Lord Haw-Haw attacking his typewriter with gusto or shouting in his usual voice against "that plutocrat Chamberlain".' By that improbable method, he evolved his attempts at the grand manner of English historical writing:

As the eighteenth century gradually unfolded itself, two
serious conditions began to develop. The first was the
decline not merely of the aristocracy but, little by little, of
all values that could not be correlated with pounds,
shillings, and pence. Strange it is that a century so prolific
in poetry, conversation, belles-lettres, and every form of
culture should serve but to herald the drab, remorseless,
materialistic industrialism that was already looming
impatiently in the offing. Yet in the long tale of history, it

has ever been so. The brilliant Augustan period of Roman literature, in which men of creative intellect scaled heights of achievement hitherto unprecedented in the history of Western Europe, was but the blazing afternoon before the twilight of Constantine and the utter darkness of the centuries that followed him.

What emerges from this is less Macaulay or Carlyle than William Joyce, the clever undergraduate who hopes that his readers will not reflect that industrialism was well rooted in the eighteenth century or that a good deal of European creativity was pre-Augustan. But the theme of Joyce's history of England was one of aristocracy and nobility corrupted and overthrown by plutocracy, first by Whig materialism and then by 'international finance'. The victims of this system had been the workers of England. Joyce holds forth on the plight of the unemployed and the miners, the women used as beasts of burden by Victorian coal-owners, in a manner that would have warmed the heart of many a left-wing radical.

Turning to the recent past, he fastens upon the poverty of England in the 1930s with the zeal of one who had, after all, insisted that National Socialism was socialist as well as nationalist. He quotes examples from *News Chronicle* reports to show the misery of the means-tested dole by which millions of people lived in the British Isles. With that, the ghost of Macaulay is laid to rest and there rises the street-corner orator, denouncing the spiritual guardians of a social system which oppresses and degrades its victims: 'Then the clergymen of England, the pompous Cardinals, the bloated Bishops, prostitute the name of Christ from the pulpits where they preach, by their mealy-mouthed claim that this is a Christian war against Germany.' No longer confined by pastiche Victorian prose, Joyce lashes out with characteristic relish against the religious denominations of England:

If ever a cortege of Pharisees deserved to be blasted by Almighty God, it is that train of lolling, rolling, over-fed, grimacing, craw-thumping, nasally booming hypocrites who said that the people of Germany had to be freed from Hitler to taste the joys of democracy.

These, wrote Joyce, were the spiritual leaders who condoned a social system in which eight pounds of mincemeat must provide a meal for two hundred Cardiff schoolchildren, already suffering from dietary deficiency. This was the system under which a couple returning from their honeymoon found that their wedding presents and all their possessions but a mattress had been taken by the bailiffs to cover the debts of their landlord. The bailiffs were said to be 'perfectly in order' and the goods were on their way to the sale room. This, he concluded, was the system which Britain sought to impose upon Germany.

Truth, half-truth, and falsehood were finely balanced in *Twilight over England*. The technique is one as old as the forensic oratory of Cicero or Demosthenes. First soften up your reader by listing the evils of the opposite system and then present the alternative, made to appear wise and humane by the omission of its far greater evils.

But Joyce also revealed a good deal of himself to his readers. Despite his two marriages and his affairs with women, despite the ease with which he brought violence to the aid of his political beliefs, his moral sensitivity was offended by what he defined as pornography. And like so many puritans of his type he saw or scented pornography where most other people had failed to find it. He was to hear with equanimity of the massacre of millions of innocent men and women in the name of National Socialism, the naked bodies of the slain piled in a ghastly hecatomb. But the appearance of a bathing beauty photographed in a newspaper filled him with moral contempt for the society which would tolerate such degeneracy.

Not only the *Sunday Pictorial* but also the *Daily Mirror* were listed in his category of 'the most pornographic and pornological papers in England'. The paradox is not uncommon. The portrayal on a television screen of a couple making love may provoke petitions and demands for 'cleaner' entertainment from those who are not moved to speech by boxers doing one another irreversible brain damage or by a wild animal being torn apart in the course of what is politely termed a 'country sport.' The anomaly in Joyce's case was far more extreme. He was offended by what he saw or imagined that he saw in such newspapers, yet the 'cleaning up', as he termed it, of his intellectual or racial enemies with sticks or knuckle-dusters – perhaps even their deaths – was, as he said, something that he looked forward to. In his Utopia, there could be no place for the sale of erotica when shops were needed to stock rubber truncheons and daggers.

Demands for censorship on the grounds of obscenity are rarely as simple as they represent themselves. They frequently constitute a slight enough disguise for political intentions. Certainly this was the case with Joyce. The crime of the two newspapers he named in his book was not merely in their pin-up pictures, though he cited these: 'Each issue tries to surpass the former in exhibiting the pectoral and fundamental aspects of woman.' William Joyce, who learnt the truth of Belsen or Dachau without the least remorse, shrank from the ultimate indelicacy of printing such words as 'breasts' or 'bottom'. Moreover, a phrase like 'the pectoral and fundamental aspects of woman' bore the stamp of his scornful pedantry.

But the greater wickedness of such newspapers and their contents was political as well as moral. They were guilty, as he put it, of 'stimulating hatred of Hitler and sexual activity at the same time.'

From this it was a short step to reminding his readers that the exploitation of such women was the work of his racial enemies and that the *Jewish World* had 'admitted' eighteen years earlier that three-quarters of the white slave trade was in such hands. Once again, outrage at the insult to sexual purity proved an unconvincing disguise for Fascist ideology.

At the level of personal apologia, one passage in *Twilight over England* sums up Joyce's ideals and pretensions with particular suggestiveness. It describes one man's experience of humble birth, of military training, of being shot at by his own people as well as by the enemy, but also of being chosen by divine providence to lead his political movement from obscurity to power. It might almost have been a romanticised vision of Joyce's experience in Ireland and England. That the parallel appealed to him and inspired him was never in doubt. But it was of Germany that he wrote, in her political and economic ruin after 1918:

That Germany was not hurled back into the chaos of 1648

and beyond, was the work of the man from the village of Braunau, born of poor parents educated in hardships, and trained as a soldier in the trenches – shot at first by the enemy, and then by his own countrymen – shot and chosen by God to take the world through the greatest revolution since the Renaissance.

By Joyce's interpretation of his own history, there were parallels in their lives. He looked up, as if to an elder and wiser brother, to an almost superhuman perfection of William Joyce. He saw in the form of Adolf Hitler a hero of Byronic pretensions and Napoleonic achievement, and knew that something of himself was reflected in the superman.

But the political philosophy of William Joyce was, like so many, of the simplest and cheapest. He insisted that politics and statecraft were subjects amenable to reason and intelligence, no less than chemistry or physiology must be. Then he denied other men the use of their reason or intelligence in such matters upon pain of imprisonment, torture and death: 'No man in his senses would suggest that questions of chemistry and physiology should be decided by popular vote.' In an age of reason, it seemed that democracy was bound to be out of fashion: 'As is shown in National Socialist Germany, the will and feeling of a whole nation can be expressed in the personality of one man.'

Joyce ended his book with a vision of the post-war world, 'when we smile grimly on the charred fragments of what was once the Power of Judah.' It was to be a time when Hitler and Germany extended the hand of friendship to Britain, though not apparently to any others among the conquered. 'The defeat of England will be her victory,' Joyce concludes, adding more ominously that 'her people will have to suffer much' in the attainment of it.

Though the book ends with a hymn to the brotherhood of Germany and England, to the glory of Hitler and God, it is almost as if Joyce was by then talking to himself. For whom had he written *Twilight over England*, other than the German Foreign Office which had paid him 10,000 marks to do the job? It was unlikely that copies would reach England during the war or that they would be permitted to circulate even if they arrived. Indeed, his political testament was never to appear in England. But in Germany there was unlikely to be a mass audience for a book in English which dealt with such specifically English obsessions.

In the Wilhelmstrasse, the book was checked and checked again for passages or allusions that might have been embarrassing to the government if printed. At the time of its appearance, Germany and the Soviet Union were still allied in their non-aggression pact. At length the text, with minor alterations, was approved and the book was printed in its edition of 100,000 copies by the Italian-owned Berlin publishing house of Internationaler Verlag. The sale was not rapid. Yet there was an audience that was in a literal sense a captive market for English language publications. It consisted of the growing number of inmates in camps for internees or prisoners of war. Here, if ever, there were recruits to be won to the Nazi cause.

With so many copies to get rid of, the distribution to the camps began as soon as the book was published in September 1940. By then their population was dramatically larger than it had been when the work was written seven months earlier.

While *Twilight over England* was in the press, Joyce's career as a propagandist received a new impetus. Early in 1940 the Reichsrundfunk had set up the Büro Concordia to co-ordinate broadcasts to those countries with whom Germany was at war. The general policy of the broadcasts was not to be pro-German but, rather, to be conspicuously patriotic. It was not difficult. After all, Joyce believed that he was acting in the best interests of England. He was the mirror image of those European refugees who worked for the propaganda services of the BBC in their broadcasts to Germany and eastern Europe.

It had long been a theme of the German broadcasts, as it was of the BBC equivalents, that the ordinary and decent people of the 'enemy' nation were as much the victims of their corrupt and cynical leaders as were those against whom they fought. To turn people against these 'real enemies' was a first priority. The Berlin-based New British Broadcasting Service – the NBBS – was first monitored on 25 February 1940, having then been on the air for several days.

Berlin

The Büro Concordia went one step beyond the BBC, however. It tried to give the impression that some of the broadcasts were actually coming from a secret transmitter within the country receiving them. Bands of patriots were taking matters into their own hands. An air of conspiracy and patriotic revolution was to be encouraged. Though its broadcasts were preceded by 'The Bonnie Bonnie Banks of Loch Lomond' as a signature tune and ended with the National Anthem, it was not likely that many people would believe that the NBBS originated anywhere but in Germany. On the other hand, it was impossible to be certain. Upon that uncertainty, the Reichsrundfunk and the Büro Concordia sought to build. In Europe, the Nazi-sponsored Voix de la Paix was transmitted close to the French frontier before the Wehrmacht's assault in the west. There was some plausibility in the suggestion that it might be the work within France of Communists or the extreme right, both groups opposed to the war as a matter of principle.

As hostilities gathered momentum in the late spring with the German invasion of Norway, Joyce and his colleagues were able to refine and improve the techniques of propaganda. A new radio programme was cheap and easy to operate. In addition to the NBBS, the British Isles became the recipient of 'Workers' Challenge', which advocated a people's revolution against Chamberlain and Churchill, and 'Radio Caledonia' which urged the Scots people to demand a separate peace with Germany if England persisted in fighting on. There was even a station broadcasting from Hamburg as the 'Christian Peace Movement', arguing the immorality of war and the case for pacifism.

No one could deny that Joyce had served Goebbels and the Ministry of Propaganda well. The neutral Americans thought his individual broadcasts the most interesting and, on 22 April 1940, *Life* magazine rated him as a smash hit. Very few people in the United States heard his broadcasts on short-wave radio. He was better known from the extracts printed in some of the major newspapers. In England the BBC, which was assumed to make copies of his talks, was surprised by the number of people who wrote and asked for transcripts of them. All these requests were refused.

Transcripts were later made, but that was the work of Inspector Hunt and the Special Branch, with a view to indicting Joyce after the war.

So far, the personal recognition by his masters had been limited to one box of cigars from Goebbels and another from Goering. But that was soon to change. On 2 July 1940 the temporary renewal of his British passport, made in August 1939, expired. A stranger arrived at Joyce's office and introduced himself as an officer of the Gestapo. Despite the shudder that this was apt to produce, he had come merely to inform the Joyces that their application for German nationality had at last been processed and that their papers would be ready for collection in due course. Due course expired on 26 September that year. Joyce had his reward. He was a German citizen, and for the future he owed no allegiance to any other nation. For a British citizen to take the nationality of the enemy nation during war was an act of treason by English law. But if Joyce had never been anything but an American, there was no crime in becoming a German while the United States was still neutral.

Before he officially acquired his new nationality on 26 September 1940, the face of Europe had been changed. Hitler's offensive in the west altered more than the political or military geography of a continent. The nature of Joyce's broadcasts and those of his colleagues changed in tone and content as Manstein's columns broke the Allied armies in France. There was an end to comic dialogues and shrewd innuendo. A new peremptory harshness coloured the voices from Berlin, better suited as an accompaniment to the Stuka sirens of the dive-bombers over neutral Holland and Belgium as well as in the skies of France and England.

'Lay down your arms! Resistance is useless!'

CHAPTER 9

The speed and totality of German military success in 1940, between the invasion of Norway on 9 April and the armistice with France on 22 June, did not find the Büro Concordia lacking in support. The opportunity offered to Joyce and his colleagues was demonstrated in the BBC's confidential report of March 1940, *Hamburg Broadcast Propaganda: A Summary of the Results of an Inquiry into the Extent and Effect of its Impact on the British Public during Midwinter 1939/40*.

The report was based on interviews with a random sample of 34,000 people. Of every six interviewees, one was a regular listener to William Joyce and four listened to him from time to time. The figures were unexpectedly high and not made more palatable by the discovery that it was the politically better-informed and the young who listened to Hamburg regularly. These were also identified as people who did not easily believe in the myth of the British empire united against a common enemy but, said the report, who knew quite well that a good many of its people had no enthusiasm for such a war. They were also ready 'to give Hitler credit for certain pre-war achievements in the social field.' In this group of intelligent listeners, the right sort of broadcasts from Berlin might have won sympathy and even converts. There was not much comfort for the BBC in the two listeners out of six who never listened to Hamburg, for they did not listen much to the BBC either.

In the questionnaire, the sample was asked the snap question whether they had listened to William Joyce's broadcasts the day before. A quarter of them said that they had. What was it that attracted them, specifically, to listen to Lord Haw-Haw? The interviewees were allowed to give more than one answer; 58 per cent thought his version of the news so fantastic as to be funny, 50 per cent heard so many other people talking about his views that they liked to keep up with them, and 38 per cent found his voice and manner amusing. But to a significant minority, he was not merely an entertainment: 29 per cent wanted to hear the German point of view, 26 per cent wanted the news that the BBC did not give them, 26 per cent liked his anecdotes, 15 per cent thought he was a good broadcaster, 9 per cent listened to him because the BBC news was so dull, and 6 per cent admired his cleverness.

As well as answering the questions, the interviewees were allowed to write a comment of their own on the broadcasts. Such comments varied widely, but 17 per cent agreed that the Hamburg broadcasts contained 'grains of truth' which they could not presumably get from the BBC, and 15 per cent thought the Hamburg broadcasts rubbish.

In the light of his eventual fate, it is interesting that no more than 4 per cent of the sample felt dislike or anger towards Haw-Haw, and that even fewer of those questioned – what the report calls 'only a handful' of the 5,000 answers in this section – suggested that it was unpatriotic to listen to him. By the spring of 1940, the report added, 'The entertainment value of the broadcasts, their concentration on undeniable evils in this country, their news sense, their presentation, and the publicity they have received in this country, together with the habit of listening to them, have all contributed towards their establishment as a familiar feature in the social landscape.'

That was certainly true. Not long after the confidential report was compiled, a new variety show opened at the Holborn Empire. It was called *Haw-Haw*.

After the Dunkirk evacuation, the collapse of the Chamberlain government, and the fall of France, there was less to be entertained by. Propaganda on both sides entered a new phase.

Joyce relied upon a double attack. In the first place, as the danger of a German invasion appeared to grow in the summer of 1940, those stations like 'Workers' Challenge' and 'Caledonia' continued to urge national minorities and the proletariat to take up arms against the government of 'Mr Bloody Churchill'. The time had come to overthrow the entire worm-eaten structure of capitalism. But the suggestion remained that the broadcasts were the work of patriots somewhere in England. 'The fact that we are British must be clear from every word we broadcast.' Ironically, Joyce was in the process of acquiring German nationality. But this brave resistance movement was assumed to be moving its transmitters around the British countryside, just ahead of the trackers. 'You'll probably 'ear us again tomorrow night,' announced the Cockney voice of Workers' Challenge, 'but it's getting 'ard. The police are always on our 'eels nowadays.'

Joyce himself joined this patriotic and revolutionary campaign on 15 June 1940, as the Germans occupied Paris. Rebellion had become a moral duty. 'Whatever disturbances may take place in consequence of our revolt, they will be utterly negligible in comparison with the bloodshed, slaughter and devastation that we should be saving our country by so acting.' The NBBS supplemented this by assuring its listeners that sabotage was rife in England, that animals due for slaughter as human food were in the last stages of foot-and-mouth disease, that forged Treasury notes were circulating widely, and that even tinned meat had been poisoned by German agents before it left Argentina.

The revolutionary propaganda of the patriotic kind, broadcast by the NBBS, urged listeners to demonstrate against the war in Downing Street and to hiss Churchill when he appeared on the newsreels. At other times, they were exhorted to horsewhip the prime minister and his supporters, to break the windows of officials during the black-out and to organise 'a campaign of frank terrorism for the good of Britain'.

The clandestine broadcasts of the imagined patriots and workers were aimed consistently against a 'shameless, indecent, rotten and demoralised ruling class'. But this was combined with an attempt to undermine the morale of the listeners by other means. There were first-aid instructions on how to dress the more fearful types of wounds which would soon be commonplace when the Luftwaffe's bombs began to fall on every town and city. There were hints on the use of strait-jackets, needed to restrain the considerable number of people who would go mad under the ordeal of days and nights of bombing in the concrete claustrophobia of public air-raid shelters.

Much was made of a Fifth Column already active in Britain and numbering thousands of men and women. The Luftwaffe endeavoured to aid this deception by dropping maps and equipment, as well as empty parachutes assumed to have been used to bring Nazi agents into the country. Most of the deceptions failed outright, as when the empty chutes were found in standing corn with no tracks leading from them. But some of the threats were much nearer the mark. The aerial torpedoes whose delivery was promised as the means of London's destruction were not far removed from the V-1 flying bomb.

Joyce was not, on the whole, much interested in the games and tricks of military deception. On the other hand, he believed wholeheartedly in rousing the British people to revolution and, unlike the tricksters, he meant every word that he said.

But his own broadcasts suffered from a fatal division of purpose. On the one hand he was the patriotic revolutionary. But just as easily he could become the German fanatic who loathed England, its people, and all that it had done. This was never clearer than in his broadcast of 2 August 1940. It was transmitted from Radio Bremen at the peak listening time of 10.15 p.m. and repeated on the following day from Zeesen. His topic was 'Britain's Cowardice in War'. It was not calculated to do anything but antagonise and alienate those who heard him, for his target was the ordinary soldier as much as the leaders of army and government. With his adversary apparently laid low, Lord Haw-Haw became the sneering and vaunting Nazi at last. Gone was all the wit and even the good humour of the dialogues between Smith and Schmidt as Joyce described the battle for France:

> What was England's contribution? An expeditionary force which carried out a glorious retreat, leaving all its equipment and arms behind, a force whose survivors arrived back in Britain, as *The Times* admits, practically naked. No doubt the soldiers fled according to orders; no doubt they found themselves utterly at a loss to cope with

Berlin

> German dive bombers and other engines of modern
> scientific warfare. But whatever excuses may be found for
> their plight, the solid fact remains that the men who made
> the war were reduced to boasting of a precipitous and
> disastrous retreat as the most glorious achievement in
> history. Such a claim could only besmirch the proud
> regimental standards inscribed with the real victories of
> two centuries. What the politicians regarded, or professed
> to regard, as a triumph, the soldiers regarded as a bloody
> defeat from which they were extremely fortunate to escape
> alive.... The glorious RAF was too busy dropping bombs
> on fields and graveyards in Germany to have any time
> available for the Battle of France.

But Joyce's disparagement of the BEF was mild by comparison
with the savage contempt that he reserved for Churchill. One
section of the broadcast, announced as 'The British Lion at Oran',
described the sinking of the French fleet by the Royal Navy to
prevent Vichy surrendering it to the Germans:

> The heroic might of the British suddenly showed itself at
> Oran. That inspired military genius, Winston Churchill,
> discovered that it was easier to bomb French ships,
> especially when they were not under steam, than to save
> the Weygand line. If it was so hard to kill Germans, why
> not, he reasoned, demonstrate Britain's might by killing
> Frenchmen instead? They were beaten and would be less
> likely to resent it.

Throughout the broadcast Joyce represents the sinking of the
French ships as a sneak attack: 'Besides, if they did not think that
the British forces would fire, the operation would have certain
great military initial advantages, which a genius, such as Churchill,
was bound to perceive.' In the last section of the talk, Churchill is
portrayed as the ogre whose aircraft have bombed German
ambulance planes on the runway and slaughtered the civilians of
Hanover. The RAF pilots must fly too high to distinguish civilian
from military targets, otherwise they would be annihilated by the
superior power of the Luftwaffe.

The transmission concluded with a sentence in which Joyce

summed up the whole thrust of Nazi propaganda in the period before the expected invasion was launched: 'The people of England will curse themselves for having preferred ruin from Churchill to peace from Hitler.'

Whether or not they cursed themselves, it appeared that Joyce himself cast them into outer darkness. For the future, the joke was over. During the next two or three years the sly and shrewd exchanges of Smith and Schmidt were replaced by a contempt for Britain and its people which was sometimes sneering and sometimes snarling, according to the circumstances. Only in the spring of 1945 did the tone become plaintive and misunderstood.

It is, of course, easy to be self-righteous about William Joyce and to overlook the fact that propaganda by the BBC and other British agencies had a manner that now makes one wince. It was perhaps this which encouraged listening to Radio Hamburg. Even to those who did not subscribe to the 'Bloody Baptist Cant' view of the BBC's tone, the organisation was not always attractive. Even in the post-war period, with its monopoly gone, the corporation was still to present a self-satisfied and self-caressing character in public debate.

There was, in its wartime bulletins, a style of delivery that suggested the tough-chinned, tooth-gritting sports commentator. Like our man in the grandstand at Aintree, one of its commentators gave eye-witness accounts of Battle of Britain dog-fights – 'There he goes ... *smash!*' as another pilot was brought down. The satisfied truculence of bulletins that began with such announcements as, 'The so-called unsinkable battleship *Bismarck* went down this morning,' was not shared by those on the British ships who watched the terrible last moments as men spilled into the water from the capsized leviathan and many more men and boys trapped in the hull were drawn to the darkness of a worse death below the ocean.

A propaganda war does not leave either side with clean hands. Though the Reichsrundfunk may have emerged the dirtier, its British counterparts were not above organising German refugees to broadcast to the Wehrmacht units and naming particular soldiers with accounts – true or false – of the destruction of their homes and the maiming of members of their families.

The natural xenophobia of the English thrived on this call to arms in the war of words. 'You know what morale is, sonny?' asks a stalwart in the propaganda film *Went the Day Well?* in 1942. 'Yus,' says the eager child, 'It's what the Wops ain't got.'

One of the most puzzling aspects of Joyce's broadcasts was the degree of information he appeared to possess about recent events in almost every locality of the British Isles. It was said that he had mentioned complaints that Orpington High Street was in need of widening – and he promised that the Luftwaffe would attend to it. He was said to have referred to the canteen of a particular factory as a target for one of the next German raids and advised the pontoon school who used it to find other accommodation. And, of course, he was supposed to know all the church clocks that were either slow or had stopped.

How could he know so much? The rumours spread and even those who had been sceptical of the existence of a Fifth Column in England began to believe that there was one in every town and village. *Went the Day Well?* is a good illustration of the zanier levels of official thought. It runs closer to the scenario of *Duck Soup* than to the events of the war. The German invasion is preceded by an inexplicable parachute drop of all the enemy's most impeccable English language speakers, disguised as a regiment of Royal Engineers, on a village so removed from the proposed assault. In reality, they would have been hopelessly cut off from their own army and far removed from anywhere where they might do much good. The local inhabitants in the film consist of loyal citizenry with a seasoning of one or two well-heeled Fifth Columnists to keep the plot moving. However absurd such scenarios may seem, the fiction of a Fifth Column suited both sides. To the British government it was a means of keeping the population on its toes and to the Nazis it seemed a way of undermining the collective British nerve.

In July 1940 the press, which had lately dismissed Lord Haw-Haw as a joke, urged its readers to regard him as a public enemy and a danger to the country. The *Daily Mirror* founded a short-lived 'Anti-Haw-Haw League'. Duff Cooper, Minister of Information and one of Joyce's targets, sanctioned the use of vigilantes to listen for defeatist talk. They were ungratefully dubbed 'Cooper's Snoopers' and soon disowned. But prosecutions were brought against two men who repeated remarks which they alleged Lord Haw-Haw had made on the air.

They did him too much honour. He knew very little more than any other European who bothered to scan the British press and listen to the BBC. Even during wartime, the contents of the English newspapers were known to the Germans almost as quickly as to their English readers. London editions would probably not reach Berlin, via neutral Stockholm, until the day after their publication. But the German Embassy in Dublin had almost instant access to them. As for remarks about a high street that needed widening, pre-war knowledge would do. Church clocks were more likely to be in need of winding or not working than running fast. And it would not take the wisdom of Solomon to guess that there was a card school, somewhere or other, in a large works canteen, or to know that pontoon was the most likely game to be played there.

But despite the ridicule and odium that soon attached to Cooper's Snoopers, there was at least one source in England from which Joyce had gathered a little information. On 7 November 1940, at the Old Bailey, Anna Volkov stood trial for offences under the Emergency Powers (Defence) Regulations Act. She was a Russian *emigrée* whose father had been the last naval attaché at the Imperial Embassy in London. Since then, she and her parents had run the Russian Tea-Shop in Kensington, an establishment which prided itself on serving the best caviare in town. Anna was naturalised in 1935 and set up as a dress-maker. She was a fanatical anti-Semite who attributed the 1917 revolution to Russian Jewry. In collaboration with Tyler Kent, a cypher clerk at the United States Embassy who had lately received seven years imprisonment for his crime, she had made copies of confidential messages between Churchill as First Lord of the Admiralty and President Roosevelt. These were to be sent to Berlin through certain neutral embassies in London sympathetic to the German cause.

Berlin

Kent's most important service had been the unauthorised copying of the documents and the passing of them to the Italian Embassy in London, before Italy's entry into the war. The company he kept had brought him under suspicion, if only because Miss Volkov's crusade drove her to fly-post walls during the black-out with anti-war leaflets known as 'sticky-backs'. The tone of these posters was typified by the New Year Resolution which she had printed for 1940:

> We appeal to the working men and women of Great
> Britain to purchase the new Defence Bonds and Savings
> Certificates, thus keeping the war going as long as possible.
> Your willing self-sacrifice and support will enable the War
> profiteers to make bigger and better profits and at the
> same time save their wealth from being conscripted. Lend
> to defend the rights of British manhood to die in a foreign
> quarrel every twenty-five years. Don't be selfish. Save for
> shells and slaughter. . . . Be patriotic. Come on the first
> five million pounds.

Ironically, as Miss Volkov bustled about in the dark, she was in close proximity to members of the Communist party with their own sticky-backs which proclaimed much the same sentiments. However, she was also reported as saying that when England was incorporated in the Third Reich, it was her ambition to be the British Julius Streicher.

On 10 April 1940, Miss Volkov handed her last letter to the woman who was to take it for her to the Roumanian Embassy. The envelope was addressed to 'Herr W. B. Joyce, Rundfunkhaus, Berlin'. The rarely used second initial was but one indication that she had been a friend of the Joyces before the war and a member of the British National Socialist League. Not surprisingly, she had been under surveillance since then. This time the female courier who appeared to take the letter to the Roumanian Embassy was an agent of MI5. Though the letter was sent on its way to Joyce, it was first opened and read. Under the insignia of the Right Club and the initials 'P. J.' for 'Perish Judah', she gave her advice on the public appetite for his broadcasts.

> Talks effect splendid but news bulletin less so. Palestine

good but I. R. A. etc. defeats object. Stick to plutocracy.
Avoid King.
Reception on mediums fair but B. B. C. 376 tends to
swamp, while B. B. C. 391 and Toulouse try squeeze
Bremen and Hamburg off air at times.
Why not try Bremen at 500?
Bremen 2 on longs very weak. Needs powerful set to get.
Here Kriegshetze [haste for war] only among Blimps.
Workers fed up. Wives more so. Troops not keen. Anti-
semitism spreading like flame everywhere – all classes.
Note refujews [sic] in so-called Pioneer Corps guaranteed
in writing [not?] to be sent into firing line.
Churchill not popular – keep on at him as Baruch tool and
war-theatre extender, sacrificer Gallipolli, etc. Stress his
conceit and repeated failures with expense lives and
prestige.
Butter ration doubled because poor can't buy – admitted
by Telegraph – bacon same. Cost living steeply mounting.
Shopkeepers suffering. Suits P. E. P.
Regret must state Meg's Tuesday talks unpopular with
women. Advise alter radically or drop. God bless and
salute to all leaguers and C. B.
Acknowledge this by Carlyle reference radio not Thurs. or
Sun. Reply same channel same cypher.

There were enough references in this to identify the friendship
between Anna Volkov and Joyce before the war. 'Meg', whose
Tuesday chats for women were proving unpopular, was Margaret
Joyce. The leaguers who were saluted were any members of
Joyce's British National Socialist League who might be with him in
Berlin. C. B. was Christian Bauer, his German contact in London
before 1939. P. E. P. stood for Political and Economic Planning,
regarded by the Fascists as a Jewish-run organisation.

The letter contained a hurried postscript:
If possible, please give again sometime in the week, the
broadcast which the German radio gave in German about
three months ago, namely:
The Free Masons' Meeting in the Grand Orient in Paris,

1931 (?) where Lord Ampthill was also present.

It is now very important that we hear more about the Jews and Free Masons. P. J.

MI5 allowed the message to pass to the Roumanian Embassy. A few days later. Joyce's broadcast acknowledged it as Anna Volkov had asked. 'We thank the French for nothing,' he said, 'Where is their Shakespeare? Who is their Carlyle?'

Anna Volkov's trial at the Central Criminal Court was held in camera and under strange circumstances. German bombers attacked the city several times during the proceedings. When the sirens sounded, judge and jury, prisoner and counsel, were obliged to go down together to the cellar which served as an air-raid shelter. And there, with robes and such formality as could be managed, the hearing was continued. In the end, it took the Old Bailey jurors twenty-five minutes to find Anna Volkov guilty of the charges against her. Mr Justice Tucker sent her to penal servitude for ten years. In the course of the trial he had occasion to denounce William Joyce as a traitor, whom Miss Volkov had sought to aid. This was a matter of some significance, since Mr Justice Tucker was to preside at the trial of Joyce himself five years later.

There was no evidence that, apart from Anna Volkov's suggestions to him, Joyce received any voluntary assistance from the country at whom his propaganda was aimed or from the millions who listened to his broadcasts. For the rest, he relied upon reports from the Italian Embassy before Italy's entry into the war, and from the British press, to whose comments he quite often referred. More embarrassingly, he was the recipient of a good deal of questionable information from Goebbels's Ministry of Propaganda which destroyed whatever credibility his version of the news might otherwise have enjoyed.

For the most part, he relied upon second-hand reporting, common sense, and a good deal of elementary guesswork. Even Anna Volkov's letter described the situation in England as she wished it to be rather than as it actually existed. But she was right about one thing. There were problems for many people about hearing Joyce at all. In the BBC survey, 22 per cent of those questioned said that they never listened to Radio Hamburg or any of the other German stations, because their wireless sets were simply not powerful enough to pick them up.

The autumn of 1940 marked the turning of the tide in the propaganda war. Fewer people in England listened to the German broadcasts – or at least fewer admitted to doing so. In the circumstances of the blitz that began in September, it was neither fashionable to listen in, nor any longer a joke. And though the blitz seemed to Londoners to be all one way, the bombs were now falling on Berlin as well.

For Joyce, the autumn was also a moment of personal success. *Twilight over England*, published in September, was later issued in a German-language edition and then in Stockholm in a Swedish translation. He gave a copy to the Berlin correspondent of CBS, William Shirer, and also dedicated one to his Glasgow-born German mentor at the Rundfunkhaus, Eduard Dietze, 'With the best respects of Faust to Mephistopheles.' But Joyce was no Faust, nor did he need the encouragement of the devil to carry out his work.

Shirer, in exchange, gave him a copy of Brett Rutledge's new novel *The Life and Death of Lord Haw-Haw*, based on an entirely inaccurate account of Joyce's career but showing that his fame had already crossed the Atlantic. The two men encountered one another frequently, since the CBS broadcasts went out from the same Charlottenburg studios as Joyce's talks.

On 25 September 1940, Royal Air Force Bomber Command began to attack Berlin at 11 p.m. and continued until 4 a.m., the longest raid of the war until that date. Shirer found himself in a cellar of the Rundfunkhaus, sheltering with Joyce and his wife, under the orders of armed guards. The CBS correspondent had noted in August that Joyce had 'shown guts' during the first air-raids, he and the girl secretaries being the only ones not to rush for cover.

On this occasion, Joyce produced a litre bottle of schnapps which he, his wife and Shirer consumed in a tunnel leading from the shelter. 'Haw-Haw can drink as straight as any man,' Shirer wrote, 'and, if you can get over your revulsion at his being a traitor, you find him an amusing and even intelligent fellow.' From the cellar they went up to Joyce's room, opened the blinds and sat in darkness, watching the yellow flashes of anti-aircraft guns and bombs lighting up the night sky.

At that time Joyce appeared a heavily-built man, taller than his five and a half feet, 'with Irish eyes that twinkle and a face scarred not by duelling in a German university but in Fascist brawls on the pavements of English towns.' To some, the scar that might have suggested gangsterdom in England, evoked more honourable possibilities under the codes of Prussia. Those codes had assumed a new significance for Lord Haw-Haw that day. When Shirer asked to whom Joyce referred when he spoke of 'we', the answer came back with a snap: 'We Germans, of course!'

He had, technically, been a German citizen for a matter of hours. Like almost all those who encountered Joyce, Shirer saw nothing to his 'philosophy' but a pathological anti-Semitism and a hatred of capitalism that a Communist might share. More chillingly, the American journalist had seen Joyce standing in the snow and haranguing the studios' SS guards on 'the necessity of liquidating all Jews everywhere'.

His new masters had embarked upon the obscene realisation of that objective, so far as lay in their power. Would Joyce the orator be able to confront its reality with enthusiasm or even equanimity? His apologists would suggest that he flinched from it but he was, in the end, unmoved. Yet the downfall of the man and his ideas had already begun. On that September night of the RAF attack on Berlin, Shirer concluded that Joyce realized 'he has lost most of his hold on the English people' and that he was increasingly restless at 'the inane things which Goebbels makes him say'.

It was not in his nature to recant, nor to desert the cause which had won his allegiance. He was obliged to proclaim the coming of German victory, as the entry into the war of Russia and finally the United States made such a thing first improbable and then inconceivable. Later, after he had been captured by the British in May 1945, he claimed to have recognised long before the illusion of the German victory which he continued to preach until the opening of that final year. 'After Russia and the United States had entered the war ... it seemed probable that with these two powerful allies Britain would succeed in defeating Germany,' he told his interrogator. It was not a possibility he dared or wanted to admit until the very last days of the Third Reich. In the end, during those last days, he could do no more than argue plaintively that the western powers would regret their defeat of Germany, as they came face to face with their true enemy in the shape of burgeoning Soviet imperialism. But that ultimate change of heart lay more than four years in the future.

CHAPTER 10

Those in England who imagined Lord Haw-Haw living in the style of patrician affluence which his voice suggested, through the gratitude of influential Nazi patrons, were themselves dupes of a romantic vision of the well-paid traitor. He was provided with a generous allowance of cigarettes and schnapps but routine luxury went little further than that.

Nor was domestic life much improved by the long hours and claustrophobic ambiance of the studios. Though his marriage was to survive the years in Berlin, it was no secret that both he and his wife found temporary attachments. As in any capital during general mobilisation, there was a shortage of eligible men. Joyce was an object of curiosity and attraction to the secretaries at the Rundfunkhaus and in the Kantstrasse where an office was found for his other work. Though he scarcely aspired to affluence, he was allowed treats by his mentors, rather like an indulged child. Perhaps this aura of privilege made him appealing to a number of women whom he encountered. War and mortal danger were traditionally a time for casting aside restraints, of which sexual scruples were among the first to go. Joyce received his rewards at the caprice of his employers. These included holidays in Germany and, as the frontiers of conquest expanded, in occupied territories like Norway and Luxembourg. He might take with him the girl of his choice. There were drinks and meals at the Press Club and the use of an official car from time to time.

He was remembered in Berlin as a smartly dressed man in a tailor-made blue suit, the same in which he was later to be tried and hanged. As a gesture of proletarian solidarity, he also wore a German worker's peaked cap. But there was a certain pallid grossness about him, where he had once seemed burly, betraying the subterranean life of the enclosed and windowless world at the Rundfunkhaus. Long hours of work were combined with bad food, heavy smoking and too many rounds of drinks in the nervous comradeship of the expatriate broadcaster. Perhaps he was like Faust after all, beginning to pay the price of his bargain even before it was due.

But there was more to his personal decline that this. Joyce was too intelligent a man to suppose, despite the material presented to him by the Ministry of Propaganda, that there could be a better outcome than stalemate in the war. By the end of 1941, the possibility of a German defeat grew to probability as the Axis powers faced the alliance of Britain, the Soviet Union, and the United States. Nor did Joyce have any doubt as to what would happen to him if the British and their partners won in the end.

He foresaw his own fate, even in his preface to *Twilight over England* during the winter of 1939–40. A preface, wrote Joyce, was usually no more than a flourish of the author's egotism. But his was a special case:

> When, however, the writer is a daily perpetrator of High Treason, his introductory remarks may command from the English public that kind of awful veneration with which £5,000 confessions are perused in the Sunday newspapers, quite frequently after the narrator has taken his last leap in the dark.

That leap in the dark, with the noose still slack about his neck until the rope sprang taut, was never far from his thoughts in the years that followed. 'The Sign of the Hanging Judge' was the name he gave to the cupboard of bottles in his offices at the Rundfunkhaus and the Kantstrasse.

Little by little, as the fortunes of war turned against the Third Reich, the crusading exhilaration of his early broadcasts developed into a perverse and resentful dogmatism. He worked under strain and to the limit of his capacity. Though he gave up the pretence that stations like Workers' Challenge and the Christian Peace Movement were patriotic underground organisations in England, he still broadcast on their behalf. 'Mr Bloody Churchill' was judged an epithet more likely to appeal to the working-class who had suffered from that politician's repressive measures many years before. And the best thing for the workers to do with the Minister of Food, Lord Woolton, was to 'kick his backside and sling him out'. Joyce with his usual zeal for direct personal violence went on to suggest that if a deputation of workers were to visit Woolton and beat him up badly enough to put him in hospital for a fortnight, 'he'd be as much use to us there as anywhere else.'

These more aggressive broadcasts were a constant reminder that behind the Macaulayan stylist of *Twilight over England* there still stood the street-fighter with his knuckle-duster and the embittered soap-box orator. But now the sneering and rasping were more evident in his private life. Margaret Joyce left her husband in 1941, rousing his still more vindictive fury at this 'betrayal' of the cause to which they were jointly dedicated. In August 1941 they were divorced, he alleging her adultery and she complaining of his cruelty.

But despite the difficulties of their life together, they were no more satisfied when apart. Six months later, in February 1942, they were remarried. Though it was by no means the last separation between them, they were to be reunited in extreme adversity and remained so until Joyce's death on the scaffold.

To those in England who still listened to Radio Hamburg and its sister stations, German propaganda broadcasts were synonymous with Lord Haw-Haw. That he was William Joyce had been positively established by the BBC with the broadcast of 2 August 1940. Special Branch and MI5 had made the identification long before that. By the time that his name was announced as commentator, some months later, the same identification had appeared in reports of parliamentary debates and in the British press. Indeed, Joyce was denounced as Lord Haw-Haw in the House of Commons as early as 23 May 1940 by the Member for Wolverhampton, G. le M. Mander.

But he was not the only potential star of the Reichsrundfunk, however much his vanity was touched by rivals near the throne. There was, for example, a promise of first-rate propaganda value in John Amery, who was twenty-seven years old when the war broke out. He was the scapegrace son of a leading Conservative politician, Leopold Amery, who had been First Lord of the Admiralty and then Colonial Secretary during the 1920s. Amery senior was more famous still for having stood up in the House of Commons on 7 May 1940 and quoted at the Chamberlain government the words of Cromwell to the Long Parliament, 'You have sat too long here for any good you have been doing. Depart, I say, and let us have done with you. In the name of God, go!'

But John Amery's single obsession was anti-Communism. Having been declared bankrupt in England in 1937, he went to Spain, travelled through Europe and was in San Sebastian when the war began. By 1942 he had made his way to Berlin. His chief employment was in recruiting British prisoners-of-war to form a Legion of St George, or a British Free Corps, to fight as a unit of the SS against the Soviet Union.

Dr Hesse of Hitler's personal staff, and the German Foreign Office saw in Amery a useful addition to the Büro Concordia. But in no time at all he had disappointed them and enraged William Joyce. This was in part a matter of personal resentment. Joyce, the fighter for National Socialism who bore scars to prove his loyalty, thought himself about to be supplanted by this well-born wastrel whose only asset was a name famous in English political life. For his own part, Amery saw the foreign service of the Reichsrundfunk as having been carved up between 'William Joyce and his friends and Baillie-Stewart and his'. Broadcasting services, even under more favourable conditions, are apt to interbreed a difficult species of bureaucrat-cum-theatrical-person. It was no less true at Charlottenburg than anywere else.

Worse still, Amery was enthusiastic only for the defeat of the Soviet Union. He thought Joyce's broadcasts were counter-productive and told the Büro Concordia as much. He insisted, in his own words, that it was 'quite insane to carry on as they did calling the British "the enemy" and so forth.' While Joyce fulminated at the manner in which his work was to be cast aside by this young patrician dilettante, Amery went on with breathtaking arrogance to lay down conditions for his own co-operation: 'I told Dr Hesse that I was not interested in a German victory as such, that what interested me was a just peace where we could all get together against the real enemies of civilisation.' As it happened, this was a path later to be followed by Joyce, when all others were closed to him. But in 1942 he was still in full flood on the subject of Churchill's brutality and the need to put Lord Woolton in hospital. A just peace was not part of that scheme.

Amery would work for the Büro Concordia only if permitted to write as he wished, without censorship. After consideration of this ultimatum, the Ministry of Propaganda gave its consent and Amery scripted about ten broadcasts. Despite his refusal to denounce England as the enemy, these talks were given in a style which one English listener, C. E. Bechhofer Roberts, later decribed as 'screeching, incoherent rodomontades'. Then, ever the *prima donna* in such matters, Amery made an uncompromising objection to Joyce being allowed to continue his broadcasts. 'I tackled Hesse on this subject,' he wrote, 'pointing out that it was absurd for me as an Englishman to talk about us all getting together if, five minutes later, from the same station, another Englishman was to yell out abuse of my countrymen.' Amery's sense of political reality had never been very acute. Now he had fatally overplayed his hand – and Joyce knew it.

The truth was that the Rundfunkhaus by 1942 was less the voice of the Third Reich and National Socialism than a greatly amplified Tower of Babel. The Ministry of Propaganda stood firm and tried to control its awkward *protégés*. If it allowed Amery such latitude, perhaps it was only because he had been taken to prisoner-of-war camps and permitted to give the absurd impression that he was a lately-appointed British Foreign Secretary. Alas, he had been dismissed from office almost at once for trying to conclude peace with Germany. Recruiting for the British Free Corps, Amery handed out leaflets in the camps which gave the impression that a considerable number of British prisoners had seen the light of reason and were fighting shoulder to shoulder with Germany against 'the common enemy'. 'We are British. We love England and all it stands for. Most of us have fought on the battlefields of France, of Lybia [sic], Greece or Italy, and many of our best comrades in arms are lying there — sacrificed in this war of Jewish revenge. ...' Like the British National Socialist League, the Free

Corps was able to suggest the ranks of dedicated patriots moving forward implacably in the stuggle of light against darkness. And like the League, it consisted in truth of a couple of dozen individual oddities.

It was clear that, despite Joyce's fears to the contrary, he stood in no danger from such rivals. The Ministry of Propaganda sent the ultimatious John Amery to address Fascist meetings in France and elsewhere. Later still, after the capitulation of Italy and the restoration of Mussolini in his puppet republic on Lake Garda, Amery was packed off there. He was to be captured by the partisans and handed over to the Allies at the end of the war. His demands had been impossible during his weeks in Berlin. His broadcasts proved far from satisfactory, and his policy of a peace with England in order to make common cause against the Soviet Union was ill-timed. Only once, after the plot to assassinate Hitler in June 1944, did Amery make another broadcast of any significance. He was then at Gatow, near Berlin, and the long silence had led to rumours of a dark fate at the hands of his Nazi keepers. 'At Hesse's wish I spoke a speech on the radio once more, because he said it was being thought I was a prisoner of the *Gestapo*.'

By no means all the English-language broadcasters in the Reichsrundfunk were committing treason or breaking any law of their own nation. Francis Stuart was an Irish novelist of some reputation who had been teaching literature at Berlin's Humboldt University. In 1942-3 he agreed to make broadcasts on behalf of the German government, aimed at an Irish audience but also available to some listeners in the United Kingdom. His intention was to correct the bias caused by Ireland's dependence upon British newsreels in the cinemas and a preponderant influence of British press and radio. Since Ireland was not at war with Germany, there was nothing illegal in this action. Ironically, however, Stuart was born in a British dominion of British parents, while Joyce had been born in America of American parents. But time and political change had given Stuart the protection of Irish citizenship.

Norman Baillie-Stewart continued to broadcast for his adopted country but his star also faded in the harsher brilliance of Joyce's street-practised rhetoric. His remarks about Joyce were not calculated to do much for the harmony of the foreign section at Charlottenburg. Baillie-Stewart described him as 'a thug of the first order'. This was apparently borne out by Joyce's continued readiness at the age of thirty-eight or thirty-nine to use his fists as necessary. Both by disposition and training, his was the voice that offered to fight the biggest man in the house. He was even arrested and charged with sub-treason after a fight in an air-raid shelter during the last year of the war. Baillie-Stewart's aristocratic resonance of name was the result of changing it from Wright by deed poll in the 1920s. But he could afford a certain patrician disdain towards the gutter politics of Lord Haw-Haw. For his part, Joyce was not likely to let his colleagues forget that Baillie-Stewart's knowledge of German and Germany was so slight that he had at first been persuaded to spy by a couple whose names were, literally, Herr Fruit and Fraulein Pear. Though he was used for a while as the voice of the genuine officer and gentleman by the Reichsrundfunk, and then by von Ribbentrop's Foreign Office as a translator, Baillie-Stewart was eventually allowed to leave Berlin and make his home in Vienna.

Among the other expatriates was an elderly woman, Margaret Bothamley, who prepared scripts and broadcast them for Goebbels's Ministry of Propaganda. She, like Amery, was motivated solely by her hatred of Bolshevism. To prove this, she hung pictures of George VI and Queen Elizabeth on her walls, protesting that she had the best interest of her country at heart. For the most part, the pictures on the wall of the mess in the British Free Corps and elsewhere were of that latter-day 'King Over the Water', the Duke of Windsor, for whom Joyce had fostered considerable sympathy before and during the war. 'In our barracks at Pankow and Hildesheim as well as Dresden,' wrote one of the British SS trainees, Alfred Vivian Minchin, 'we had a photograph of the Duke of Windsor, whom we all admired as he was also a rebel. We all recognized him as the King of England. When we had parties we always toasted the Duke of Windsor.'

Despite National Socialist theories of racial purity, carefully adapted to include the Japanese within the pale, all nations and continents were fair game for propaganda. Elsa Gertrude

Brietzmann, born in England though her father was German, specialised in broadcasting from Berlin to India, on the topics of 'The hated British regime' and 'The Great Indian Revolution'. She called upon the subject people to 'unite to deliver a crushing blow to British imperialism'. But she and her type were the small fry of treason. Joyce alone survived of the most famous names among the propagandists of Charlottenburg.

Yet he had disciples of a kind. John Amery's visits to prisoner-of-war camps to recruit for the British Free Corps were greeted by jeers and heckling. Joyce, on the other hand, became known through the distribution in the camps of *Twilight over England*. In his visits, he gained no more recruits than Amery, but while twenty or thirty volunteers would hardly launch a British division of the Waffen SS, a handful would be a useful addition to the voices of Workers' Challenge or the Christian Peace Movement.

Among those who were persuaded by Joyce's book or the lure of life outside the camps, there was only one officer, Pilot Officer Benson Freeman, who agreed to write scripts for 200 marks a week. Warrant Officer Hughes was an RAF air-gunner who also made recordings for Joyce. Guardsman William Griffiths, at his trial in 1945, insisted that he and others were obliged to continue this work once they had begun it because Joyce threatened them with deportation to a concentration camp from which they would not return alive. Walter Purdy claimed that he had twice tried to kill Joyce, once with a booby-trapped hand-grenade and once by placing three grenades in a suitcase next to him on a train journey. The grenades failed to go off. Purdy, junior engineer on HMS *Vandyke*, had been taken prisoner at Narvik and was a wholehearted supporter of Nazi propaganda. He had been a member of the British Union of Fascists before the war. Before long, he had become the voice of one of the patriotic radio stations, 'Radio National', which with increasing absurdity once again pretended to be secretly located somewhere in the British Isles. His scripts included such features as 'The Air Racket' and 'Jewish Profiteering in War'. Purdy was to be sentenced to death for treason in December 1945 but was reprieved a few days before he was due to go to the gallows.

Berlin

Some of the other volunteers worked for Joyce on grounds that had little to do with National Socialism. Pearl Vardon was a Jersey schoolmistress who fell in love with an officer of the German occupation force. When he was posted to Berlin in 1943, she went with him and worked as a radio announcer. That such cases as hers should have been visited with the full rigour of the law and a term of imprisonment is some indication of the zeal for retribution felt by the victors in 1945.

Purdy and one or two other volunteers were of some use to Joyce. Most of the rest were of no more value to him than they were in the Waffen SS. In practice this mattered nothing. It was Joyce alone who commanded and held an audience. By the end of 1941 that audience was a good deal smaller than it had been eighteen months earlier. All the same, if English listeners took the trouble to tune in to Radio Hamburg, they expected to hear Lord Haw-Haw. Nothing less.

In July 1942, after almost three years of service to the Reichsrundfunk, Joyce received the confirmation of his superiors' satisfaction with his work. He was appointed 'Head Commentator in the English editorial department of German Broadcasting Stations for Europe'. The contract referred to him as 'William Joyce, *alias* Wilhelm Froelich, of Berlin'. In such a position he was supreme among the English-language broadcasters and subject only to 'the plan of distribution of business prepared by the Foreign Directorate'.

His salary was to be the equivalent of about £60 a month, at a time when half that amount in England would have been regarded as a living wage. In addition he was to get a Christmas bonus and overtime pay when 'shift or Sunday extra work is done for service reasons'. From time to time he received a fee for other services. In February 1942, for example, he was on holiday with a girl-friend in Luxembourg. While there he made four broadcasts for the German-controlled Radio Luxembourg and was given a payment of 200 marks, about £10. He was to be the best-paid of the broadcasters, and, far more important, he was acknowledged as the English voice of Berlin.

Dr Winkelnkemper, Foreign Director of the Reichsrundfunk, wrote to him on 26 June 1942 to confirm the appointment. Joyce's main duty was 'to prepare political comments in the English language for our news service, in accordance with the directions of the superior authorities and suggestions by the directors of the group of countries.' Not even Joyce was to be let off the rein by the Ministry of Propaganda. 'I also ask you', wrote Dr Winkelnkemper 'to examine the news services from the language point of view and to allocate the announcers in concert with the editorial chief on duty.'

In view of his 'extended duties', Joyce was to be released from the 'news announcement service'. He had star billing at last. In future it was other men and women who announced him by name to the listeners. The letter from Winkelnkemper ended with a paragraph of appreciation and promise: 'Having regard to your extended responsibility and your many years of efficiency as an announcer and commentator, I am considering a readjustment of your remuneration. You will hear further on this matter shortly.'

In England, there was growing belief and indignation that Joyce had sold his country for money as much as from principle. To add insult to the injury he had done, it seemed that he was also being paid by the British government. His entitlement to such money came from an agreement whereby the government paid £10 a month as a means of livelihood to every British citizen interned in an enemy country. The money was distributed by the neutral 'protecting power' of those citizens, which in this case was Switzerland.

On 4 February 1942, the Foreign Secretary, Anthony Eden, was confronted by demands in the House of Commons as to what had happened in the case of William Joyce, 'a British subject interned in German territory and employed by the German broadcasting authorities.' Eden was asked 'if he would take steps to stop such payments to Joyce and like traitors forthwith.' As it happened, Joyce had never received money from this source and parliamentary honour was satisfied.

But even at this stage of the war, there was a curious ambivalence of view about news of the enemy and news from the enemy. For example, on 1 January 1942, *The Times* published Hitler's New Year message *in extenso* and without immediate comment, as a major item of news. It also gave information about the propaganda broadcasts from Hamburg. In the same issue the paper informed its readers that, 'The German wireless announced that its news broadcasts in English at 10.30 a.m. and 12.30 p.m. would be discontinued from today.' In the early stages of the war, the times of the German broadcasts in English had been given.

The nature of Joyce's treason in repeating the same message of Hitler's as *The Times* had done was not in revealing the contents of it to innocent ears but in doing so from Berlin via Hamburg. After his capture in 1945, British newspapers gave the impression that it was the sardonic gloating of his tone rather than the country of origin which required that the law should make an example of Lord Haw-Haw. And in this he gave them every assistance. But however virulent his propaganda, had he truly broadcast it from clandestine transmitters on British soil, the crime of which he was eventually convicted might not have been treason. The *Daily Worker* campaigned as scornfully as Joyce against Britain's part in the war before Hitler's attack on the Soviet Union. The paper was closed down by the government but there was no question of indicting its editor for high treason.

In Germany, as well as in Nazi-occupied Europe, listening to enemy broadcasts had been a criminal offence. In England, though prosecutions had been brought in 1940 against those who repeated what they had heard in Joyce's broadcasts, listening to the transmissions themselves had been perfectly legal. Though this libertarian attitude towards freedom of speech was the more commendable, there remained something incongruous about being allowed to listen to a man but to merit imprisonment for repeating to anyone else what he had said. After the ill-judged experiments of 'Cooper's Snoopers' and the overturning of certain convictions on appeal, such prosecutions were discontinued.

In Charlottenburg, now that Joyce's position was established, he was built up by the Reichsrundfunk as a voice of political and strategic authority. His programme was to be called 'Views on the News', announced for him as a major feature of the evening's output. He was virtually free of censorship. Indeed, he had been so for some time. Whatever reservations he might have as to the material provided by Goebbels and the Ministry of Propaganda, he was at liberty to make his own comments upon it. That remained so until the last days of confusion and catastrophe at the end of April 1945.

In one respect Joyce remained – and remains – an enigma. He was well aware of the existence of concentration camps in Germany. According to those who claimed that he threatened them when they refused to broadcast for him, he was under no illusion as to the fate of detainees consigned to such places. What, then, of his vaunting anti-Semitism?

From his wife there subsequently came a story of Joyce's first encounter in Berlin with an old man wearing a yellow star stitched to his dark suit, by order of the Nazi regime. It was evident to Margaret that her husband was deeply, if not lastingly, affected by the sight of what anti-Semitism now meant. But the Kastanienallee was not to be a Damascus Road. The instinctive sympathy that Joyce felt for one old man at that moment meant no more to him in the long run than the human pity which an anti-monarchist might feel for an hour or two while watching a performance of *King Lear* or *Oedipus Tyrannus*.

The virulent anti-Semitism of Joyce's Pimlico street oratory had been tempered by prudence in the broadcasts from Charlottenburg. He never ceased to remind his listeners that the war had been brought about in the interests of Jewish international finance, but his grosser epithets were reserved for Churchill, Woolton, Duff Cooper and their colleagues. Before the end of his life, the atrocity of Belsen, Dachau and the other camps was public knowledge. Joyce's response, however feeble, was without remorse or repentance. While in the condemned cell at Wandsworth, he conceded that the camps were not run by 'the best type of man'. But, he added, most of the inmates were of a type beyond the conception of British imagination. In the desperate final months before a defeat, faced with the problems of assembling and moving supplies under constant attack, neither British nor Germans would have given first priority to keeping alive 'a hostile political or criminal substratum'. How, in any case, could thousands of deaths be prevented in prison camps where typhus already had a firm grip?

It was the standard defence offered by Nazi apologists after the war, perhaps because it was the only one with a shred of credibility. It depended on the outlandish assumption that most of the men, women and children who died were of a criminal type as likely to be in prison in England as in Germany – and on the assertion that only Allied bombing prevented supplies from reaching the camps. But those, like Joyce, who offered such excuses were also driven to believe in them. How else could he reconcile the bright hope of National Socialism with the hideous implementation of its dictates? It was human error and not Nazi idealism that had caused the tragedy. It was also the fault of an entire race for being congenitally 'criminal'. He never wavered in his anti-Semitic beliefs. In death as in life, said his posthumous message read by the BBC, he defied the Jews. It was the first article of a pitiless creed. To acknowledge the terrible wrong endorsed by his wartime Fascist views required a greater spirit than Joyce and was to be found, for example, in Ezra Pound. But Pound's politics and personal life were a compound of contradictions, in any case. His attacks on Italian radio against Roosevelt and the Jewish influences surrounding him did not alter the fact that Pound numbered Jews and Gentiles alike among his own friends. For the horrors of Nazism in its treatment of European Jewry, he admitted shame and dismay.

It was little consolation to those who suffered to know that Joyce in his private life was an amiable companion, a witty fellow, and even a source of personal kindness. But indeed the figure of the old man in the Kastanienallee moved his sympathy. Joyce was at one level like the boy who enjoys watching on the cinema screen the defence of the ranch house, so long as the Indians are mere horizon figures who drop down as the guns are fired. For the camera to close in on the shattered chests or bleeding limbs would be to spoil the game. His political and racial targets were to him like the horizon silhouettes.

No less than politicians of all persuasions he was subject to the corrupting influence of categories. It is easier to manipulate and control those who can be persuaded to think of themselves and others in such terms. The people, the proletariat, the bourgeoisie, women, racial groups, have a place – to the exclusion of any individual – in the politics of self-interest and the politician's route of advancement. Apart from his attacks on individual English leaders, Joyce wrote and talked in terms of just such groups. The pattern of his broadcasts followed this. There was to be 'Views on the News' for the middle class, 'Workers' Challenge' for the sons of toil, 'Radio Caledonia' for the rights of one racial group, and Margaret's talks for women.

Most people know better than politicians or political orators of Joyce's stamp that individuals and not categories make up the texture of their lives. But since the October night in a Lambeth alleyway, the contemptuous insertion of the razor in the corner of his mouth and the vicious cut back to the ear, whether the act of a Jew or Gentile, the Jewish race was to pay the price of extermination for Joyce's injury. If his resolve weakened, he had only to study his own face in the mirror in order to excite its rebirth. There were to be no exceptions in the matter of vengeance, for the world of categories does not permit them. Hence the shock, as much at an aberration in the law of politics as an instinct of human sympathy, at the sight of one lonely and elderly man shuffling through the winter day in the Kastanienallee with the yellow star of premeditated murder stitched to his dark suit.

CHAPTER 11

The downfall of William Joyce was at the same time pathetic, grotesque and ludicrous. He was once again the street-fighter cornered in the blind alleyway of fanaticism and unreason. Alone, as his enemies drew closer, he could only run deeper into the shadows. At a very little distance rose the blank wall that ended all hope of escape. It was this image, rather than a Wagnerian scenario of the Twilight of the Gods, that most aptly symbolised the three years remaining to him after he had signed his contract with the Reichsrundfunk. His talk of dying on the barricades in Berlin with two bullets saved for himself and his wife was to remain talk and nothing more.

In 1940 Joyce had entertained his listeners with comic imitations of Churchill's voice on the air and had almost chortled in his triumph at the foolish measures which the British were taking to repel a German invasion:

So bombs at two shillings a time, home-made in accordance with Lesson Seven, are to be used against the German Stukas.... Home-made bombs, dead dogs and lady finger-breakers are expected to defend England against the forces which wiped out the Maginot Line in a few days!

As the blitz began upon southern England, he had assured his audience of worse to follow:

No wonder American correspondents are not allowed to see the damage which the German attacks have already caused in Britain. However, what has been done is but a pale shadow of what is to come.

By the beginning of 1942, his manner had changed. He still retained the professional *élan* of the propagandist but he swayed unpredictably between blustering confidence and the plaintive logics of the misunderstood prophet. Then, on 5 July that year, even before the high tide of German military success was turned at Stalingrad and El Alamein, Joyce switched his emphasis from promise of attack to invincibility of defence. He talked of the planning for an Allied Second Front in Europe. 'Germany would more cordially than ever welcome such a false move on the part of the enemy,' Joyce assured his listeners, adding, 'I am doubtful whether the British government will risk any invasion of Europe this year.' It was a tone of uncharacteristic caution on his part, hardly justified by events. The German army had occupied Sebastopol and was overrunning the Caucasus; Rommel had taken Tobruk, destroying 230 British tanks, and had entered Egypt. In August the enthusiasm for a Second Front was, in any case, to be checked by the casualty toll in the miscalculation of the Dieppe raid.

For the next year or so Joyce's temperament grew increasingly erratic, as much in his broadcasts as in his private life. His marriage and his affairs with women made demands on his emotions which he was constitutionally unable to meet. Puritanism and promiscuity seemed the warring hag-riders of his sexuality. But, despite his amiability in casual meetings, he appears as one of those people who can sustain a love affair more easily than a friendship. There was, of course, no permanence in these attachments to other women during his marriage. The puritan and the sensualist were ultimately placated in the National Socialist hero, by means of Nietzsche's advice that the 'Bitch Sensuality' would whine for a piece of spirit 'if a piece of flesh is denied her'. Better, then, to indulge the flesh and save the soul. The product of St Ignatius Loyola College, disgusted by bathing beauties in the Sunday papers, kept sex at the level of need.

There were still thousands of unattached young women in Berlin, as in any great city at war. What charm the personality of William Joyce held for them is not immediately evident. He was, of course, articulate and dominating. He was brutal in his political diagnosis and a thug in the view of his acquaintances. But far more violent and vicious criminals than he have little difficulty in finding attractive and willing sexual partners. It would be tempting to think of Joyce as the psychopathic cad, like Ronald True or Neville Heath, for whom the nice girl proverbially falls. But there is a flaw in that hypothesis. However greatly his enemies might detest and revile him, Joyce never thought of himself as a cad. He was armed invincibly by self-righteousness, true to a burning vision of political idealism. In this he was as far removed as he could possibly be from the mercenary or callous seductions of the ladykiller. That he should be regarded as a criminal at all seemed to him the preposterous malice of Europe's self-destroyers.

In his broadcasts he walked the plank of necessity. His commentaries were at the mercy of every new and unfavourable turn in the course of the war. At one moment he was warning the British that Germany would not give in on easy terms. Then he would suddenly announce that Hitler was winning the war and would knock out all the Allied powers combined. To some extent he was the mere purveyor of what Goebbels and the Ministry of Propaganda offered him by way of news. But the tone of his pronouncements grew increasingly neurotic and inconsistent. It was quite clear that German hopes of winning the war had receded almost to invisibility by the end of 1942, and yet he was expected to clutch at every straw as if it portended a change in the fortunes of the conflict. Worse still, as time went by, he was required to present German reverses as victories in disguise. If the British or the Americans won a battle, their advance would only lure them closer to the main weight of the Wehrmacht which waited to crush them once they came within its reach.

When the Allied invasion of Sicily began in July 1943, Joyce described it vaguely as 'an attack from the Mediterranean which in fact took the form of a landing in Sicily'. He added, 'If that indeed were the plan it can already be described as a failure.' A moment later, as if having been handed the latest report, he announced, 'From the Sicilian theatre of war comes the news that the Anglo-American forces have failed to increase the extent of coastline which they hold.' He sounded like a man ad-libbing and making a fatuous mess of it. Presently, hedging his bets, he concluded that even were the invasion of Sicily to succeed, no one would count it as a true Second Front. He quoted Herbert Morrison in support of this. Many of those who heard him at this stage of the war swore that he was drunk at the microphone. Meanwhile, the crumbs of Nazi comfort doled out by the Ministry of Propaganda grew smaller by the day.

That Joyce drank heavily was common knowledge in Berlin and it is hard to imagine that some of his reports were the work of an intelligent man in possession of his faculties. The incoherence and downright nonsense in such broadcasts as the Sicilian commentary bore witness to the deadly combination of schnapps and Joseph Goebbels.

In the longer term, one banana-skin after another lay in wait for the once self-assured figure of Lord Haw-Haw. As the Sicilian campaign continued, the drawling sardonic voice proclaimed, 'Churchill seems to have entertained some crazy notion that if only he could deliver a blow on Italian territory, Italy would collapse. It is evident already that the whole Italian nation is united as never before and inspired with the ardent determination to defend the Fatherland.' Two weeks to the day after this broadcast, Mussolini's Fascist regime collapsed. Within three months, Italy had declared war on Germany. It was one of the best comic turns that the Haw-Haw show had ever put on. But most of the audience had long since left.

Yoked absurdly to the mirage of Axis triumphs, he showed a convert's faith in Hitler's personal invincibility. 'I will only say that German victory is certain,' Joyce shouted into the microphone on 4 September 1943, as the Allies landed in Italy and the first of the three Axis powers made its unconditional surrender. 'The German people know that while many blows are yet to be struck, the final blow will be struck by Adolf Hitler.'

Intellectually, Joyce could be shrewd if not profound. He had been trained in logic by the Jesuits at Galway. Therefore he was not, on the whole, prey to delusions of this sort. But in his personal life and his political allegiance alike he walked his plank, pretending it was a main highway, while his adversaries watched with amusement and growing expectation. He must now talk nonsense or else not talk at all. In the unreal world of Charlottenburg, away from daylight and the opinions of ordinary people, it seemed that he could make even the nonsense appear plausible.

As a propagandist, he was naturally better equipped to make capital out of the future than the present, to deal with events that might take place rather than to explain away the dispiriting contents of Goebbels's press releases. Throughout the early months of 1944, Joyce warned against the appalling casualties that an invasion of northern Europe must entail for the British and the Americans. By now his predictions were being made to a casual audience, principally those who picked up his voice by accident while trying to tune the needle from one BBC programme to another. They did not need to be told that the invasion of France would prove a difficult and risky business. But they too were walking a narrow and predetermined path to the promise of victory.

To celebrate Christmas 1943, Joyce's 'Views on the News' had taken the theme 'Invasion of Europe will bring Allied disaster'. To attempt a landing in France, he insisted, was the one mistake that could lose the war for the Anglo-Americans at a stroke and make even a negotiated peace impossible. And if such a Second Front were to succeed, only Soviet imperialism would be the beneficiary. 'Can the ordinary British soldier understand', he inquired on 4 January, 'why he should have been expected to die in 1939 or 1940 or 1941 to restore an independent Poland on the old scale, whilst today he must die in order that the Soviets may rule Europe? Surely it must occur to him that he is the victim of false pretences.'

Leaving his few listeners in the British army to ponder this, Joyce turned to the civilian audience: 'After the collapse of the Second Front the whole of the British people will want to know what compensation they can expect on the score of their sacrifices.'

As the spring passed, he returned frequently to the same theme. The German High Command hoped keenly that the Allies would try to land in France. What had appeared in 1942 and 1943 to be Soviet or Anglo-American successes were merely tactical withdrawals of units by the Wehrmacht to reinforce the Atlantic wall. A mighty force was being assembled to smash the Allies once and for all in the great battle of the west. What more did Stalin need for his purposes than 'a catastrophic defeat for the British forces... a general weakening of Britain, the effects of which will last for many decades and possibly for generations?' It was to be the worst of 1914–18 all over again: 'That is why Stalin is requesting the British to walk into the German parlour.'

His manner betrayed him as what he was – the bar-room pugilist who starts a fight by putting up his fists and dancing in front of his adversary, calling out, 'Hit me! Hit me! Go on, hit me!' But the absuridty was in the tone of his remarks rather than what they predicted. Though Joyce's warnings might be belittled by hindsight, he was not without justification in expecting an Allied *débâcle*. The proposed fifty-mile D-Day line running from the east bank of the Orne to the mid-point of the Cherbourg peninsula, which had been the first objective of the Normandy invasion, remained in reality a number of separate beach-heads and isolated airborne landings. The American assault at Omaha Beach came close to total failure and nowhere was the D-Day objective reached. Combined with the wrecking of the Mulberry harbours by storms a few days later, a co-ordinated and committed counter-attack by the Germans might have put an end to the venture. In that case, as Joyce and his enemies alike saw it, the Americans would have been reluctant to attempt another such assault in Europe. They would have committed their main strength to the Far East. German reinforcements would have been despatched to the Russian Front and the whole issue of the war must again have been in doubt.

In the event, if the invasion of Normandy did not go as well as it might, it still went well enough. There was only a brief period in which Joyce was able to hail it as the very thing the German High Command had hoped for. He insisted to his listeners that the luring of the fly into the parlour would prove to have been the Fuehrer's master-plan. But then, as the news from France grew worse and not even the most credulous Nazi could imagine that the 'holocaust organised at Stalin's request', as Joyce called it, was going to take place, he was saved in the nick of time by the first V-1 flying bombs falling on south-east England and on London itself. He changed the direction of his broadcasts at once. Secret weapons, not the course of the campaign on the ground, would determine the outcome of the war.

Berlin

'Bombardment by a new device of centres essential to the British war effort!' he announced as his headline on 17 June 1944. He even went on to hint that the humane leadership of the Third Reich had held back from such horrors until its hand was forced by the Normandy invasion. 'The action was long delayed, but who can deny that the moment selected for it was chosen appropriately from the military point of view?' Lord Haw-Haw promised his listeners that Germany had 'more secret weapons than one'.

This at least was true. Germany had two secret weapons rather than one. The V-2 rocket was launched against England in September 1944. Briefly, Joyce came into his own again as he had not done since 1940. In order that the Germans should not be able to target the rockets on the basis of where previous ones landed, the British government imposed a news black-out on the V-2 assault. This lasted for some weeks, though the inhabitants of south-east England and London particularly knew by their own eyes and ears that something dreadful had been unleashed against them. They swore that it travelled faster than sound. The explosion would come without warning. Only then did one hear the ghostly sound of its engine approaching through an empty sky. But while the BBC kept silent, Lord Haw-Haw and his colleagues obliged these anxious listeners with accounts of the whole of southern England in flames.

The V-2 attack lasted for eighty days, until the German retreat put England out of range. After that, the fantasies of Goebbels and Charlottenburg ran riot. Everything in Joyce's imaginings now turned to Germany's advantage. The plot against Hitler's life that summer had already proved to be a blessing in disguise, he announced. It unearthed traitors in the High Command who had deliberately held back reinforcements in the battle for France. The entire Home Army had been 'kept from the fronts by those persons who have paid the just penalty and were instantaneously crushed on 20 July.' That was why the Allies appeared to be doing so well. Now those units were speeding to the front to turn the tide of the war in the west.

The increasing desperation, or alienation from reality, in Joyce's 'Views on the News' was illustrated by his broadcast on 30 August

1944. Everywhere, in the Rhône valley and in the west, the invaders of France and the French who aided them were being halted or repulsed. As though it were a victory to rank with Alamein or Stalingrad, he revealed that a force of German tanks had just recaptured the town of Briançon from local 'terrorists'.

> Generally the position in France is regarded by Allied propagandists in one way and by me in another. I can well understand their display of solid satisfaction at the gains in ground which the invading expeditionary forces have achieved during the last few weeks. They would not be human if they did not rejoice at the retirement of the German forces, and from these withdrawals they are deducing inferences which are not only out of conformity with the facts, but which represent, I must say, very bad propaganda. Without specifying in detail their flamboyant predictions, I can sum them up by saying that they promise the complete collapse of Germany in the immediate future.

He sounded like a man with nothing to say, hoping for a miracle. But Joyce assured his listeners that it was nonsense to believe that 'as the fifth year of the war draws to its close, the Reich has exhausted its resources':

> If you had lived in Germany during the first six months of the fifth year of the war, you would have wondered why such a high and comfortable standard of living was being maintained; why so many people were engaged upon tasks which were not essential to the concentrated prosecution of the war. The answer is that the government of the Reich was not in any way neglectful of its duty or oblivious to existing potentialities, but it was thought well to hold large reserves in hand.... In brief, Germany is in a position not only to defend itself, but with the aid of time to win this war. The chief purpose of German strategy is to gain this time.

As Joyce made his promise of German victory, the Red Army entered Bucharest. Within a month they were in Yugoslavia. Five days after the broadcast, the British liberated Brussels and six days later the American army crossed the frontier into Germany near Trier.

Berlin

The transmission ended with his ritual denunciation of Churchill who 'has renounced all British interests in Europe. And those of his people who are not blind now realise that the pretext for this war was far removed from the cause of it, namely the subservience of the so-called democratic politicians to their Jewish masters.'

After this final peal of animosity, Joyce's assault was over. Another Englishman's voice said quietly, 'You have just been listening to "Views on the News" by William Joyce. Thank you for your attention.' Radio Calais, which had relayed the Charlottenburg transmission, was now within striking distance of the Canadian army. In Berlin itself, as the signal faded from the speakers of radio receivers in England, the first bombs of the summer night began to fall.

There was, however, one grain of truth which Joyce had magnified to monstrous proportions. The belief that German industrial power had been shattered by aerial bombardment was a delusion of the Allied propagandists. Only a small proportion of the bombs throughout the war fell anywhere near specific targets. Whatever the assertions of the strategists, both sides for most of the time bombed civilians. To break the morale of civilians who operated machinery was more valuable than to destroy the machinery itself. It was dislocation, not destruction, that hampered German industry. Despite the pictures of ruin and rubble, 80 per cent of that industry survived the war.

It did not alter the outcome in the least. Joyce, who had elaborated upon fact and probability in 1940, was now driven back upon sophistry. He needed only the hint of a remotely possible industrial resurgence by the German armaments manufacturers in order to transform this into certainty. But the very language and style of his broadcasts gave the game away. Now he spoke of 'deducing inferences' and 'conformity with the facts'. Four years earlier he had talked of Stukas and drums of mustard gas.

In February 1941 Joyce had been registered as a military reservist and issued with a military passport. His nationality was given as 'German, formerly English', and his religion as 'Believer', which usually indicated a nominal Christian not a member of any religious congregation. He was liable for service under the command of Military District Headquarters, Berlin X. Though never called upon to defend the city, he was issued with this passport on 12 April 1941.

It was not likely, whatever the military situation, that Joyce would have been taken from his duties at the Rundfunkhaus. But like all able-bodied civilians he was conscripted into the Volkssturm, as the prospects for the Reich darkened in the autumn of 1944. The Volkssturm was the German counterpart of that Home Guard which he had dismissed with such scorn when it was organised in England during the autumn of 1940. When asked for details of any previous military experience, Joyce replied laconically that it had been in the British army, the Worcestershire Regiment. But this was not to disqualify him from registration for military service to his chosen country. His certificate of membership described him as belonging to the District V Battalion, Wilhelmplatz 1, with effect from 21 December 1944. It was not before time. The Red Army had overrun Roumania, Bulgaria, half of Poland and Hungary, and had crossed into German territory in East Prussia cutting off the port of Memel. Six million men, twice the German strength, and 90,000 tanks, three times the German number, were assembled 300 miles east of Berlin.

Though the radio audience for Lord Haw-Haw diminished, his legend continued to grow. Hitler, it was said, had decorated him personally with the coveted Iron Cross. The truth was less sensational. On 1 September 1944 he had been awarded the Kriegsverdienstkreuz, the Cross of War Merit, First Class. Though given for services to the war effort, it was a civilian decoration rather like the OBE. There were a large number of such awards made to bureaucrats and public servants on a routine basis. That Joyce had done more than most to earn it was not in question. However, it was not presented to him by Hitler, nor even by Goebbels. The certificate accompanying the decoration was issued from Hitler's headquarters and was signed by the Fuehrer himself. But it was presented to Joyce in the Rundfunkhaus by a senior member of the Foreign Directorate.

In the bitter winter of Berlin the bombs of the Allied air forces fell night and day. The Rundfunkhaus was not destroyed but its operations were hampered by the constant raids. Windows and walls were blown in, there was dust and rubble everywhere. As in most official buildings there could be little heating. This was in part caused by the shortage of fuel and in part by minor damage to the system which put it out of action. The repeated bursting and leaking of pipes from the impact of explosions, as well as the cutting off of water when the mains were hit, made the central heating useless.

Joyce continued to broadcast the material and advocate the policy of the Ministry of Propaganda. As a matter of tactics, there was now an attempt to make trouble between the British and the Americans. So Joyce duly informed his listeners, just before Christmas, that their half-American leader Churchill had sold the empire to Wall Street financiers in 1940 for 'fifty-eight tubs, misnamed destroyers'. Such was the nature of Lease-Lend. Though the tone of his broadcasts altered in the final months of the war, he never lost his personal contempt for Churchill. One of his favourite stories was to describe why the naval battle of Jutland, in the First World War, had been classified neither as a defeat nor as a victory. Churchill, as First Lord of the Admiralty, said Joyce, had first of all deliberately allowed it to be considered as a defeat. The result of this was that British government stock went down on the market. Churchill and his friends had bought it up cheaply and quickly. Afterwards the First Lord had revised his assessment of the despatches. Jutland had been a naval victory after all. British stock rose handsomely upon this assurance. Then the rascals who had been involved in the speculation sold out at a splendid profit.

But Joyce's broadcasts in December 1944 and January 1945 were also part of a military strategy on Hitler's part. A major defeat of the less battle-hardened Americans, endangering the position of the British army to the north, might kindle hostility in the alliance and revive the hope of a separate peace in the west. Accordingly, von Rundstedt launched the last major offensive of the Wehrmacht, through deep snow in the Ardennes. The aim was to break through on a sixty-mile front, swing north across the Meuse and take the port of Antwerp. The Allied armies would be split in two, the

British effectively cut off. There was a chance, according to this argument, of a long military stalemate and an armistice with the Anglo-Americans.

The 'Battle of the Bulge' was the largest pitched battle in the history of the United States, involving some 600,000 American troops. Launched on 16 December, the German attack went well for almost a fortnight, advancing for some fifty miles across Luxembourg and Belgium. Perhaps the British could be persuaded that their partners were letting them down. On 7 January, the voice of Lord Haw-Haw knowingly assured the people of England that 'the German command dictates the course of events in the winter battle in the West.' He mocked 'the myth that the Reich will be overwhelmed by immense masses of British and US troops, employing irresistible quantities of arms and equipment.'

It was as if his masters had deliberately chosen him to be the recipient of a custard-pie in a macabre political slapstick. Even as Joyce made his broadcast and his boast, Hitler had decided to cut his losses in the Ardennes attack. Orders were being prepared for the advanced units to be pulled back the next morning.

That Joyce should have been exceptionally exhausted and irritable in the New Year of 1945 was not surprising. There was to be no disaffection between the western Allies to end the war on that front. Far worse, the Red Army was thrusting towards Berlin with a speed that terrified many of the inhabitants. Three weeks after Joyce's Ardennes broadcast, the Soviet tanks were not 300 miles away but 40, already across the Oder and occupying the town of Küstrin on the nearer bank. To the recipients of Nazi propaganda, these were the Asiatic or Mongol hordes who would bring looting, rape, and butchery in their wake. There was a frantic resolve to defend Berlin to the last on the one hand, and a terrible despair on the other. The survivors, it seemed, might envy the dead. Women, and men too, began to take their own lives rather than fall into the hands of the barbarian invaders. Stories spread of atrocities already committed by the Red Army in the first of the German towns that had been captured.

The nerves of Berlin's citizens had been tried for several months by a constant bombardment that brought the long ordeal of the

Berlin

western front in the last great war to the suburbs and fashionable streets of the capital. At dawn, the British bombers turned away and the sirens sounded the 'all clear'. The fires faded in the morning sky and towers of smoke rose from the working-class industrial areas of Moabit and Wedding, as well as from suburban Steglitz and Schöneberg to the south. And then, with scarcely a break, the warnings sounded again as the American bombers came over to continue the destruction by day. That spring the sky was constantly veiled by a yellow dust of plaster drawn up into the air from shattered buildings. There was glass underfoot almost everywhere and many streets were blocked by the mass of rubble. On 17 January, Adolf Hitler had gone down to the air-raid shelter of the Reich Chancellery to set up his headquarters. Apart from three brief appearances above ground, he never again moved from this so-called Fuehrerbunker during the three and a half months before his death.

Hitler in his bunker and Joyce in the studio from which all light and sound of the world had been excluded, shared something of the same habitat. One manoeuvred armies that had ceased to exist and the other talked of victories that had never taken place. It was as if the real world now lay in the mind's prison of an insulated bulb-lit cell while on the battlefield the tanks, troops and planes performed a chessboard ballet at the players' command. Chess was the one intellectual recreation Joyce permitted himself in his London years.

But reality was not to be denied for ever. Its light penetrated the shattered walls and blasted windows of Charlottenburg. As the Red Army prepared for its final assault on Berlin, the voice of Lord Haw-Haw ceased at length to talk of an inevitable German victory.

For Joyce, the welcome death would have been in the last and bravest street-fight of all, against a sub-human Bolshevik army in the Wilhelmplatz. But only the greatest in the land were permitted to stage their personal *Gotterdämmarung*. At the beginning of March, it had become almost impossible to co-ordinate the propaganda services at Charlottenburg. Many of the buildings needed immediate repair if they were to be used again. The studio equipment, if destroyed, could no longer be replaced. Joyce was not destined to die fighting the Mongol hordes. He was to suffer the indignity of evacuation to a place of rural safety near Oldenburg, not far from the Dutch frontier. There, away from the grand Wagnerian apocalypse, he was to sit out the brief remainder of the war in tranquillity.

As for Berlin, where he had enjoyed a fame among his English listeners second only to that of the leaders of nations, William Joyce had seen it for the last time.

CHAPTER 12

Despite the predicament of the German army on the eastern front, the Anglo-American advance had not progressed much beyond the Rhine before the end of March. Though there was a constant threat of air attack by strafing from fighter aircraft, a considerable area of north-west Germany was not in imminent danger of being overrun. Even at the end of hostilities on 7 May much of the north-west coast and the German base of the Danish peninsula – including Emden, Bremerhaven, Kiel and Flensburg – had not been reached by the invading armies. Control of the air waves in Schleswig-Holstein and on the coast of Lower Saxony remained in German hands until the capitulation and beyond.

Once again, it was dislocation rather than destruction or hostile advance that proved the greatest difficulty. Trains ran erratically, if they ran at all. Mechanised transport of any kind was soon the privilege of the military and political hierarchy. Road and railway alike were natural targets for the machine-guns of Allied fighters. Above all, there was no clear sense of what was going on or where the future of the Büro Concordia might lie.

By the end of March the Joyces were lodged in the little town of Apen, among the open fields and flat roads of the former Grand Duchy of Oldenburg. It was not far from Bremen or Holland or the sea. From this remaining haven, the transmissions of 'Views on the News' continued to go out across the North Sea. But long before the end, the broadcasts had lost almost all relevance and interest for their English audience. A few listened because it was their duty to monitor such transmissions and others found a fascination in hearing the trapped and embittered traitor still ranting in his lair. Most who listened to him now swore that they could hear the drink in his voice as easily as they might have smelt it on his breath. His broadcasts conveyed the melancholy tones of a prophet unheeded. Quietly and without further malice, he informed the people of England that they must rue the day when they turned away from his warnings of the past six years. He spoke increasingly of a future in which he would have no part.

From time to time a message clicked out on the teleprinter in the makeshift offices in rural Apen, as if to show that the beleaguered Nazi heroes in Berlin had not entirely forgotten their servants. There was an instruction, said to be from Goebbels, that the Joyces must not be allowed to fall into the hands of the Allies. But how was that to be prevented when the whole of Germany seemed about to fall into those hands? Plans were discussed for spiriting away William and Margaret Joyce by U-boat to the Irish Republic, where they would presumably be safe from capture or extradition. Joyce was the son of an Irish-born father and on such grounds he might appeal for asylum in the republic. At least he could contest the claims of British law over him. But in the last days of the Third Reich there was no U-boat available for the expedition and the officials of the Ministry of Propaganda were soon too busy saving their own skins in Berlin to give much further thought to Joyce. At last there remained only the possibility of an escape through German-occupied Denmark to neutral Sweden.

Joyce and his wife were escorted to Hamburg and registered in a hotel there for a week or so. Joyce was given a false passport in the name of Wilhelm Hansen, on which Margaret was also entered. It was not a forgery, in the sense that it was a genuinely-issued passport in the name of the alias chosen for him by the Hamburg Gestapo. To make it seem more plausible, the passport was pre-dated 'Hamburg, 3 November 1944'. According to the details, 'Hansen' was a German citizen, though born in Ireland, at Galway, on 11 March 1906. He was a teacher of languages, now living in Hamburg. It was as much as the Ministry of Propaganda could do to help him in his escape. Before leaving Berlin, Joyce had been paid three months' salary in advance, so that he might be able to live for some time while on the run. It was possible to change a little of it for Danish banknotes. For the rest, if German currency became worthless in the aftermath of war, Joyce and his wife would have to manage as best they could.

During these days at Hamburg, 'Views on the News' continued to go out. But now the broadcasts had only a single theme. Hitler was the friend of the west. The Fuehrer had shown his good faith by standing fast in Berlin and commanding the remaining power of the Wehrmacht in the battle to save Europe from Soviet conquest. Adolf Hitler now fought for England as surely as he fought to save Germany itself. Hitler and Goebbels, said Joyce on 24 April, were 'directing the fanatical resistance of the tough and valiant Berliners in the fight for every street corner, every heap of ruins, every cobblestone in that city, greater than ever in the invincible majesty of its ruins.' And on 30 April, in his final broadcast, he spoke of the German people in the same terms: 'In this hour of supreme trial they seem to understand the European position with a clarity which is, unfortunately, denied to the people of Britain, and they realise that the great alternative lies between civilisation and Bolshevikism.'

Whatever sneering and snarling there had been in the earlier broadcasts was absent now. Joyce spoke without animosity or even regret in the quiet voice of exhaustion and obsession. Though he had not changed his racial views, they found no place in this final appeal. Ironically, in his warnings against Soviet imperialism, he anticipated the very phrases and ideas which were to become common coinage of Allied politicians and military leaders in the next two or three years.

On 28 April news reached the Büro Concordia that Mussolini had been put to death by his Italian partisan captors. On 30 April Hitler committed suicide in the Berlin bunker, followed on 1 May by Goebbels, whom in the future Joyce always referred to affectionately as 'my old chief' or 'the gallant little doctor'. Not until 9.30 p.m. on 1 May, against a background of solemn Wagnerian motifs and the slow movement of Bruckner's Seventh Symphony, did German radio inform its listeners that the Fuehrer had fallen, fighting to the last against Bolshevism, in the battle for Berlin. Joyce, in his broadcast of the previous day, had spoken of 'the numerous and wild rumours which naturally spread like wildfire in circumstances of the present kind.... Any fool or any fraud can manufacture them at will.' Now rumour was replaced by actuality, except for the suggestion that Hitler had died at the hands of the Russians rather than by his own.

Joyce knew nothing of the details when he made his final broadcast. Ironically, as he explained to his listeners, in the past twenty-four hours he had been obliged to rely on BBC news broadcasts as his main source of information.

Whatever the truth about Hitler's death on 30 April, the military situation in north-west Germany was beginning to change by the hour. The Allied armies were now three days from Hamburg and it was time for the Büro Concordia to be dispersed. At the beginning of May there was still sanctuary to be found in the territory of Schleswig-Holstein where Admiral Doenitz had become head of state on Hitler's instructions. Flensburg, the new seat of government near the Danish frontier, was still almost a hundred miles beyond the final battlefront when hostilities ended.

A last mad gaiety on the part of the members of the Büro Concordia was not at all out of keeping with what was going on about them. The events of April 1945 in the shrinking enclave of Nazi dominion grew increasingly surreal. Among the ruling caste there was apprehension and dismay at the retribution that the Soviet invaders might exact. At the same time, there was a frantic air of saturnalia among this same class, more suited to the celebration of a great victory than to national destruction. The deaths of their leaders, one by one, had the effect upon the followers of parental authority being removed from the nursery. Food and drink became available to the Büro Concordia in unexpected quantities. Stores that must otherwise be lost were broken into. There was festivity in the spring air, a carnival of irresponsibility in defeat. Even back in Berlin, in the Fuehrerbunker itself, men and women gave themselves up to bacchanalian indulgence, as the citadel of National Socialism was given to the flames. Tension and inactivity sought their predictable forms of release. Dr Ernst-Guenther Schenk – appropriately an authority on stress – gave testimony of this in his accounts of the drunkenness and haphazard copulation in the Chancellery building while the Red Army units fought their way towards it, street by street. Dr

Berlin

Kunz's black leather dentist's chair in Hitler's headquarters 'seemed to have a special erotic attraction', he wrote, 'for the wilder women... Still it came as a bit of a shock to me to see a German general chasing some half-naked signalwoman between and over the cots.'

The final celebrations of the Büro Concordia were a good deal more sedate than the cavortings in the dentist's chair. By now the American advance was less than fifty miles away with no effective German units intervening. While documents and records were burnt in the yard outside, the survivors of Charlottenburg ate, drank, and were merry beyond any justification except that of nervous exhaustion. Commander Leonard Burt, who was later to interrogate Joyce and other defendants, described their account of the festivities:

> He and his fellows had what must have been a sort of macabre 'end of term' party. They were all drunk and crushed and yet uncowed.... When the party was at its wildest, they broadcast their final messages.

It is agreed by all accounts that William Joyce was drunk when he broke off from the party to go and make his last Hamburg broadcast. Yet there was a sinister sobriety in the message that he delivered. Millions of people in Britain, he suggested, must be thinking with relief, 'Ah well, it will soon be over now. We can at long last get back to peace and do something constructive for a change.'

In his farewell to them, Lord Haw-Haw assured the victors of their error. It was impossible that Germany could resist militarily for much longer – 'Germany is sorely wounded but her spirit is not broken.' On the other hand, the triumphant British must face 'a great and bitter struggle' in the Far East. But the destruction of Germany and the Pacific war were nothing compared with the threat now directed by Joseph Stalin at the heart of western civilisation. Joyce reminded his listeners of the 'cause' that had brought England and Germany into conflict. He made it sound little more than a misunderstanding between friends:

> How modest, how harmless does Germany's request for the return of Danzig seem in contrast to the immense

acquisitions of the Soviet Union and the further ambitions of the Kremlin. Stalin is not content with Poland, Finland, the Baltic States, Roumania, Bulgaria, and Eastern Slovakia. He wants the whole of Central Europe, with Norway, Turkey, and Persia thrown in. And if these territories fall to him, his lust for aggrandisement will only be stimulated still further. He sees now the Bolshevik dream of a world proletarian revolution changing into a substantial prospect of baculine politics.

To the British empire, Joyce held out the prospect of certain destruction as Soviet influence grew in the Near and Middle East. He cited the means by which the Kremlin had unilaterally imposed its own terms of peace on Bulgaria and had set up a 'Red Junta' to rule Austria, without consulting its western Allies. 'The terrible war through which we have just been passing is but the prelude to a struggle of a far more decisive kind.'

A good deal of what he predicted was soon to appear true to many of his listeners. Indeed, the greatest disadvantage to the argument was that it should have been put forward by Lord Haw-Haw, whose reputation was that of practising falsehood on system. But despite the wartime image of Stalin as a fatherly and beaming 'Uncle Joe', there was a rumour of a different kind circulating in England during the spring and summer of 1945. It was said that Churchill had feared the Soviet advance would not stop at the agreed line through Germany. He had therefore ordered a contingency plan, whereby the surrendered German weapons should be reissued to those who had formerly borne them, if the Red Army refused to halt at its given objectives. In that event, according to the rumour, the western Allies and their former enemies would fight 'shoulder to shoulder' against Bolshevism, as the propaganda of the British Free Corps had urged.

The significance was not in any foundation of truth upon which the rumour relied, but in the fact that such a story should have circulated and seemed plausible when the war in Europe had scarcely ended.

Throughout his final broadcast, Joyce insists that the sole cause of war in 1939 was the German wish that the city of Danzig –

racially and politically German and part of Germany until 1919 – should be returned by Poland. He summed up the British reaction to this request: 'If Germany grows too strong, we shall be in deadly danger.' The consequence of such misunderstanding was now to be written large on the post-war map of Europe.

> And if the Soviet Empire adds to its strength from week to week, if the Red Hand extends to the Near and Middle East, will the danger to Britain be less deadly than if a Germany, with no outlet whatever to the sea, with no outlet to Asia, had peacefully acquired minor gains of territory with historical or racial justification?

The argument still showed Joyce's intellectual sleight of hand. His was the voice of the friendly pickpocket, urging his victim to part quietly with his wallet in the street, rather than have his house ransacked by a gang of desperadoes. A year before the Danzig question, Hitler had described the Sudetenland as 'the last territorial demand I have to make in Europe'. But more persuasive than territorial expansion were the images of recent history – of Nazi atrocity in the camps themselves or the notorious public execution of a hundred men and women by a single machine-gunner on 15 December 1941 in St Wenceslas Square, Prague, when Himmler himself had fainted at the sight of so much blood.

That the last words of Lord Haw-Haw to his listeners have an uncomfortable edge of truth to them forty years later does not disguise their moral dishonesty. He had often added a dash of truth to his most preposterous falsehoods. Now, for the first time, he could gain his effect by telling the truth and omitting the lie. He concluded with a prophecy for Britain:

> Such is the attitude of the Red dictator who menaces the security of the whole world, and whose power to-day constitutes the greatest threat to peace that has existed in modern times. Britain's victories are barren; they leave her poor, and they leave her people hungry; they leave her bereft of the markets and the wealth that she possessed six years ago. But above all, they leave her with an immensely greater problem than she had then. We are nearing the end of one phase in Europe's history, but the

next will be no happier. It will be grimmer, harder and
perhaps bloodier. And now I ask you earnestly, can Britain
survive? I am profoundly convinced that without German
help she cannot.

Such was the final message. It reduced the whole of the war to a
political tiff over the city of Danzig. Yet Joyce might have thought
himself vindicated. Four years after his final broadcast there was a
new Federal German Republic and two years after that the NATO
Allies made provision for a new German army to counter the
Soviet threat. Joyce in his broadcast overlooked the nature of the
war and of the Nazi regime. Yet at the end he was more plausible
than he had ever seemed. Given such material at an earlier stage of
his career, he might have made a considerable impact.

Joyce signed off with a final defiant 'Heil Hitler!' It was either an
indication that the story of Hitler's death had not yet reached the
Büro Concordia or else it was a final salute to a hero whose fall
most be imminent. Though rumours of the Fuehrer's death had
been circulating for some days, it seems impossible that a message
confirming the suicide which took place at 3.30 p.m. could have
reached the Büro Concordia by that evening.

But as soon as that news became known, by radio and by
telegram from Goebbels in the bunker to Doenitz in Schleswig-
Holstein, the last mad weeks of the Third Reich began. William
Joyce was part of the bizarre fiction by which the regime
continued to exist in areas of Germany for two or three weeks
after the war ended. Even after General Jodl's military surrender to
Eisenhower near Rheims on 7 May, the Reich continued to
administer those areas not overrun by the Allies. Its power was not
dissolved until 23 May. For a little while, Joyce and his wife could
hide. In the days following Hitler's death, Himmler tried to set up a
government at Luebeck on the Baltic. But the true succession went
to Doenitz with instructions that both Himmler and Goering
should be excluded from the new administration. It was not their
crimes which made Hitler exclude them from the succession but
the suspicion that they were treating with the western Allies.

So the place of government was transferred to the old Naval

Training School at Flensburg, the furthest refuge from the battleline in German territory. In this dockyard town with its medieval Nikolaikirche, its kiosks along the quays and shopping streets, its tree-shaded fiord with little yachting harbours, the court of the new Reichschancellor and his rivals assembled. Here, in the first days of peace and the last days of his own freedom, lived Lord Haw-Haw.

Soon after the recording of his final broadcast, on the evening of 30 April, he and his wife had been driven from Hamburg to Flensburg in an SS staff car. It was the first stage in a possible escape to neutral territory. There was little to stop the Joyces passing from Germany into German-occupied Denmark, which indeed they were soon to do. Then, from Copenhagen, they would cross the narrow straits to Stockholm and gain sanctuary.

They reached Flensburg and crossed the frontier into Denmark. But by this time the dislocation of transport and the political uncertainty were far worse than they had known in Germany. It was said that a British occupation force had landed somewhere in the north. The fugitive Nazis were met by a mass of refugees coming the other way. Harbours along this coast were crowded with ships that had brought terrified German civilians from the Baltic coast and the path of the Red Army's advance.

When it was clear that there could be no escape to Sweden, Joyce insisted on returning the short distance across the German frontier to Flensburg. In so doing, he probably made a grievous miscalculation. By remaining where he was he would have been subject to Danish jurisdiction, against which he had committed no crime. By returning, he put himself under the government of the British military occupation.

Despite what it had suffered at the hands of Germany, Denmark retained a liberal constitution in matters of political opinion. It was not likely to extradite a man if the offence with which he was charged appeared to be political. The French novelist Louis-Ferdinand Céline, author of *Voyage au bout de la nuit*, owed his liberty and possibly his life to the Danes in 1945. A pre-war Fascist sympathiser and wartime supporter of Vichy, Céline had fled from France to Germany during the liberation, and escaped to Denmark in the last days of the war. On 19 April 1945 a warrant for his arrest had been issued in France. Like Joyce, he was to be charged with treason.

At the request of the French government, Céline was arrested in Copenhagen and application was made for his extradition. The Danes delayed this, on the grounds that his offence appeared to be of a political nature. After a year's detention in Copenhagen, Céline was set free on parole. Four years later the case against him was dismissed by the Danish courts. In 1951 he returned to France, at a time when the post-war treason trials were over and, in many cases, had begun to seem suspect. Even his trial *in absentia* had been delayed until 1949, with the result that he was not sentenced to death but to a term of imprisonment, a fine, and the confiscation of his property. By the time that he returned to France, he had benefited from an amnesty extended to those Frenchmen who had fought for their country in the First World War.

Perhaps William Joyce might have been less fortunate. Yet his offence was certainly political – the charge of treason was identical to Céline's – and there was the vexed question of his nationality. The Danes might be less easily convinced that he was not American, or Irish, or even German. At least the case might have dragged on long enough, as it did for Céline, to allow the immediate thirst for post-war vengeance to be slaked. Even in France, by 1949 or 1950, wartime crimes were not a matter for the public executioner or the firing-squad.

Moreover, there was just a possibility that the Danes might have interned him as 'Wilhelm Hansen', accepting the extra passport as genuine. In that case too he might have remained out of British hands until the time of post-war vengeance was over. The Danes had no particular interest in Lord Haw-Haw and he might have been able to merge with the other internees. His disappearance need not have surprised the British authorities in Germany. If he could not be found, it would be assumed that he lay dead somewhere under the ruins of Berlin or Hamburg. Though his voice was familiar to tens of thousands of people he had the advantage, for a fugitive, that very few of these people knew what he looked like. They imagined him as the languid blue-blooded aristocrat rather than the razor-scarred Fascist street-fighter.

But, for better or worse, Joyce decided that he and Margaret would return to Flensburg. It was to prove for the worse.

As *The Times* was soon to report, the returning travellers managed to find a room for the next ten days in the station hotel at Flensburg. Around them the government of the post-Hitler Third Reich was taking shape. Admiral Doenitz and his 'cabinet' occupied the Naval Training School. Heinrich Himmler and an SS bodyguard arrived in town to set up headquarters from which the former Reichsfuehrer proposed to exercise his power. No matter if the war was over, the SS would still be in control of Flensburg. Himmler had already been a secret negotiator through Count Bernadotte, which led to his exclusion from the succession by Hitler. But now there was practically nothing to negotiate about, as German control shrank to the base of the peninsula and the occupied territories of Norway and Denmark. Moreover, Doenitz and his government were already in place. The new Fuehrer informed Himmler that there was to be no place for him. Three days after the war had ended, Himmler and his SS entourage left Flensburg, the former Reichsfuehrer discarding his familiar pince-nez in favour of a Long John Silver eye-patch.

The war in Flensburg came to an eerie conclusion. There had been comparatively little bombing or any sign of hostility. Joyce, from his hotel, was able to view the crowded decks of the refugee ships in the port. Doenitz had announced the military surrender of the Third Reich. There was nothing to do but wait for the first units of the British army of occupation to arrive. Meantime the familiar Nazi uniforms and functionaries controlled the town.

One day a ship docked without refugees on its decks. The Royal Navy had begun to land the first detachments of the British army. A few buildings, including the station hotel, were taken over. The rest of the British troops patrolled the town in groups and continued to live on the accommodation vessels in the port. There seemed no great animosity between the victors and the vanquished. Flensburg, with its markedly Danish appearance, was physically and emotionally remote from the scenes of Nazi triumph and atrocity.

Turned out of their hotel, the Joyces found lodgings with civilians near the town. As J. B. Priestley said of Bournemouth, it had not been too bad a war for Flensburg. Set in the middle of a prosperous farming area, it had immediate supplies of food not available to the shattered cities of Germany or the towns overrun in the great military offensives of the spring. Rations were short but life was not intolerable.

As the days passed, it seemed that there was little interest in 'Wilhelm Hansen' the displaced person. Among millions of others perhaps he could lose himself after all. At this stage it was Margaret who posed the greater danger. She did not speak German well and would be detected at once as a foreigner. Joyce, with the story of his Irish birth, might just get away with it. In any case, the army of occupation was still looking for the Nazi leaders and constructing a form of administration. The arrest of Lord Haw-Haw was not a first priority. And however much he might be disliked, it was by no means clear what crime he could be charged with.

As it happened, 'Lord Haw-Haw' was arrested more than once. The first claimant to the title in the Büro Concordia was Norman Baillie-Stewart. When the Russians entered Vienna, they looted his flat of everything that seemed valuable but left his papers undisturbed. These provided the substance of the case against him. Baillie-Stewart himself was arrested while wandering, cold and hungry, in the mountains. He was incongruously dressed in Tyrolean costume. Proud of his German nationality and the work that he had done, he insisted that he was the only genuine Haw-Haw. William Joyce was a mere thug with no claim upon such nobility.

Another week passed. Joyce attracted no suspicion, though he passed the patrols of British soldiers and even spoke to some of them. Did they not remember his voice? Or had they perhaps never had the chance to listen while they were on active service?

Whether he could get away with it for long enough – or whether he cared sufficiently about the future to attempt it – was open to question. The days of glory were over and the prospects of Joyce in the post-war world were poor in the extreme. Fascism as he had known and advocated it, was dead. There would be other forms of oppression from the right and left of the political spectrum, there would be echoes of Nazism here and there. But National Socialism was dead as the Holy Roman Empire or the dynasty of the Bourbons.

On the evening of 28 May, Joyce was walking through a wood which overlooked the harbour. He was alone. Ahead of him he saw two English officers who were apparently gathering firewood. They belonged to the Reconnaissance Regiment of the Royal Armoured Corps. Their vehicles were drawn up near Flensburg and the crews were preparing a meal. One of the officers was Captain Lickorish and the other was Lieutenant Perry. Joyce could have passed on his way without attracting their attention. Instead, he waved a hand, speaking to them first in French. Then he called out helpfully in English, 'There are a few more pieces over here.'

He was walking away again when the two officers overtook him. Lieutenant Perry said, 'You wouldn't happen to be William Joyce, would you?'

The question was almost superfluous, for as Captain Lickorish said later, he had already recognised the voice as 'that of the announcer or speaker on the German radio'.

Joyce stopped and began to put his hand into his pocket. He was looking for the passport which identified him as Wilhelm Hansen. But these were days when a fanatical Nazi might reach for his poison phial or his gun rather than surrender. Five days earlier, Himmler had committed suicide in the presence of his captors by biting on a cyanide capsule. A more resolute Nazi might choose to go down in an exchange of bullets.

As Joyce reached into his pocket, Lieutenant Perry snatched his own revolver from its holster and fired low. The explosion in the wood brought others running in that direction. But at such close range the bullet had entered Joyce's right thigh, passed out of it into his left thigh, and passed out of that as well. He fell to the ground, crying out, 'My name is Fritz Hansen!'

That he should have got the first of his assumed names wrong was not surprising in the moment of being shot. Captain Lickorish described what happened next. 'I, thinking the same as Perry, that he was armed, rushed over to get his weapon from him and searched him at the same moment and found two passports on his person. He was unarmed and was wounded in the leg.'

The first passport was a German civilian document in the name of 'Wilhelm Hansen'. The other was a military passport in the name of William Joyce. Lickorish bound up the bullet wounds and got a jeep to take his prisoner to the Danish frontier post not far away. He took the two passports and handed them to the Guard Commander.

As Joyce was carried away, he assumed that it was a poison phial rather than a gun that Perry thought was in his pocket. 'I suppose', he said contemptuously, 'that in view of recent suicides you will expect me to do the same? I am not that sort of person.'

It was perhaps as well for his *sang-froid* that he remained unaware of the fully irony of his fate. Lieutenant Perry, who had fired the bullet into him, was Jewish.

The press reported that Lord Haw-Haw had been 'seriously wounded' during his capture. He was certainly a stretcher-case and arrived next day at Lueneburg Hospital, close to British Second Army Headquarters. At the news of his identity, soldiers crowded round the vehicle. Joyce was lifted out on the stretcher. His hair had been cropped and his features appeared thin and wasted. This was in part because his false teeth had been confiscated, for fear that they might contain an ingeniously concealed capsule of cyanide or some other poison. Except at the Old Bailey and on the morning of his execution, he was never again allowed to wear clothes with buttons on for fear that he might use them to commit suicide. Tapes were provided instead. The press photographs from Lueneburg showed him surrounded by uniformed soldiers who looked on with impassive curiosity. A few taunted him with their own versions of 'Jairmany calling! Jairmany calling!' He spoke once to them, in a sneer that a million listeners would have known instantly: 'In civilised countries, wounded men are not peepshows!'

But the Lueneburg peepshow was a mere prelude to the grand spectacle of justice and retribution that was about to begin.

Part Three

RETRIBUTION

Behold the Pale Criminal has bowed his neck:
from his eye speaks the great contempt.
                Friedrich Nietzsche, *Thus Spake Zarathustra*

CHAPTER 13

Despite the manner in which the case was to develop, Joyce's fate had by no means been decided when he arrived at Lueneburg Hospital. Three Attorney-Generals were in office during the proceedings against him. Sir Donald Somervell served in the last days of the wartime coalition. He was succeeded by Sir David Maxwell Fyfe in Churchill's 'caretaker' government until the election of July 1945. The main burden fell upon Sir Hartley Shawcross, Attorney-General of the incoming Labour government.

Writing in 1946 on the legal aspects of the case, C. E. Bechhofer Roberts reported that the Director of Public Prosecutions had suggested indicting Joyce for high treason but that each Attorney-General had received the proposal with 'incredulity'. There did not appear to be sufficient grounds or evidence for the charge. If any proceedings could be taken against him, they would more reasonably be based upon breaches of the wartime Defence Regulations. But as the newspapers and the voices of government demanded justice, the three Attorney-Generals 'studied the proposition with increasing interest ... in the end professional repugnance had changed to enthusiasm.' England was to have a major war criminal of its very own.

The interrogation began two days after his arrival at 74 General Hospital, Lueneburg. Margaret Joyce had been arrested shortly after him and was now also held in custody at Second Army Headquarters. Joyce himself was visited first of all by Captain Scarden of the Intelligence Corps. One of Scarden's jobs, a fortnight earlier, had been to search the Radio Luxembourg broadcasting station. Among other papers, he had found a receipt for 200 Reichsmarks, the payment dated 10 February 1944. The money had been paid to the credit of William Joyce, who was then staying with a girl-friend at the Hotel Alfa in Luxembourg. During this holiday he had given four talks for Radio Luxembourg at 50 marks a time.

On the morning of 31 May 1945, Captain Scarden appeared at Joyce's bedside. His introduction was unceremonious. He gave his name and at once came to the purpose of the visit: 'I am charged with the duty of making inquiries into the activities of British subjects employed by the enemy during the course of the war. There is abundant evidence to show that you have been working for the German broadcasting services, and it is proposed to present a case to the Director of Public Prosecutions.'

Captain Scarden, in his flat policeman's prose, informed Joyce of the procedure which the investigation would follow. As yet, no accusation had been made and no charge brought against him. The authorities had every reason to delay this until some preliminary decision had been taken on the question of his nationality. Among Joyce's papers Scarden found a birth certificate. It apparently confirmed that the suspect had been born in New York in 1906. Was it genuine? Was the prisoner the same William Joyce as the man referred to in the certificate, for the name was not in itself uncommon?

Scarden cautioned Joyce, but it was scarcely necessary. The suspect was a compulsive talker. On the question of his nationality, Joyce seemed vague: 'I understand, though I have no documents to prove any statement, that my father was American by naturalisation at the time of my birth.' Then, in a potentially damning admission, he added, 'We were always treated as British during the period of my stay in England, whether we were or not. In 1940 I acquired German nationality. I believe the date was September 26th but the certificate of naturalisation is not in my possession.'

By lunchtime Scarden had got all that he needed on the subject of Joyce's nationality. He withdrew to the officers' mess and came back that afternoon to find his prisoner anxious to make a full statement. Joyce dictated to him a long self-justification, describing his political upbringing and beliefs, his admiration for the 'constructive work which Hitler had done for Germany'. and his conviction that 'a war between Britain and Germany would be a tragedy, the effects of which Britain and the British Empire would not survive.' Of his present situation he had little to say:

> I know that I have been denounced as a traitor and I
> resent the accusation, as I conceive myself to have been
> guilty of no underhand or deceitful act against Britain,
> although I am able to understand the resentment that my
> broadcasts have, in many quarters, aroused. Whatever
> opinion may be formed at the present time with regard to
> my conduct, I submit that the final judgment cannot be
> properly passed until it is seen whether Britain can win the
> peace. Finally I should like to stress the fact that in coming
> to Germany and in working for the German radio system,
> my wife was powerfully influenced by me. She protests to
> the contrary, but I am sure that if I had not taken this
> step, she would not have taken it either.

Captain Scarden read the statement over and gave it to the prisoner to sign. Then he left the ward, where Joyce lay on his bed and considered his prospects, his false teeth once again impounded by the authorities.

The news of Joyce's arrest was followed in England by a newspaper clamour which reminded readers what a sneering traitor he had been. He had even sneered – or snarled – at the soldiers who crowded round the ambulance to have a look at him as he lay on his stretcher. A few members of his family were quoted as having disparaged or disowned him. Who, after all, would choose to be related to Lord Haw-Haw? In the first weeks of summer, Fleet Street promised him a homecoming he would not easily forget.

At another level, the government itself had to decide his future. It would be hard to show that he was a British subject. Surely, it would be even more difficult to convict an American citizen of treason, when the acts complained of had not even been committed on British soil. Moreover, since September 1940, he had technically been a German citizen. To be sure he had had a British passport for some years before that date. But he had not been entitled to it and had made no use of it during the war.

All this suggested that he should be treated as almost all the other prisoners of his kind would be. By charging him under the Defence

Retribution

Regulations, his nationality would be irrelevant, and he could be sentenced to fourteen years penal servitude. But would public opinion accept this? If the press could be believed, the British people would not stand for anything less than a treason trial and the execution of Lord Haw-Haw. He was their only war criminal of consequence and they were entitled to some satisfaction after all that they had suffered from him.

So ran the argument. Joyce was transferred from Lueneburg to the British military police detention barracks at Brussels. He and Margaret were held separately there. Indeed, their separation was soon to be almost complete. While he was taken to England, she was kept in Brussels during most of the time that his trial and appeals ran their course.

The worst outcome from the government's point of view would be to put him on trial for treason and then see him acquitted. By then it would be more difficult to bring other charges. The public might stand for that even less easily than for a non-capital conviction. It might break the reputations of the ministers or law officers involved, if Lord Haw-Haw walked down the Old Bailey steps a free man.

Before he was brought back to England, it was decided to alter the law on treason. The Treason Act (1945) received the royal assent the day before he was flown from Brussels under guard. Its purpose was to bring the law up to date by making the procedure in trials for treason the same as in trials for murder. It seemed a sensible way of clearing out archaic procedural lumber and making the whole thing more easily understood by the modern man. But it also changed the law in one detail that made a difference of life and death to William Joyce.

Treason had been the blackest of crimes. Because of this, the law of 1695 required at least two witnesses to an act of treason, or else two acts of treason each vouched for by a separate witness. This safeguard was now abolished and in Joyce's case the prosecution offered only one clear act of treason vouched for by one witness.

Having tidied up the law, the government was able to have Joyce flown from Brussels without complications. Had he arrived earlier, objections might have been made by his lawyers that he had not been charged under the old statute.

Commander Leonard Burt of Scotland Yard's Murder Squad had been seconded to Military Intelligence with the rank of Lieutenant-Colonel. With three armed guards, he was to bring William Joyce back to face justice. His prisoner was fetched from the detention cell, wearing the blue suit that he had had made for him in Berlin during the days of his prosperity. He looked thin and downcast to this escort, but by this time he was able to walk again rather lamely. Burt told him that he was to be taken to England and charged with treason. Joyce seemed unmoved by the news. His guard ordered him to go back and collect his belongings.

An RAF Dakota had been detailed for the flight. Though Joyce could walk with the aid of a stick, his escort was obliged to lift him on to the plane. For the next hour or so, the commander and his prisoner were confined together in adjoining seats of the aircraft, 'talking as if we had been boyhood friends'. It was one of the oddest confessional moments in Leonard Burt's life. But during the flight Joyce was treated with the charity shown to a dying man, however distasteful his past conduct or opinions may have been. Soon after the plane took off, he asked if the pilot would fly a little off course, over a military cemetery of the First World War. He was allowed this indulgence, as if he had been a sick child asking for a treat.

He and Burt sat together, not far behind the pilot, while the three guards took their places at the rear. Joyce was in the window-seat, 'thin, shabby, scar-faced, and lame'. Burt gave him a cigarette and watched him smoking. Of all the traitors whom he brought back, he wrote, 'Joyce was the one I liked best for his courage and his blazing sincerity. He said to me as the Channel glinted below us: "I have the courage of my convictions. I can stand up to the consequences".'

Burt's professional reputation was that of the sympathetic interrogator. In this case, he gathered little beyond a repetition of Joyce's political views and an account of his arrest. To those who thought that Joyce was glad to have been captured and to have his fate decided, his remarks to Burt might be a disappointment. 'The wood near Flensburg,' he said confidentially. 'If only I'd kept my mouth shut!'

Retribution

But he also tried, constantly and self-hypnotically, to justify the cause for which he had fought and would die.

'I tried my best,' he said presently. 'in the last year before the war I warned the people of England. Every day, every day I spoke to them, at street corners, in clubs, anywhere, everywhere. They were blind and deaf. They wanted war, and race suicide. I still think I was right. You'll see it proved soon enough, now that Germany is destroyed and Communism stronger than ever.'

He spoke like a man who would not be present to witness the consequences. According to Burt, Joyce had thought about and rejected the possibility that he might save his life by virtue of his American birth: 'It didn't impress him very much. He was sure he was for the rope.'

The two men talked and smoked until the first outlines of the English coast came mistily into view. One of the guards got up and came forward with his autograph book, suggesting that Lord Haw-Haw might be good enough to write something in it. He handed the book to Burt, who passed it on to Joyce. A moment later it came back with an entry in firm clear script: 'We are about to pass over the white chalk cliffs England's bulwark. It is a sacred moment in my life – and I can only say whatever my fate may be – God bless Old England on the lee.' Presently he lit his last cigarette before the plane touched down and turned again to Burt.

'She had nothing to do with anything I did,' he said. 'I know you won't try to pin anything on her.'

Burt did not need to ask the identity of the woman referred to.

The plane landed and Joyce was lifted down. He walked awkwardly away between his escorts to be confronted by a nondescript middle-aged man in a grey suit.

'I am Chief Inspector Bridges of New Scotland Yard,' the man said quietly. 'I shall arrest you and take you to Bow Street, where you will be charged with high treason.'

Joyce looked at him without malice or resentment. 'Yes,' he said, 'Thank you.'

He was driven to Bow Street at once under armed police escort and the charge of treason was read to him.

'I have heard and taken cognisance,' he said. 'Today I shall not add anything to the statement I have made to the military authorities.'

So far as the police and the courts were concerned, William Joyce was never to add another word, except to say 'No, sir' three times on Monday morning to the magistrate who asked him if he had a lawyer, or any questions to put to the witnesses, or objected to being remanded in custody. And last of all, he was to plead 'Not guilty' at the Central Criminal Court. He gave the impression as he landed in England, on that Saturday afternoon of 16 June 1945, of great weariness after all that had happened. It was as if he wished only to be left alone. In the case of Lord Haw-Haw that was a favour which neither the press nor the public proposed to grant.

CHAPTER 14

In 1945, for the first time in almost six years, the people of London were able to spend the summer free from the danger of enemy action. Yet the city to which William Joyce returned had been altered by the blitz to a place of strange perspectives and dramatic views. The area round the Old Bailey had been flattened by the bombs, so that the pillared building rose from a vast wasteland of grass and wild flowers. Some of the courts had been destroyed and then sealed off by makeshift walls of brick. Like many public buildings the Central Criminal Court remained almost dark inside throughout the day because of the black-out paint used to prevent light showing through the glass.

Though the war in Europe was over, the fire-blackened shells of city buildings and the deserts of rubble still looked much as they had done in the immediate aftermath of the Luftwaffe's bombardment. The people too bore the marks of their ordeal. If William Joyce looked pallid and thin and shabby, he was a match for most of those who now waited with interest for his trial.

Forty-eight hours after leaving Belgium, he appeared at Bow Street magistrates court on Monday 18 June. News and rumours of his arrival in England led to a crowd of would-be spectators arriving, hours before the hearing, to queue for seats in the public gallery. There was room for only a handful of them. Behind Bow Street rose blocks of old tenements. Their tenants rented the higher windows to press photographers who might be able to take telephoto pictures of Joyce at exercise in the yard of the court during the lunch-hour. Before the chief magistrate, Sir Bertrand Watson, he was charged with treason and remanded in custody for a week. Now that the case was *sub judice*, the press had to bide its time in commenting on Lord Haw-Haw. But it had already created the necessary impression of him in the public mind. He appeared on remand again on 25 June and then, three days later, he was commited for trial to the July Sessions of the Central Criminal Court.

He had no money to pay for his representation. Under the Poor Prisoners' Defence Act, he was entitled to legal aid. At his appearance on 25 June he was defended by a solicitor experienced in criminal practice, C. B. V. Head. Mr Head went directly to the point, arguing that there was no case for his client to answer. Joyce had been a United States citizen until September 1940 and then became a naturalised German. It was legally and logically impossible for him, while he was in Germany, to commit treason against the King of England to whom he owed no allegiance whatever once he had left the British Isles.

A matter of this importance could hardly be decided by a magistrate. Joyce must stand his trial at the Central Criminal Court. For the defence, Head briefed Gerald Slade, KC, the Recorder of Guildford. At fifty-four, Slade had made a considerable reputation in the civil and criminal courts as a defender in cases which turned upon subtle points of law. Derek Curtis-Bennet, KC, another experienced criminal lawyer, and James Burge, who was Deputy Judge Advocate in the RAF from 1941 until 1944, completed the team of Joyce's counsel.

It was impossible to say who would lead for the crown. A general election was then a week away, though its result was not to be announced until 26 July, when the votes of servicemen overseas would have been received and counted. The Attorney-General of the new government would be Joyce's prosecutor. In the event, this was to be Sir Hartley Shawcross KC, one of the most distinguished of the new generation of lawyers and prosecutor at the Nuremberg War Crimes Tribunal.

There was less urgency than had been supposed. Joyce was not, after all, to appear at the Old Bailey in July. Because so much depended upon evidence from New York, the defence applied for a postponement until September. The birth certificate was already available but that would not be accepted as evidence without some support. Proof would be needed that the William Joyce in the dock was the same William Joyce whose name appeared on the document. Witnesses would also be needed to support the story of his father's naturalisation.

The most important of these witnesses could no longer be called. Joyce's father had died in 1941 and his mother in 1944. The house in Underhill Road, East Dulwich, had been virtually destroyed by a German bomb. It seemed that defence witnesses and new copies of the documents might have to be brought from America.

Though the press was now prevented from commenting directly on the case until the proceedings were over, every development was reported in great detail. Fleet Street remained second to none in its zeal for post-war retribution. The *Daily Mail* was among the leaders, conveniently forgetting its pre-war encouragement of Fascism. The *Evening Standard* published readers' letters on the theme of post-war vengeance. One of these was from a lady who suggested that after the conviction of the surviving Nazi leaders, they should be hanged as a public spectacle – upside down in a row across the Thames. The technical complexities of this form of execution were not allowed to dim the shining example of her moral anger. Another of the paper's letters was from a lady who advocated making a film of the hanging of Goering, which could then be shown at all the cinemas. People would 'enjoy' watching it, she wrote.

The popular press offered such sentiments as though they were typical and proper. What the public actually thought was another matter. It was scarcely worth carrying out a survey of opinion on the few and comparatively unimportant traitors brought to judgment in England. But a survey was undertaken in a far more important case in France. Marshal Pétain, leader of Vichy and one of the principal collaborators with Hitler, was tried for treason in the summer of 1945. Before this, the French opinion poll IFOP asked its countrymen whether they thought Pétain should be punished for concluding an armistice with Germany in 1940 and acting as Vichy head of state.

The result was instructive: 32 per cent of the sample thought he should be punished; 58 per cent thought he should not; 10 per cent had no opinion. In the event, he was condemned to death, though this was commuted to life imprisonment. According to the opinion poll, only 3 per cent of those questioned thought he deserved a death sentence. Though the circumstances were unlike, both this and the BBC's opinion survey in the case of Lord Haw-Haw suggest that ordinary people were less vindictive than their masters, whether in government or in the press.

In that summer of 1945, England had one other potential traitor who, had he been brought to trial, would have eclipsed William Joyce. P. G. Wodehouse, then almost sixty years old, was still living in his villa at Le Touquet when the town was taken by the Germans in 1940. With other British civilians he was consigned to Loos prison and then taken by cattle truck to a camp in Poland. Like all civil internees, he was freed from the camp when he was sixty, though not repatriated. The United States was still neutral and the CBS correspondent in Berlin invited Wodehouse to give three radio talks to his American public. He did so, describing his experiences in prison in such terms that another prisoner-of-war commented, 'Why the Germans ever let him say all this, I cannot think.... Wodehouse has probably been shot by now.'

Despite Air Marshal Boyd's prediction, Wodehouse had more to fear from the British. It was said that 'his Nazi captors persuaded him to broadcast from his Upper Silesian prison appeals to his British countrymen to surrender to the Madman of Berchtesgaden.' This was complete nonsense. But it was small wonder if his countrymen during the war, perhaps goaded by denunciations from columnists like Cassandra of the *Daily Mirror*, were smashing the windows of shops which dared to display the traitor's books. So, at least, it was said.

What did English people truly think of Wodehouse? When he was found in Paris, in 1944, Malcolm Muggeridge was the intelligence officer who became his minder. On a visit to London, Muggeridge was persuaded to inquire of Wodehouse's English agent how the novels had done during the war. Watt informed him that there had been 'record sales' and an unfailing demand. Not a single pane of window-glass had been broken. On the other hand, the search for possible traitors was gaining in enthusiasm and there was what Muggeridge called 'a mood for sacrificial victims'. He concluded that 'Wodehouse might well have fared ill if he had come before a British court at that time.'

Of the traitors who now faced their trials in London, few had been of much use to the Nazi cause, however grandiose their intentions. Most were the remnant of the British Free Corps – the former Legion of St George – recruited from the prison camps. Never more than a handful, only one or two had seen combat anywhere except in the bars and brothels of Berlin. There were also those men and women who had broadcast for the Reichsrundfunk, almost all civilians. For the most part they had been no more than announcers. Of the rest, Norman Baillie-Stewart had applied for German nationality before the war and had acquired it in 1940. He was technically as capable of treason as Joyce but the matter was not pursued. Though he was given a prison sentence under the Defence Regulations, he was not tried for treason. It was predictable that John Amery was tried as a traitor. It would look bad for the new Labour government if he seemed to be let off lightly just because he bore a name distinguished in British political life.

It was in this post-war climate that William Joyce waited in the hospital of Brixton prison for his trial to come on. He was able to walk about without sticks, though his hair had now been cropped as the result of a scalp infection. A few other prisoners, who regarded their own crimes of theft or assault as morally superior to his, bombarded him with missiles and insults while he was exercising alone in the yard. His visitors, including his brother Quentin and John Macnab who had been his ally in the National Socialist League, found him cheerful enough. He passed his time reading novels, playing chess and writing letters. Not until November was Margaret brought from Belgium and confined in Holloway prison, as if bureaucracy had contrived the petty inhumanity of keeping husband and wife apart deliberately during the short remainder of his life. After her return, she was permitted to visit him.

Perhaps because, as Commander Burt said, Joyce 'knew he was for the rope', he seemed to regard his trial with detached fatalism and schoolboy facetiousness. 'It will be amusing to see if they can get away with it,' he said to one of the guards, referring to the defence that his lawyers were preparing. He spoke as if their lives, not his, were at stake. His own he regarded as already lost. Towards the Attorney-General, whom he nicknamed 'Hotcross' for his busy and energetic manner, he showed neither hostility nor malice.

When Head, his solicitor, visited him in Brixton one day, Joyce was suddenly struck by the thought that he might find himself tried before a predominantly Jewish jury. Head assured him that his counsel would have the right to challenge jurors, if he thought they were Jewish.

'How does one know them?' Joyce asked.

'Oh,' said Head, 'when they take the oath they put on a hat or put their hand on their head.'

A glint of amusement appeared in the prisoner's eyes.

'Well,' he said, 'if six of them do it, wouldn't it be a good idea if I took the oath the same way?'

Among the many disadvantages of punishing murder or treason by death was the opportunity it gave to criminals of Joyce's kind to show wit and courage that won admiration from their very enemies. From the moment of his capture he appeared courteous, helpful, and appreciative of all that was done for him. He became the very thing that there had been no sign of in his broadcasts or pre-war campaigning, likeable. It was particularly those who guarded or served him in the few months that were left who found it impossible not to admire him, despite what he had done. He drew incalculable strength from the knowledge that he had committed no crime by his own morality. Had the war ended differently, his conduct might have made him a hero. It was luck, not justice, that caught him in the end. He saw it as his duty to be true to his National Socialist faith and to give an example to all who watched him in his ordeal. In this, his memory for an apt quotation came to his aid. He later told his friends that as he stood in the dock and heard sentence of death passed upon him, he drew strength and example from the seventeenth-century lines of Andrew Marvell, describing Charles I on the scaffold:

> He nothing common did nor mean

Retribution

> Upon that memorable scene.

The notion of Marvell being conscripted to bolster the morale of Lord Haw-Haw might seem distinctly odd. But the man who came to judgment at the Old Bailey on Monday 17 September 1945 was no less the clever and eccentric English undergraduate than the Fascist preacher and the sardonic apologist for the Third Reich.

Joyce was driven under armed police escort from Brixton to the Old Bailey early on that September morning to face his trial for high treason. The building was still darkened where missing windows and skylights were boarded over. Black paint had not yet been removed from the remaining glass.

Long before his arrival a queue of several friends and a good many enemies had formed at the entrance of the public gallery. Few of those who waited patiently in the autumn sunshine had any chance of being admitted. But the old hands knew that the spectators admitted in the morning would have to leave their seats when the court rose for lunch. By standing patiently in line, the next group in the queue would be admitted for the afternoon sitting.

Very few of them were allowed in at any time. The trial of Lord Haw-Haw had caught the imagination of the world's press. Part of the public gallery was reserved for its representatives. Ordinary men and women had little prospect of being admitted, but a good many more seats were reserved for distinguished guests, invited by the Common Council of the City of London. They included diplomats from foreign embassies, senior officers from the three services, and influential figures in British public life – or at least those who had influence enough to get a seat.

The police officers in the case sat at the solicitors' table, accompanied by a number of men not in uniform, the anonymous representatives of MI5. At either end of the counsels' bench sat the Attorney-General, Sir Hartley Shawcross, and Gerald Slade for the defence. A shelf had been fitted in front of this bench to hold the considerable number of legal volumes whose authority was to be called upon during the case.

Presently there were three taps on the door behind the judge's bench, 'like the signal in a French theatre for the raising of the curtain,' said Bechhofer Roberts. The mutters of conversation died away and the entire assembly rose to its feet as Mr Justice Tucker in scarlet robes and wig entered with the aldermen and sheriffs. He bowed to the aldermen, clerk and counsel, and the bows were returned. Then Sir Frederick Tucker, as he was known outside the court, sat down, permitting the onlookers to take their places again. In his hands he carried the traditional white gloves – an eighteenth-century precaution against the contagion of gaol-fever – and the piece of cloth known as the Black Cap. It was noticed that he tucked this behind the books on his desk so that the prisoner should not see it during the proceedings.

The choice of Mr Justice Tucker to preside over the case was an interesting one. He had already described William Joyce as a traitor while sitting in judgment on Anna Volkov almost five years earlier.

As if it had been a routine case of theft or assault, the clerk said loudly, 'Put up William Joyce!'

There was a stillness of expectation as those in the courtroom heard the prisoner's footsteps on the stairs from the cells and then saw him emerge in the dock between his warders. He bowed to the judge and, in the pause before the clerk spoke, he gave a smile and a wave to his brother and several friends in the public gallery. The harsh radiance of the electric light in the darkened No. 1 Court was merciless to William Joyce, wrote Rebecca West. His hair was still cropped and the glare of the lights made the misshapen nose and the razor-scar more evident. He still walked with nervous energy, though rather awkwardly as a result of the bullet wounds received four months earlier. He was a shorter and slighter figure than his radio presence had suggested. Very few of his listeners had had the least idea of what he looked like. In the flesh, Lord Haw-Haw presented an incongruous appearance to the public gaze.

The press could not quite make up its mind whether to present him as the swaggering Nazi or a shabby and insignificant little gnome. The swaggering Nazi would have sold more copies but shabbiness was nearer the truth. Guilty or not, he had to be made contemptible by virtue of his appearance alone. 'He was a not very

Retribution

fortunate example of the small, nippy, jig-dancing type of Irish peasant,' wrote Rebecca West in the *New Yorker*, putting him down at the outset. Had she been right, Joyce would not have been standing in the dock of the Old Bailey.

The charges of treason were read out. He had three counts to answer. First, he was charged with treason throughout the war for his broadcasts from Germany. Second, he was charged with treason for taking German nationality while England and Germany were at war. In law, it was treasonable for a British subject to do so. Third, he was charged with treason for his broadcasts between 3 September 1939 and 2 July 1940, the period of the war before his British passport had expired.

When the charges had been read, the clerk of the court asked him, 'Are you guilty or not guilty?'

'Not guilty,' said Joyce.

To the disappointment of those who had queued so long for the public gallery, they were the only words that he spoke during the whole of the case. Indeed, they were his last public utterance.

CHAPTER 15

When the jury had been sworn, Sir Hartley Shawcross rose to open the case for the crown. Youthful in appearance, neatly dressed and with great physical presence, he had a baritone subtlety of voice and command of his audience that a West End actor might have envied. Indeed, his portraits issued to the press were not of the formal and stolid full-face kind by which an older generation of lawyers had been known. The newly-appointed Attorney-General was seen in theatrical profile, his 'Photo by Yevond' equally appropriate to the Old Bailey or the Old Vic. He was only eleven years younger than Gerald Slade who led the defence. But Mr Slade, with his wing-collar and patriarchal moustache, and the solid intelligence of his sharp eyes and bald dome, might almost have been the Attorney-General's Victorian grandfather.

Each of the legal gladiators had his characteristic strengths. In the case of Sir Hartley Shawcross these included an even-tempered urbanity and courtesy towards his adversary, an impression of fairness and fair play, as if he were content merely to put the facts to the jury and might be quite happy to see William Joyce go free, if that proved to be the outcome. It would have been easy, and fatal to William Joyce, to underestimate the resilience of the Attorney-General's skill. Gerald Slade, by contrast, was a great debater. He would take the key points of the defence and then refine them until they seemed unanswerable in their simplicity and common sense.

It was as well that Gerald Slade possessed such qualities. His was an uphill fight against prejudice and legal argument. This trial was to be a reversal of the usual situation, where the prisoner is entitled to the benefit of the doubt. Because the facts about Joyce's conduct were not in dispute, he was guilty unless Slade could prove otherwise. Yet throughout much of the case, in the face of the

Retribution

judge's apparent lack of sympathy, Slade had the better of the argument.

The Attorney-General rose and opened his case to the jury. With complete fairness he told them that they must put from their minds any knowledge or feelings they had about the prisoner. But in explaining this, he carefully reminded them of what it was they must now forget:

> 'It may be even perhaps that in those dark days of 1940 when this country was standing alone against the whole might and force of Nazi Germany, that some of us may have heard, or thought we heard, his voice on the wireless, attempting as we may have thought to undermine the morale of our people. And perhaps at that time some of us formed feelings of dislike and detestation at what he was doing. And perhaps later on some of us heard with a not altogether unnatural satisfaction that he had been apprehended and was to be brought to trial.'

There was a chilling professional skill in this quiet opening. Not a word had been said to which the defence could object. Sir Hartley Shawcross rightly impressed upon the jurors that they must put prejudice from their minds. Posterity must see that the proceedings were conducted 'in the best traditions of English law'. But in order to accomplish that, he must recall the moral justice of that prejudice. He did his duty. But what William Joyce had been was never plainer than at that moment.

Sir Hartley pointed out that an alien would not normally owe any allegiance to the British crown and therefore could not be guilty of treason. A German soldier fighting for his country against Britain could not be held guilty of treason to King George VI. But it was central to English law that an alien who put himself under the protection of the crown owed a duty of allegiance. The Attorney-General cited Sir William Blackstone's *Commentaries* of 1765–9: 'So long as the Prince affords protection to his subject, so long that subject owes a debt of allegiance to the Prince.' Whether or not Joyce was born in New York of United States parents was something for the defence to prove:

> 'If that is true ... it would mean that at all times material

to this case the prisoner was an American citizen, owing
no natural duty of allegiance to the British Crown, but
still capable as an alien of placing himself under the
protection of the Crown, of clothing himself with the
status of a British subject and thereby acquiring and taking
upon himself an obligation to be loyal and faithful to the
British Crown.'

The case for the prosecution consisted of two arguments. In the
first place, an alien who lives in the United Kingdom is subject to
its laws and owes allegiance to the protecting monarch. In the
second place, the holder of a British passport enjoys that protection
even after leaving the country. If Joyce were a British citizen, he
owed allegiance to the king throughout his life. If he were an
American citizen, then he owed allegiance until his British passport
expired on 2 June 1940. Even in Berlin during the war, holders of
British passports were under the care of the neutral 'protecting
power', which in this case was Switzerland. A British passport
entitled them to that safeguard:

'He would have been entitled, had he so desired, to call
upon that neutral power for whatever assistance or
protection he might have required. The Crown say that in
these circumstances he had not merely clothed himself with
the status of a British subject, he had, so to speak,
enveloped himself in the Union Jack, secured for himself
the greatest protection that he could secure.'

The image of William Joyce enveloped in the Union Jack was
central to the Attorney-General's opening speech. It was his case in
a nutshell. Yet he summarised the events of the past ten years and
reminded the jury of the way in which Joyce had fled the country a
few days before war began in 1939, 'thinking, no doubt, that he
was deserting the sinking ship.' Sir Hartley did not need to add that
it is rats who, proverbially, desert ships in those circumstances.
'Nor did this man, who had protested to love this country so dearly
and to be ready to draw the sword in favour of it, lose much time
in associating himself with our enemies.'

Quiet and balanced though the tone of the speech might seem,
sentence after sentence and phrase upon phrase were lethal to

Retribution

William Joyce. That he was deceitful, contemptible and hypocritical appeared the least of his vices. Indeed, the speech held the jury's attention so closely that it was easy to forget that it might be a total irrelevance. All these things mattered only if William Joyce was British and owed allegiance to the British crown. Presently the Attorney-General sat down and left it to his juniors to examine the first of the prosecution's witnesses.

There were seven witnesses in all and six of them did little more than confirm facts and documents already beyond dispute. Gladys Winifred Isaac produced the records of the University of London OTC. These included Joyce's letter of 9 August 1922, describing himself as born in America of British parents. Harold Godwin, of the Passport Office, produced Joyce's application form of 4 July 1933, on which the nationality had been entered as 'a British subject by birth'. Gerald Slade tried to make some progress in cross-examination by suggesting that when Joyce applied for a passport renewal in August 1939 he merely wished to get to Germany and had no desire to put himself under British protection thereafter. That he was the possessor of the passport until 2 July 1940 was the result of a Foreign Office practice whereby passports were renewed automatically for a year. Joyce had no wish to be protected by it after 18 September 1939, nor did he apply for protection of any kind. Instead, he applied for German citizenship. Was not renewal for a year the minimum allowed by the rules? But he was wrong on this. Mr Godwin explained that passports were sometimes renewed for only a few months.

Captain Lickorish described the arrest of Joyce near Flensburg. Captain Scarden gave evidence of the interrogation at Lueneburg Hospital and read out the prisoner's statement. Chief Inspector Frank Bridges of New Scotland Yard gave formal evidence of charging Joyce after he had arrived in England under military escort. Samuel Salzedo, a translator, went through the German documents produced by the prosecution and described their contents.

None of this could affect the outcome of the case. The one witness for the prosecution whose appearance caused a stir of interest was Inspector Albert Hunt of Scotland Yard's Special

Branch. He alone gave direct evidence of an act of treason committed by the prisoner.

In the event, if Hunt's evidence had been discredited, there was surely no testimony offered by the crown upon which Joyce could have been convicted of treason. The entire country knew that he had broadcast for the Germans, millions of its inhabitants had heard him. But no further evidence of that was offered by the prosecution in court.

Hunt could only say that he was stationed at Folkestone from 3 September until 10 December 1939 and that he heard Joyce speaking on the radio 'either in September or early October'. He recognised the voice from pre-war meetings of the British Union of Fascists and the National Socialist League. However, he now admitted that he had never actually spoken to Joyce and that the statement in which he said he had was inaccurate. Someone had left out the word 'not'. But he had recognised Joyce in that one radio transmission. It was the broadcast in which the speaker claimed that the Luftwaffe had destroyed Dover and Folkestone, though in fact no bomb had yet fallen anywhere in the British Isles.

This was the most important evidence of any of Joyce's activities which the crown chose to present. A few months earlier, before the new Treason Act became law in June 1945, it would have been inadmissable without a second witness to corroborate it. There was no corroboration of Hunt's evidence. He could not say on what day – let alone at what time – he had heard the broadcast. He did not even remember in which month he had heard it. Nor, when asked in cross-examination, could he tell the station which had broadcast the so-called news. 'I do not know,' he said, 'I was just tuning in my receiver round the wavelengths when I heard the voice.'

It was at least questionable whether the Ministry of Propaganda in Berlin, or Joyce himself, could have been daft enough to put out a story so far removed from any possibility of truth. Was it not fantastic, Slade asked Inspector Hunt, to suggest that a town like Dover or Folkestone had been destroyed at that stage of the war?

'Not necessarily,' said Hunt. 'It could have been destroyed.'

Slade persisted in his next question. Was it not a fantastic statement?

Retribution

'Well, it was really,' said Hunt, changing his ground with improbable rapidity.

It was on the uncorroborated evidence of one broadcast, whose date and origin were unknown, whose precise content and authorship could not be verified, that Joyce went to the gallows. To be sure there were papers showing that he was under contract to the Reichsrundfunk in 1942 but by then he was a German citizen. The BBC identified his voice in August 1940. But by then his British passport had expired and he enjoyed no further protection from it. The only further evidence against him was the workbook which recorded his employment as an announcer for the Reichsrundfunk. But no other person, even of British nationality, was indicated – let alone convicted of treason – on such grounds as that.

Such was the case for the prosecution. It had opened with a skilful address to the jury but the evidence which the seven witnesses had presented was less than conclusive – unless, of course, Joyce had been right in his letter to the OTC when, at sixteen years old, he claimed to be British and proud of it.

There was only one complete answer to the charge of treason but, if valid, it made William Joyce a free man. He had never been a British citizen, though he had lived in the country for thirty years, twelve of them in what was now the Republic of Ireland. So long as he lived under the protection of British law, he owed allegiance to the monarch, as any foreigner does in such circumstances. But the moment he left the country, whether for Germany or anywhere else, the protection and the allegiance ceased.

There was no doubt that this was, fundamentally, the legal position. Gerald Slade's first task was to show that Joyce was and always had been a United States citizen.

Slade began by suggesting that the charges against Joyce should be dismissed without more ado. There was no more justification in arresting Joyce and bringing him to England for trial than there would have been in doing the same with Ezra Pound, an American who had broadcast for Mussolini. If anyone had a right to try Joyce, it was probably the Americans. Even here there was a difficulty. Joyce became a German citizen on 26 September 1940. It was a valid transfer of allegiance in British and American law, as well as German. By the time that the United States entered the war, neither it nor its British ally had any call upon Joyce's loyalty. 'I submit to your lordship as a matter of law,' said Gerald Slade, 'that there is no case to go to the jury.'

Whether or not the British public would stand for such arguments, it seemed that Mr Justice Tucker was unlikely to do so. William Joyce had broadcast repeatedly and unrepentantly on behalf of the Nazi regime, undermining British morale by every means at his disposal. He was the representative of a brutal and vaunting tyranny that sought the downfall and subjection of a country in which he had lived for thirty years and whose nationality he claimed to share. By the ordinary rules of conduct, it could not be disputed that he had betrayed those whose fellow-citizen he claimed to be. Was it to be tolerated that he should now escape through the net of law which held him and wriggle his way to freedom?

The judicial wig and robes may be unkind to certain men who wear them. There are judges who appear like little old ladies in nightgowns and others who are transformed into sheep. The strength of Sir Frederick Tucker's profile might have been modelled from the bust of a Roman general and his attitude was that of robust common sense in the guise of law. He listened with scarcely veiled scepticism to Gerald Slade's finely-spun argument. His eyelids were of a heavy appearance, as if he might at any moment lower them and continue to watch the proceedings through their slits. Five years before, he had denounced William Joyce as a traitor. Why should he change his opinion now? He began a series of interventions. These proved helpful, though not invariably so, to the prosecution and deadly to the defence.

As Slade was building proof of Joyce's American nationality on the New York birth certificate, Tucker intervened.

'It only becomes evidence when there is some evidence of the identity of the prisoner with the person described in the certificate.'

Without witnesses to the birth or upbringing of William Joyce the certificate was worthless. But Slade turned the tables on Tucker with admirable forensic sleight of hand. The law presumes that a man cannot remember his own birth and therefore that his mere statements about it cannot be accepted as true in a court of law. 'In the absence of this birth certificate,' said Slade, 'there is no evidence that he was born within His Majesty's allegiance except, of course, the man's own statements which I am submitting are not evidence at all.'

So far as the first two counts of the indictment went, both assuming that Joyce was British, judge and prosecution were hoist by their own objections. If the birth certificate was not evidence, then there was no proof of his nationality whatever and no foundation to the charges of treason.

But Hartley Shawcross rose and intervened, citing East's *Pleas of the Crown* as a precedent to show that a defendant was presumed to be British unless he could prove otherwise. Mr Justice Tucker ruled that the present evidence, 'if uncontradicted', would entitle the jury to conclude that Joyce was British.

The prisoner in the dock, wrote the *Daily Mirror* correspondent, 'sat unconcernedly, hands folded, while a legal battle developed.'

Having failed to win his client's freedom by an initial *coup de main*, Slade began the long struggle to win judge and jury to his point of view in the face of massive public hostility. With tireless patience, he demonstrated the simplicity of the legal position. To be a British citizen by birth, Joyce must either have a British father or have been born in British territory. The judge ruled that the birth certificate was not sufficient proof. Very well, the defence would call witnesses to establish that Joyce had been born in the United States and they would furnish proof of his father's previous naturalisation.

It seems curious that the prosecution should have fought so hard, and in the face of the evidence soon forthcoming, to maintain that Joyce was British. That they did so was surely an indication of how uncertain was their hope of conviction on the third count. This charged Joyce only with treason between 18 September 1939 and 2 July 1940, while his fraudulently obtained British passport was still valid. But, passport or not, it was far from clear that an American subject in Germany could be guilty of treason against England, a country which he had left and to which he had no intention of returning. Moreover, the evidence of treason during that period amounted to the uncorroborated and extremely vague recollections of Inspector Hunt and the Reichsrundfunk workbook issued to Joyce.

The workbook proved little beyond its own existence. Joyce had presumably made some unspecified broadcasts from Berlin. So had P. G. Wodehouse, which indicates how easily the novelist might have found himself in the dock at the Central Criminal Court if matters had turned out a little differently in 1945. As it was, Joyce was to be hanged and Wodehouse to receive a knighthood.

Slade explained patiently to the jury the list of witnesses they would hear for the defence and the proof that would be offered of Michael Joyce's signature on the papers relating to his naturalisation. By this time, however, it was late in the afternoon and Mr Justice Tucker intervened to adjourn the case until the following morning, Tuesday 18 September. The jurors were not to be kept together under surveillance for the night but were allowed to return to their homes. 'But make sure that although you are allowed to separate, you do not discuss this case with anybody or allow anybody to discuss it with you, please.'

When the day's proceedings ended, Joyce bowed stiffly to the judge as he did at the beginning and end of every hearing. Still somewhat bemused by the publicity they had enjoyed since that morning, the jurors went their separate ways. The press, though straining the leash to say what it thought of William Joyce, was still forbidden from expressing its feelings. However, the first day's hearing at the Old Bailey received maximum coverage, befitting the most spectacular of all the war-crimes trials that were to take place in England.

On the second morning, Gerald Slade produced the documents upon which his case would rest and described them for the benefit of the court. It took him only a little while to complete his opening address to the jury and then he began to call his witnesses.

The first of these was white-haired and almost stone-deaf, a friend of Michael and Gertrude Joyce in New York. Frank Holland, though only sixty-two, was aged beyond his years. He suffered from a tremor. He looked and sounded, said Rebecca West, like an actor playing a part in Sean O'Casey. 'I don't hear very well,' he said plaintively, when Derek Curtis-Bennett began to question him for the defence. At the judge's suggestion, defence counsel moved closer to the witness-box.

'Were you born at a place called Shaw in Lancashire on 31 March 1883?' asked Curtis-Bennett, having established the name and residence of his witness.

'Yes,' said Holland, in such a subdued manner that Mr Justice Tucker leant forward to the defence counsel.

'Is he hearing you or answering you, Mr Curtis-Bennett?'

'He is certainly answering me, my Lord. I hope he is hearing me.'

Little by little, Mr Holland's story was established. Before emigrating to New York, he had known a girl called 'Queenie' Brooke in Shaw. When he reached New York she had already married Michael Joyce. They had a child whom he had seen regularly from infancy to manhood and whom he identified as the prisoner in the dock. There was no doubt whatever that the disputed birth certificate referred to him.

On the question of Michael Joyce's nationality, Frank Holland recalled that the prisoner's father had needed a United States passport to return to Great Britain in 1909. He was quite sure of this because Michael Joyce had already left for Hoboken, New Jersey, on the start of his journey before the passport arrived. As a favour to his friend, Frank Holland took the passport to him.

Finally, Curtis-Bennett produced a photocopy of the marriage certificate of Michael Joyce and Gertrude Brooke, dating from 1905. Mr Holland recognised the bride's handwriting as that of William Joyce's mother but his ordeal in the witness-box had now reduced the quavering voice to a mumble. Only Curtis-Bennett standing close by him could catch his words, which he repeated for the benefit of the judge and jurors.

The Attorney-General made no attempt to cross-examine Frank Holland. Mrs Holland was also to have been called, this time to identify the handwriting of the late Michael Joyce. But she was too ill to appear in court. Gerald Slade therefore relied upon Edwin

Quentin Joyce, the younger brother of his client, to do this. Quentin Joyce identified his father's handwriting on various documents as being identical with that on the marriage certificate and, by implication, on the papers of American naturalisation.

William Joyce's younger brother gave the impression of a gentle and mournful soul, a quiet contrast to the figure in the dock with his ill-contained energy and volubility. Quentin described how he had seen his father burning the documents of American naturalisation in 1934 or 1935. Though it had been possible to obtain photographs of the official record from New Jersey, the original parchment with its embossed American eagle and its red seal had gone for ever. It was suggested that Michael Joyce burnt the evidence of his American citizenship at the time of William Joyce's trial with Mosley and others at Lewes Assizes. If the son had been found guilty and his alien birth established, he and perhaps the rest of his family might have been deported to the United States.

As in the case of Frank Holland, the Attorney-General chose not to cross-examine Quentin Joyce.

The remaining four witnesses for the defence appeared briefly and with the dispassion of experts who have little reason to care what the outcome of the case may be. Detective Superintendent John Woodmansey of the Lancashire police confirmed that the Joyces had been regarded as American citizens and, hence, aliens during the period of their residence at Shaw in 1917. Sergeant Bernard Reilly, long ago retired from the force, described how he had been sent to question Michael Joyce at Salthill on the matter of his nationality. William Yuile Forbes, 'an examiner of questioned documents', confirmed that the handwriting on the naturalisation documents in New Jersey was identical with that on Michael Joyce's will and on other documents signed or written by him. Last of all, Henry Stebbings, who was First Secretary at the American Embassy in London, put the final touch to the defence case. Michael Joyce had sworn the oath required for American citizenship.

'He thereupon, by American law, became an American citizen without any formal order or requirement of any description. If the Michael Joyce referred to in this document married in New York and a son was born to him after he had become an American citizen, the nationality of that son would be an American citizen by birth.'

But what of Michael Joyce's subsequent denials, after he returned to England, that he was American? 'We are all British and not American,' he had replied to the OTC inquiry. Mr Stebbings had no doubt about that either. 'If at some subsequent time the father lost the American nationality which he had acquired in 1894, according to American law there would be no effect upon the status of the son who was born in America.'

Mr Stebbings left the witness-box and returned to his embassy. It was now quite impossible for the jury to find William Joyce guilty of the first two charges of treason against him. He had first been a United States citizen, though until 2 July 1940 he had illegally held a British passport. When he ceased to be a United States citizen, on 26 September 1940, he became German. He committed no crime in English law by this naturalisation. Had he been British, it would have been treason to take German citizenship while the two countries were at war. Since he was American, he committed no crime. After 26 September 1940, it was impossible for him to commit treason against any country but Germany.

As the representatives of Fleet Street watched and listened, Mr Justice Tucker made the inevitable but sensational announcement, 'I think everybody must agree that the evidence which has been tendered is really overwhelming. That leaves us with count 3 as the only effective matter which we have to deal with.'

In other words, the jury would be directed to acquit William Joyce of the first two of the three charges of treason. The remaining count was that, as an American citizen fraudulently in possession of a British passport, he committed treason while enjoying British protection in Germany until 2 July 1940. In all the sneers and snarls, the taunting and the vituperation that had come over the airwaves from Berlin after that date, William Joyce had committed no treason – and perhaps no crime at all under English law.

Notes were passed and there was a hubbub in the corridor outside. News reached Fleet Street that Lord Haw-Haw had 'got off' on two of the charges and seemed about to get off on the other because of his American nationality. It was then, said the *Daily Mail*, that an angry crowd began to gather outside the Central Criminal Court.

At the very least, the case was now finely balanced. There was a feeling among members of the bar that the prosecution argument would never stick. In the great treason case of the First World War, that of Sir Roger Casement, the defendant had been a British subject. But to hang a man for treason to Britain who had been an American at the time of the alleged offences – and who had committed them in Germany – would surely not be easy.

Sir Hartley Shawcross faced a major difficulty which he frankly admitted to the court. Almost every legal precedent insisted that an alien owed allegiance to the British Crown while resident in Britain but that when he left the country that allegiance ceased. It was known as 'local allegiance', to distinguish it from the natural and permanent allegiance which a British subject owed. Joyce had left the country three weeks before the start of the period in which his alleged treason occurred. But as the Attorney-General soon pointed out, such legal precedents came mainly from cases of the eighteenth century, long before the modern system of passports. Did not the holder of a British passport – whether obtained honestly or by fraud – enjoy the protection of the British crown while abroad? If he did, then he logically continued to owe allegiance to the crown, even though he was an American and living in Germany during a time of war.

The trouble was that no law had ever said this was so. Passports of the familiar kind were a modern innovation and there had been few occasions for legal argument about them. The spectre of William Joyce leaving the court a free man began to trouble the minds of all those who had combined to bring him to justice.

What was to be done? The press had prepared its readers to believe that he was morally guilty. He had sneered at England in her finest and most imperilled hour. Everything about him – the best as well as the worst – was essentially English. How on earth could that drawling, blue-blooded tone be American or German – except by a clever lawyer's trick? The public would surely not

Retribution

tolerate an acquittal by means of legal technicalities. Lord Haw-Haw must not be allowed to 'cheat' – that was seen as the correct term – the hangman's noose.

It was an uneasy moment, particularly for the new Labour government. The triumph of Lord Haw-Haw might have signalled the destruction of a number of political reputations. But English law was extremely flexible. If that law could not suit the crime of William Joyce in its present form, perhaps it could be tailored to fit. The first step had been taken by the Treason Act of 1945 which made the evidence of Inspector Hunt admissible. Moreover, as the Attorney-General pointed out, there was no reason why the court should be bound to follow legal precedent. It might be time to apply the law in a new way. The twentieth century was not to be governed by the laws of the eighteenth.

'There is very little law on it,' Sir Hartley Shawcross said, when Mr Justice Tucker confessed his ignorance of how possession of a passport would affect the issue. 'I will say at once that I think that the submission I am about to make is not covered by any express authority. It is, perhaps, none the worse for that. I think it was Baron Parke who said that it is one of the incalculable advantages of our common law that it is applicable to new circumstances perpetually renewing themselves.'

It might sound as if the court was dangerously close to making up the law as it went along, in order to deal with William Joyce. But this was not so. The status of a passport in such a charge of treason had never had to be decided. It was therefore open to the court – in this case Mr Justice Tucker – to rule what the law should be.

Throughout the legal arguments, he inclined towards the prosecution case. Joyce himself said that as he listened he recalled two lines from one of his favourite English poets, John Dryden:
> What weight of ancient witness can prevail,
> When private judgment holds the public scale?

But even those who would have given the defence the benefit of the doubt could not deny that a judge must follow where logic leads him, for better or worse.

'May I, first of all, refer to two cases which at first appear to be against me?' Sir Hartley Shawcross resumed.

And, indeed, these and most of the other precedents certainly appeared to demolish his case. Time and again they confirmed that an alien's obligation to the British crown ended the moment he left the country. The crown's only hope was to show that Joyce enjoyed the protection of a British passport abroad, even though he was not entitled to that passport. And then Sir Hartley Shawcross quite fairly conceded that such protection might be 'in suspense' during a time of war. However skilfully presented, it was not a case that could be built on strong historical foundations.

As the Attorney-General began to sum up his arguments, Mr Justice Tucker leant forward and added another. What if Joyce had only intended to leave the country temporarily in August 1939 and to return after a little while? It would be absurd to say that he ceased to be resident in England merely because he took a short holiday abroad. And if he continued to be resident, he still owed a duty of allegiance:

> 'Supposing during the recent war, before Italy came into the war, an Italian subject had contrived somehow to have got out of this country for twenty-four hours and to have adhered to the enemy by some act during that twenty-four hours and then returned to this country, would he not still be guilty of treason based upon presence here, although the act was physically committed outside the country?'

If the circumstances of Joyce's case were to be fitted within the framework of treason, this was an inspired contribution. An interpretation of the law, as Mr Justice Tucker now suggested it, would probably put the rope round Lord Haw-Haw's neck. The Attorney-General agreed with the judge's suggestion, adding that when Joyce was asked the purpose of his passport application in 1933 he had put down 'holiday touring'. Joyce, said Sir Hartley Shawcross, was 'applying for facilities to leave this country and to go to various countries for a holiday tour with a view to his eventual readmission to this country.'

This was a reasonable interpretation. However, when Joyce applied for his passport renewal six years later, the purpose was no longer asked. Common sense suggested that it might well have changed. The circumstances of his departure in August 1939 hardly suggested 'holiday touring' and his application for German citizenship was not the act of a man only temporarily visiting Berlin.

It was unthinkable, the Attorney-General concluded, that a man who had been domiciled in England and whose family 'with the exception of his wife' remained behind, who declared himself to be British and who held a passport, should not owe allegiance to the crown while in Germany:

> 'I would ask your lordship to deal with the matter, and I submit it in this way under two heads. That here is a man who was resident and, indeed, domiciled, in this country ... and who left it for a period of time for a purely temporary purpose.... Secondly, on the basis that here was a man who quite independently of any continuing residence of that kind was under a duty of allegiance because of the protection of the Crown with which he had clothed himself.'

In answering this, it was the judge rather than the Attorney-General with whom Gerald Slade had to contend. He suggested that a man who takes his wife or children with him, leaving his parents and other independent relatives, has not left behind him a family for which he is directly responsible. Mr Justice Tucker refused to accept that there was evidence of Joyce being married.

Sir Hartley Shawcross rose chivalrously and pointed out that Joyce was described as a married man in his passport application. Mr Justice Tucker ruled that this was not evidence, though 'statements made by him in an application could, of course, be used as evidence against him.'

The argument continued for the rest of that September afternoon. Only once did Gerald Slade seem to lose his composure after one of the judge's interventions. 'I do not profess to have profound knowledge of criminal law or of any law at all. Your lordship is obviously right and I am wrong.'

There were, as it happened, few men at the bar or on the bench with a more profound knowledge of the law than Gerald Slade. With great tenacity and logic he displayed by the opinion of every major legal authority that an alien owed allegiance to the crown only so long as he was resident in British territory. All precedent supported that.

'Are you contending,' inquired Mr Justice Tucker, 'that residence means the physical presence in this country of the man?'

'Yes.'

'He must always be physically present in the country when he commits a treasonable act?'

'Yes.'

'Even in the case of the Italian which I put to you?'

'In that case, I should say he was not triable for treason.'

And Slade went on to cite the Treachery Act of 1940 which had been passed to cover just such cases as that of Mr Justice Tucker's Italian day-tripper. The problem with the Treachery Act, however, was that Joyce's alleged offences in the first nine months of the war pre-dated it.

Slade was still on his feet at the end of the afternoon, arguing the law as it applied in this case. When the court adjourned until the next morning, Joyce's fate remained evenly balanced. He might just win his freedom at the end of the trial. If not, there appeared an even better chance of a successful hearing in the Court of Appeal or the House of Lords. The chance of freedom shone brighter still when Slade finished his submission during the following morning.

'I have not yet decided, Mr Slade,' said Mr Justice Tucker, 'whether there is anything for the jury at all.'

If there were no case to go to the jury, then William Joyce might be a free man by teatime.

For the rest of the morning the argument over the crucial issues of residence and allegiance, passport and protection, went to and fro between the bench, the Attorney-General and Gerald Slade. The press and the spectators in the crowded No. 1 Court of the Old Bailey watched and listened as intently as if it had been a Wimbledon final. From the dock, William Joyce looked on with an air of critical detachment and even slight amusement.

At last the debate ended and it was almost lunchtime. Mr Justice Tucker prepared to adjourn.

'I shall give my ruling on these submissions which have been

Retribution

made at two o'clock and, if necessary, then address the jury on any issue that remains for them.'

'If necessary.' In other words, William Joyce would be free in an hour or two if there was no case to answer.

At two o'clock the hearing was resumed. Mr Justice Tucker gave his ruling on the legal arguments. 'I shall direct the jury on count 3 that on 24 August 1939, when the passport was applied for, the prisoner beyond the shadow of a doubt owed allegiance to the Crown of this country.'

There was a pause and the court waited.

'On the evidence given, if they accept it, nothing happened at the material time thereafter to put an end to the allegiance that he then owed.'

With that ruling, Joyce stood almost in the shadow of the gallows. There was no possibility of acquittal, for the evidence itself was not in doubt. If he had owed allegiance to the British crown while in Germany, he must hang for treason. Gerald Slade made the closing speech for the defence, casting such doubt as he could upon the evidence of Inspector Hunt. Sir Hartley Shawcross followed with an address that lasted only a few minutes. Though the summing up was long and detailed, the jury was able to retire and consider its verdict soon after half-past three. Shortly before four o'clock, there was a stir of activity and a whisper that the jurors were coming back. Joyce was escorted to the dock once more and stood there, waiting. 'His light-hearted self-confidence', wrote the *Daily Telegraph* correspondent, 'had visibly wilted.' The jury filed into the box and, in answer to the clerk, the foreman confirmed that they were all in agreement.

'Do you find the prisoner, William Joyce, guilty or not guilty on the first two counts of the indictment.'

'Not guilty, my lord.'

'Do you find him guilty or not guilty on the third count of high treason?'

'Guilty.'

Joyce, standing in the dock, pursed his lips at the verdict. In the next brief pause which followed it, he smiled at his brother and several friends in the public gallery. When asked if he had anything to say before sentence was passed, he made no response. The clerk made the usual proclamation. Then, wrote the *Daily Telegraph*, Joyce stood at attention watching 'fascinated' as Mr Justice Tucker laid the strip of black cloth over his wig:

William Joyce, the sentence of the court upon you is that you be taken from this place to a lawful prison and thence to a place of execution, and that you be there hanged by the neck until you be dead, and that your body be afterwards buried within the precincts of the prison in which you shall have been confined before your execution. And may the Lord have mercy on your soul.'

The judge's chaplain, standing close by, added his 'Amen' and the trial was over.

Quentin Joyce in the gallery crossed himself and his companions sat in an attitude of prayer. The condemned man bowed to the judge. He raised his right arm in what the press variously described as a greeting or a Fascist salute to his friends in the gallery. Then he turned smartly about – and clicked his heels Nazi-style to the ears of some reporters – before going down the steps out of sight.

It seemed that the world had seen him for the last time, though it was to hear of him again. What thoughts went through his mind as he sat between armed officers in the police car, we do not know. He did not even attack the court with a Fascist apologia when asked if he had anything to say before sentence was passed. But after he had been escorted from the Old Bailey, one of the warders on duty in the cells below the dock noticed that something had been scratched on a wall. It was in the cell where William Joyce had awaited the verdict. The scratch was a clear and unambiguous swastika.

CHAPTER 16

'"He got what he deserved," an old woman said, and that was the general view.' As William Joyce and his armed police escort drove away to Wormwood Scrubs, the *Daily Mirror* collected the views of those who had witnessed the trial. 'I am behind my brother,' said Quentin Joyce quietly, 'We await his appeal with confidence.'

Police were on duty at the major intersections as the first car and its back-up sped from central London, past the autumn trees of the park and the crowds from the tube stations, returning home among the houses and flats of Bayswater and Notting Hill. Next morning the press had its chance. *The Times* agreed that Lord Haw-Haw's wartime listeners had always thought him British through and through. 'The fact that he is, and always has been, technically an alien cannot in any degree lessen in retrospect the detestation and contempt which his conduct provoked.' Whatever the arguments in court may have been, 'If WILLIAM JOYCE had had his way the abominations of Nazism would have been fastened upon Britain and the world.'

In somewhat larger headlines than *The Times*, the *Daily Mirror* announced a continuation of the drama of treason: 'Joyce to Appeal – Gave Fascist Salute when Condemned.' Its front-page report added, 'William "Jairmany Calling" Joyce, whose gibes and sneers in Nazi propaganda broadcasts against Britain during the war disgusted the British people, is to appeal.... Legal experts predict a great battle.' The story continued on an inside page next to a feature, 'Branded at Belsen', which described how a woman had been marked in this way by the Nazi commandant, Kramer. The trials of the concentration camp guards in the British sector of Germany were now a major news story. For that reason too it was a bad time for William Joyce to have come to judgment. The *Mirror* spoke for the popular press as a whole in its portrait of the traitor:

> William Joyce, who became known as Lord Haw-Haw of
> Hamburg in the darkest days of the war when Britain
> fought on alone against the might of the Fascist dictators,
> who gloated at Britain's reverses, who dreamed and
> boasted of riding triumphant as 'Dictator of Britain' is in
> the condemned cell in Wormwood Scrubs.

The *Mirror* described how he had swayed for a moment while sentence was pronounced, 'Then he smiled, raised his hand in a Fascist salute, clicked his heels and walked down the dock steps to the cells.' The hush during the sentence was broken only by the sound of a man sobbing. It was John Macnab. 'He buried his face in his hands and wept.'

Most of the press comment was fair in substance, if histrionic in tone, at a time when some of the worst abominations of Nazism, as *The Times* called them, were still comparatively recent news. Yet there was also cant of a kind that nearly rivalled Lord Haw-Haw. The *Daily Mail* wrote with lip-smacking enthusiasm of the Londoners living close enough to Wormwood Scrubs to see the light in the condemned cell at night:

> And these people get a great kick from looking. It is a
> great satisfaction to them to know that under this light sits
> William Joyce, the man whose voice they so often heard
> jeering and taunting over the German radio during the
> dark days of the London blitz.

Long before that, there had been another voice proclaiming the delights of Fascism in 'Hurrah for the Blackshirts!' It was, of course, the *Daily Mail*, at a time when Hitler was already in power. Such features, combined with *The Times*'s leniency towards appeasement, had played a part in encouraging Fascism at home or National Socialism abroad, making it seem as if Britain might not after all go to war in support of Hitler's victims.

Most ordinary people had better things to do now that the war was over than to puzzle themselves over the fate of William Joyce, let alone try to catch a glimpse of the mythical death-cell light-bulb. In the population at large there were two feelings about his trial, which seemed to have been a very odd business. These

Retribution

feelings were not incompatible. The first was that Joyce had tried to pull a clever stroke and had failed. The second was that the forces of law had also tried to pull a clever stroke and had succeeded. A game had been played with a man's life as the stake. The man had lost. Perhaps it did not much matter. William Joyce had been the tormentor of ordinary folk during the war. If they had some sport with him now, was it more than he deserved?

However preposterously the press tried to represent a mood of stern and virtuous judgment among the people as a whole, it would be absurd to suggest that there was any sympathy for Joyce as a man. Even if justice had not been quite done, no one of consequence was prepared to step forward and appear to be his ally. Indeed, it was thought to be a tribute to the British legal system that a barrister could be found who was actually willing to represent such a creature.

In this climate, his case came before the Court of Criminal Appeal on 30 October 1945, a hearing that lasted for three days. By then there was another treason trial pending. John Amery had been indicted and had argued that he had taken Spanish nationality before the war. The case had been adjourned until the end of November in order that his nationality should be established.

Joyce had already been taken under armed guard from Wormwood Scrubs a week after his trial. As justice was done in the aftermath of war, more death cells than usual were needed to hold the culprits. An extra one had been prepared at Wandsworth during that week, so that Joyce might spend the short remainder of his life there. Without an appeal, he would die in about three weeks. In the four months since his arrest, he had not been permitted to see his wife. Margaret was still held at the British military detention barracks in Brussels. To refuse a last meeting between husband and wife before his execution would have done little for the humanitarian reputation of the new Labour government and might have engendered natural sympathy for the couple. It was also arguable that he had a right to see her before he died. Therefore, she was brought to England and kept in Holloway prison. Visits were arranged, when she was driven under escort to

Wandsworth.

The Court of Criminal Appeal at the Law Courts in the Strand was far less splendid than its name might suggest. It was a square room whose walls were lined with leather-bound volumes in red and blue and green. It might have been a gentleman's private library of modest size. There was room for only a handful of spectators, among whom were Joyce's sympathisers and supporters in the present case. Joyce and the counsel for both sides sat facing the three judges. Viscount Caldecote, who was Lord Chief Justice, heard the appeal with Mr Justice Humphreys and Mr Justice Lynskey.

It was impossible for Gerald Slade to offer new evidence or devise new arguments. He based the appeal on the simple premise that Mr Justice Tucker had been wrong at the trial in his interpretation of the law and his direction of the jury. British law could not try an alien for an offence committed abroad. The judge had been wrong in directing the jury that Joyce owed allegiance to the British crown while in Germany, between 18 September 1939 and 2 July 1940. There was no evidence that during this period he sought or could have obtained any protection from his British passport. But that was an issue for the jury alone and not, as Mr Justice Tucker had made it, a matter for the judge to decide upon and to direct the jury accordingly.

The Lord Chief Justice intervened. Was Mr Slade arguing that 'an alien can go backwards and forwards across the Channel, owing allegiance when he arrives at Dover and no longer owing it when he lands at Calais?'

'Yes,' said Slade.

Mr Justice Humphreys joined in.

'And although he is resident in this country?'

'Such a person,' said Slade, 'would not be resident in this country when not physically here.'

Moreover, he added, such a person could not possibly be regarded as a resident because, 'This country has a complete right to say to an alien, "You may not return here".'

Mr Justice Humphreys was not convinced that this could be said to a man with a British passport. He did not go on to consider what the reaction of the immigration authority would be if that passport proved to be a forgery or fraudulently obtained. Would it still confer the rights of British citizenship?

Though the appeal was based on more grounds than the question of jurisdiction, this was by far the strongest. Could the Soviet Union, for example, have a British subject arrested in Rome, deported and put on trial in Moscow for anti-Soviet remarks made in Italy? To the man in the street, that appeared to be the corollary. As for the passport, had the authorities known that Joyce held it illegally, surely he would have been charged with the offence and eventually deported as an alien.

Ominously, during Slade's argument, the Lord Chief Justice intervened again. The legal decisions and precedents quoted by the defence were all very well, said Viscount Caldecote, but 'those learned authors were not thinking of the facts of a case like this. This case exhibits new facts.' Once again, it seemed, Joyce could hope for nothing from the law as it had previously appeared. It must be tailored to fit his case.

If the trial of William Joyce has a hero, it is certainly not the defendant himself but Gerald Slade. He pursued the logic of his argument with tenacity and vigour, showing the skill of a David before the Goliath of the state. New facts could not alter the essential principle of English law, upon which his authorities were unanimous. An alien's allegiance ceased when he left the country. The fathers of English legal theory 'are either right or wrong. If they are right, Mr Justice Tucker's ruling must be wrong.'

It was as simple as that. He concluded his submission on this point with a quotation from the Victorian judge, Sir Alexander Cockburn, on the very point now at issue. In doing so, he echoed the feeling of those whose doubts had begun to grow over the wisdom or the justice of sending Joyce to the gallows. What had Sir Alexander Cockburn said? Gerald Slade repeated the words: 'Upon this point I had deemed all jurists unanimous, and could not have supposed that a doubt could exist. Upon what is the contrary opinion founded? Simply upon expediency, which is to prevail over principle.'

It was an uncomfortable moment. No one could doubt the

fairness or the integrity of the Attorney-General in doing justice to his opponent or the prisoner, though it was his duty to use his skill on behalf of the crown. Whether ordinary people would see that justice had been done, or whether the belief would grow that Lord Haw-Haw had been 'fitted up' by the English law, was another matter. If that belief prevailed, then his conviction and his death would have been dearly bought.

When Slade sat down, the Lord Chief Justice informed the Attorney-General that he need not deal with matters relating to the passport. In other words, the appeal had failed already on those two grounds. But the appeal judges required him to answer the rest of the case, 'particularly the question of jurisdiction'.

Sir Hartley Shawcross, taking the opposite view of the law, dismissed 'the slavish search for exact precedent' as being 'always a somewhat sterile pursuit':

- 'The incalculable advantage of the whole system of British law is that its principles are capable of adaptation to the new circumstances perpetually arising. The question is whether the old principles of the law of treason can be applied to the circumstances of the present case.... The historic function of his Majesty's judges in treason cases is to adapt old principles to new circumstances. There must be few cases in the past in which the reasons for applying the existing principles to new circumstances were more obvious and compelling then they are in the present case.'

As an argument, this was entirely fair and reasonable. The nature and the strength of English law lay in its adaptability. The point at issue remained whether it was wise or just to revoke, in the case of William Joyce, the almost unanimous legal opinion and wisdom of the past which Gerald Slade had cited.

Judgment was deferred on the appeal until 7 November. When it was delivered, the court's decision vindicated the Attorney-General. The Lord Chief Justice dismissed Gerald Slade's authorities. Blackstone was sharply downgraded on the rather curious basis that the late Lord Birkenhead had thought his *Commentaries* 'an elementary textbook for students'. A good deal of Birkenhead's writing was after-dinner dictation and some of it was ghost-written, for which reason this description of Blackstone was less than authoritative.

William Joyce was driven back across Waterloo Bridge through the light fog of the November day, over the river to Wandsworth and the vigil of the barrack-like death-cell. There remained only the hope of an appeal to the House of Lords.

On 16 November 1945 the Attorney-General issued his *fiat*, confirming that the case involved 'a point of law of exceptional public importance', and permitting an appeal to the House of Lords. The hearing was to begin on Monday 10 December.

The nature of these appeals and the length of time involved raised a further question. At what point would it be inhumane to keep the prisoner under sentence of death any longer? At least three months would have passed since he was condemned to the gallows. Unlike the ghoulish vindictiveness of capital punishment in the United States, where a man might be executed more than twenty years after his crime, there was an objection in the practice of English justice to keeping a man in such circumstances. Before Joyce's appeal, a murderer who had been under sentence for some months and whose case had gone to the Lords was apparently informed beforehand that this sentence would be commuted to life imprisonment, whatever the outcome of his appeal.

The arguments of Gerald Slade and the Attorney-General before the Law Lords began on Monday 10 December and ended on Thursday 13 December. There was nothing new in their contentions, though the surroundings were far more splendid than any so far provided for the trials of William Joyce.

When the House of Commons had been bombed, its members had moved into the House of Lords. The Lords, in turn, occupied the royal Robing Room. From the little gallery, provided for the press and the public, it was impossible to see the proceedings of the appeal and difficult to hear them, because they were going on underneath those who sat there. The view which the onlookers had was of the length of the empty fresco'd hall, the thrones of the king and queen at the far end, the woolsack, and a table at which a clerk sat cutting up paper with scissors, said Rebecca West, 'as if preparing to amuse an infinite number of children.' Under the gallery and invisible to those who occupied it, there was a table at which sat the Lord Chancellor in his robes and four Law Lords in lounge suits. The winter was already bitter and there was a fuel crisis. The five elderly men sat in judgment with rugs wrapped round their legs to keep warm. Counsel addressed them from the bar of the house, not entering the chamber itself. William Joyce, guarded by four warders, sat in a corner under the gallery, his face yellow with prison pallor.

Quentin Joyce and two of the prisoner's friends attended the last and most melancholy hearing of the case. The public at large seemed almost to have forgotten him. Most of the press reported his appeals in a perfunctory manner. There was, after all, little that counsel could do but repeat their arguments and, in the case of Gerald Slade, hope that the Law Lords would prove more receptive than their predecessors.

Perhaps in this there was some hope after all. From the interventions by the Lord Chancellor and by Lords Macmillan, Wright, Porter and Simonds, it seemed that they might incline more sympathetically towards the case for the appellant. Or was it merely that they knew this must be his last chance to escape the noose and so paid scrupulous attention, by their questions, to any detail that might save his life?

At length, Sir Hartley Shawcross summed up the crown's answer. He did so both in terms of law and moral common sense:

'I submit, in this important case – important because of the effect it would have in defining the position of all persons who placed themselves in the protection of the British Crown – that it would be an unthinkable outrage on the common law of this country if the crime of treason were held not to have been committed; if a person who had made his home here and enjoyed all the benefits of British citizenship, should be held, while temporarily absent from the country, not to be under a reciprocal duty of allegiance to it.'

However ingenious in argument Gerald Slade might be, it was this peroration by Sir Hartley Shawcross that rang with blunt moral conviction. The appellant was entitled to one final reply, after which judgment would normally be given. By the end of the Thursday morning, 13 December, the speeches were over. The Law Lords adjourned until 3 p.m. But when they returned, it was only for the Lord Chancellor to announce that they needed more time for their deliberations. They would convene the House again and announce their decision on Tuesday 18 December at 10.30 a.m.

The torment of anticipation under which William Joyce now lay was extended for another week. How much more time must pass before his execution became incompatible with humanity? When Tuesday morning came and the Lords reconvened, he was not present. There was a feeling that he might win his appeal. If that happened, he would probably be re-arrested on lesser charges under the Defence Regulations. But he could not be arrested within the precincts of parliament. Was it not possible that he might get outside and escape? The authorities were taking no chances.

They need not have worried. William Joyce was not to win his appeal. 'I have come to the conclusion', said the Lord Chancellor, 'that the appeal should be dismissed.'

'I agree,' said Lord Macmillan.

'I also agree,' said Lord Wright.

'I would myself allow the appeal,' Lord Porter said, the only one to dissent.

'I concur in the opinion given by my noble and learned friend on the woolsack,' Lord Simonds concluded.

But though preparations for the hanging of William Joyce could now go ahead, the Law Lords announced that they would give their reasons for dismissing the appeal at a later date. These were delivered on 1 February 1946. By then they were of no concern to William Joyce. He was to be hanged on 3 January, without knowing precisely why.

In the sixteen days between the dismissal of his last appeal and his execution, the press turned its back on William Joyce. To the world, he was almost the non-person of Orwellian political nightmare. From being an item of hot news, he became a subject which it seemed almost in bad taste to mention. On the appointed day, having announced briefly in the previous week that there would be no reprieve and that Joyce was spending his remaining hours playing chess with his warders, few papers did more than the *Daily Telegraph*, which gave five lines at the bottom of a column on an inside page to the item: 'Joyce to Hang Today.'

Quentin Joyce and John Macnab visited him and came away overawed by his courage and his example in the face of death. 'If your time comes, we shall be with you in God,' Macnab promised him. Margaret was allowed to visit him every day and then, on the morning of his death, withdrew into what was fatuously called 'a frenzy of grief', as if this were letting the side down.

As for Joyce himself, he showed how easily this ritual makes heroes of men who are in every other way contemptible. He was admirable, in this respect, and unrepentant. The determination of the law to hang him merely strengthened his commitment to Nazism. He was, in the end, not afraid to stand alone in the shadow of death and against the world. Far better had they commuted his sentence and taken away the one necessary prop of his performance – the gallows.

He was not fully reconciled to the Catholic church but he accepted a Catholic blessing from the chaplain. For the rest, he needed nothing but to be left alone. Soon after dawn on that cold and foggy morning of 3 January, he began to write his final letters.

As the last minutes ticked away, the former trooper of the Bataillon Wilhelmplatz faced death more certainly than ever he could have done in the rubble of Berlin. At the end, he was unswervingly true to his love and his allegiance.

'I salute you, Freja as your lover for ever,' he wrote to Margaret, while the hangman waited to enter the cell, 'Sieg Heil! Sieg Heil! Sieg Heil!'

It was well-nigh impossible for those who watched him not to salute his own bravery and integrity. By granting him such a death, the law and the government had made their worst mistake of all.

CHAPTER 17

Whatever the merits of the case against him or the outcome of the legal battle, no one could doubt that William Joyce was unlucky to be caught, tried and condemned at such a time. Had he continued to evade capture for a year or two, perhaps by reaching southern Ireland as Goebbels intended, it seems inconceivable that a trial at a later date would have led to his being hanged as a traitor.

His execution did not excite quite the universal satisfaction that the nation's leaders and the press suggested. On 19 December 1945, the *Manchester Guardian* put an opposing view when it remarked that 'one could wish he had been condemned on something more solid than a falsehood', and it reminded the Labour government that 'killing a man is not the way to root out false opinions.' In that it was to be proved correct. There are those in the 1980s, presently to be quoted, to whom William Joyce remains a martyred prophet.

On 9 February 1946, after the Law Lords revealed that they had dismissed the appeal for much the same reasons as the Court of Appeal itself, there was a protest in *The Times*. Lennox Russell demanded how the Home Secretary could give proper consideration to a reprieve if the grounds of the Lords' decision were not to be announced until four weeks after the man was dead?

> If present normal procedure makes it possible for execution of a capital sentence to precede the recording of the grounds on which the final judicial appeal has been dismissed, would it not be well that this procedure should be altered?

There was a further implicit question. The Law Lords had taken a week to reach their decision. Why should it have taken them another six weeks to reveal the grounds for that decision? It had the advantage, for the government, of getting Joyce hanged and out of the way before any further argument could begin. The alternative, of postponing the execution until after the judgment on 1 February, was impossible. To keep a man under sentence of death for five months and then hang him would be intolerable. Surely, they would have to commute his sentence to life imprisonment, the very thing that the government wished to avoid.

Political considerations at such a moment dwarfed the legal arguments. The twelve months that followed the end of the war in Europe were a special time. Long before the fighting ended, in October 1941, Churchill had warned the world that those who were responsible for war crimes would be hunted to the Antipodes, if necessary, and brought to judgment when the conflict was over. Nor did the end of the war appear to bring an immediate change of mood. The press and the broadcasting services encouraged people to think not so much in terms of justice as in those of vengeance.

The chamber of moral horrors which constituted the Third Reich had been thrown open for universal condemnation. Now there was to be a carnival of retribution.

Goering's comment about the farce of the victors trying the vanquished, among whom was William Joyce, contained at least a half truth. For example, the German invasion of Poland from the west was rightly condemned as aggressive war. But the Soviet Union, which had invaded from the east and divided the spoils, now sat in judgment upon its former partner in the crime.

The true objection to the Nuremberg process and its sequel was, as in Joyce's case, that they might be seen too readily as a means of reprisal. That would have been unfortunate. A full revelation of Nazi atrocities was necessary if only to shame some of the neutral politicians. Hugh Trevor-Roper has described Eamonn de Valera, at a time when the pictures of Belsen had been in every newsreel, going to the German Embassy in Dublin to express his condolences on the death of the great leader, Adolf Hitler. It was the sequel to the Nuremberg process that blighted it, when genial GI Joe became the hangman and a theatre of execution was staged at dead of night for the press, with the thirteen steps to the gymnasium gallows and the black drapes, by no means all of the victims of the spectacle

Retribution

dying quickly upon the rope.

In retrospect, a number of the trials of 1945–6 give the impression of a rush to judgment and execution before too many questions should be asked about the logic of the process or the justice of the outcome. In France, more than 6,000 men and women were condemned to death for collaboration with the Germans, let alone those who met a summary fate immediately after the liberation. George Orwell was only one of many who believed that the hunting down of 'petty rats' was largely the work of bigger rats.

The liberation of France was certainly a cause for patriotic celebration. In an arbitrary settling of scores, however, it also offered an example for justice to wink rather than go blindfold. It was a period when forms of sexual violence could be perpetrated against French girl-friends of German soldiers by those whose behaviour would earn them prison sentences at any other time. The *collabos* were fair game. Press photographs of head-shavings and the like are now less instructive for the tears and terrors of the victims than for the grinning excitement of those who surround them and the satisfied glee of the self-appointed patriots disfiguring the young women. Such retribution was without exception the work of scoundrels or misfits, whose enthusiasms had far more in common with the perversions of Nazism than with the liberation for which they purported to have fought.

In the wake of that liberation, accusations of treason or collaboration were likely to be accompanied by summary justice. All too often these patriotic denunciations were no more than the means of paying off old scores or even eliminating creditors. The accusers offered a contemporary illustration of a couplet from one of William Joyce's most frequently quoted authors: John Dryden, writing in *Absalom and Achitophel*:

> How easy still it proves in factious times
> With public zeal to cancel private crimes.

At a higher level than this, post-war justice was selective. From 1942 onwards, French Communists had fought bravely with the Resistance. Before Hitler's invasion of the Soviet Union, however, they had been willing collaborators with the occupying power.

William L. Shirer, as an American journalist with the invading German army in June 1940, found 'a surprising fraternal feeling between the French Communists and their Nazi occupiers.' The ban which the French government had imposed on the Communist daily *L'Humanité* for its opposition to the war was lifted at once by the Germans. The paper gave its support to Pétain and the armistice. On 4 July 1940, it praised the large number of Parisian workers who were making friends with German soldiers. When post-war justice was done, however, an exception was made in the case of collaboration between the Communists and the Nazi army of occupation before Hitler's attack on the Soviet Union.

Whether in England or France, the press assured its readers that the public would not stand for acquittal or pardon in the case of those who had aided the enemy. An image of 'the public' for this purpose was a convenient simplification for what the writer wished his readers to feel.

Pétain may have trodden the path of senile acquiescence and Laval may have been a Fascist turncoat. But the execution of Pétain, had it been carried out, would have alienated the vast majority of Frenchmen, while Laval's trial was widely regarded as a discredit to French justice.

For personal reasons alone, it was unthinkable to the Gaullists that Pétain should go unpunished or that his followers should be allowed to flourish in opposition to theirs. In a still more invidious form of retribution, treason trials began to appear as a convenient way of getting rid of political enemies or even political nuisances. The Breton nationalist movement, for example, had seen in the German invasion a possible means of independence from France. With the liberation, Breton nationalists were put on trial for their lives as collaborators with the Nazi occupation. In many cases the treatment of political or cultural leaders in Brittany could be described as little else than assassination. In 1947 the continuing series of Breton trials led to an intervention by the Welsh Nationalists on behalf of their Celtic cousins. Observers were sent and a report was drawn up which charged the French government with genocide. With that, the trials ceased.

England's traitors in 1945 came in two groups. There were those like Joyce who had joined the ideological battle on the German side, writing and broadcasting for Hitler's brand of National Socialism. Others, as a matter of conviction or personal convenience, had renounced their allegiance to the British crown and joined the armed forces of the Third Reich. Some had gone of their own free will and others had chosen this as the best way out of a prisoner-of-war camp.

During the period of Joyce's trial and the subsequent appeals, the cases of such defendants were heard. Only a minority of them was condemned to death and, of those who were, some were reprieved. But it seemed necessary that a few should be hanged. If that were so, there could be no more obvious choice for the gallows then Joyce himself and the man whom he had come to detest, John Amery.

Amery had been both propagandist and organiser of the British Free Corps as a fighting unit of the Wehrmacht. In answer to the charge of treason, he first claimed that he had become a naturalised Spanish subject during his adherence to Franco's side in the Spanish Civil War. His trial was adjourned until November 1945 in an attempt to establish the truth of this. On 28 November, even before Amery appeared in the dock at the Old Bailey to answer the charge of treason, his counsel was summoned to the cells. Amery had decided to alter his plea and announce himself guilty of treason. The judge first of all questioned him to make sure that Amery understood the full implication of the plea. Then he pronounced the only sentence which the law prescribed, adding, 'You now stand a self-confessed traitor to your King and country, and you have forfeited the right to live.'

If Amery hoped that clemency might be shown towards him, he was in error. He was confined in another death cell at Wandsworth prison and executed on 29 December 1945, only five days before William Joyce. His trial at the Old Bailey had lasted just eight minutes. The treason of John Amery was the next in magnitude to that of Joyce. Once he had been executed, it was hard to see how his fellow prisoner in Wandsworth could be reprieved.

Of the other broadcasters, Norman Baillie-Stewart had

renounced his British citizenship long before the war. At his trial in January 1946 the treason charges against him were dropped and he pleaded guilty to offences against the Defence Regulations. For this he was sentenced to five years' imprisonment.

Apart from Joyce and Amery, the other death sentence carried out was upon Private Schurch of the RASC, who claimed to be of Swiss citizenship. By his own account, he had joined the army in 1936 on the instructions of the British Union of Fascists, of which he was a member. He had volunteered for a front-line unit in North Africa, in order to desert to the enemy. He was captured by the Italians at Tobruk and offered his services to their intelligence officers. Convicted of treachery by court-martial in 1945, Schurch was hanged two days after Joyce, on 5 January 1946.

Whether or not a man was chosen to stand trial, whether or not a sentence of death was imposed and carried out seemed to be a haphazard business. Schurch was hanged for treachery of a lesser significance. Walter Purdy, another former member of the British Union of Fascists, was reprieved. Purdy had been captured at Narvik in 1940. He betrayed the escape plans of his fellow prisoners-of-war and offered his services to the Germans. As a broadcaster, he was responsible for such features as 'The Air Racket' and 'Jewish Profiteering in War'. When arrested and asked his place of birth, however, he replied, 'Barking and true British and never would be anything else.' In his defence, he claimed that he had only pretended to work for the Germans, had attempted various acts of sabotage against their broadcasting installations, and had tried to assassinate William Joyce on two occasions. There was not a shred of truth in any of this but, though sentenced to death on 31 December 1945, this was commuted to life imprisonment a few days before the date set for his execution.

Thomas Haller Cooper was the only other man to be sentenced to death for joining the German armed forces. He had been born of a British father and a German mother, and had been in Germany when the war began. He had first joined the Adolf Hitler division of the Waffen SS, fought in Poland and the Soviet Union, and had been wounded. Later he joined Amery's Legion of St George, which subsequently became the British Free Corps, its SS uniforms carrying Union Jack flashes. He was tried at the Old Bailey in January 1946 and sentenced to death. The Court of Criminal Appeal dismissed his appeal against conviction. Then, as he waited to be hanged, he was suddenly reprieved on 19 February 1946. It was true that he seemed more German than English and that he spoke German better than English. But more certainly than William Joyce, he owed allegiance to the British crown.

There was little logic in such decisions, except that with the deaths of Joyce, Amery and Schurch, the Labour government felt that it had let enough blood to satisfy what the press represented as public anger at wartime treason. Purdy's crime and that of Cooper may have been a good deal worse than that of Private Schurch, but Purdy and Cooper had been lucky in having their cases heard a little later.

Some twenty other defendants were sentenced on lesser charges than treason in the year that followed the war's end. A few men and women, like Joyce's friend Mrs Eckersley, were sentenced to prison terms for having worked in relatively minor capacities for the English-language broadcasts from Charlottenburg. Almost all the others were British prisoners-of-war who had been induced to join the British Free Corps. For this they were sentenced to penal servitude for periods ranging from six months to life.

It was the British Free Corps which provided the greatest source of traitors for the Old Bailey in 1945–6. But despite their SS uniforms, suggestively incorporating the Union Jack and the swastika, their numbers never seem to have been greater than twenty-six. There may have been a furtive public thrill after the war in discovering that England contributed a contingent to Hitler's élite but the truth was that they had never been of the least military use and never saw action. Indeed, they had wasted enough time and made sufficient demands on their Nazi mentors to constitute a small addition to the Allied war effort.

Not for more than 200 years had men been put to death in England or been tried for their lives on the grounds of the opinions they expressed. But the advent of radio broadcasting had given a temporary urgency to the matter. It was now possible for an ideological dissident to take up residence in enemy territory and address his countrymen as directly as if he sat at their firesides. This was not something to be tolerated as freedom of speech by the nation's rulers in 1945.

France and the United States had as good a reason to be embarrassed by this development as the British.

In international literature, Ezra Pound was the most distinguished modern poet holding United States citizenship. His disenchantment and anti-Semitism were well known before the war and some of his most famous lines from *Hugh Selwyn Mauberley* had denounced the futility of fighting Germany in the war before that. The flower of Europe had died for what Pound described as 'an old bitch gone in the teeth', a 'botched civilisation'.

When the United States entered the war, Pound chose to remain in Italy. He had made his home there in 1924 and had not the least desire to leave. In 1942 he agreed to broadcast on short wave to the United States, provided that he was not required to say anything 'incompatible with his duties as a citizen of the United States of America'. Ignoring the events of the war, his twice-weekly broadcasts denounced the rascality of Roosevelt's financial policies and the malign influence of those who advised him. The style was that of the homespun and folksy common sense in which the greatest of living American poets commended the philosophy of Fascist economics to his countrymen:

> There is no patriotism in submittin' to the prolonged and multiple frauds of the Roosevelt administration and to try to make the present support of these frauds figure as loyalty to the American Union, to the American Constitution, to the American heritage, is just as much dirt or bunkum. Doubtless the tactics of evasion will be used to the uttermost, blackmail will be used to the uttermost – but if the American people submit to either or both of these wheezes, the American people will be mugs.

Pound's anti-Semitism was less shrill and less frequently expressed than Joyce's. It might even be questioned whether the contents of the broadcasts constituted treason or permissible criticism of his government. However, he was taken into custody by the United States army during the invasion of Italy and eventually held at the military prison near Pisa. That he, by then sixty years old, was kept for weeks in a cage of metal landing strips made purposely for him was not disputed. His health broke and so, it was later alleged, did his sanity. However, he went on writing in his head the *Pisan Cantos*. In November 1945 he was flown to Washington.

Pound presented a problem for his own government. He had been charged with treason. A full-scale trial was likely to focus unfavourable world attention on Washington, for it was quite likely that he would be convicted. Would there come a day when, before press representatives, *il miglior fabbro* of T. S. Eliot's dedication of *The Waste Land* would be strapped into the electric chair and burnt alive, while the literary establishment proclaimed him as the greatest poetic genius of American modernism?

A grateful administration accepted the evidence of doctors that Pound's experience at Pisa had unhinged his mind. He was unfit to plead. They despatched him to the lunatic asylum of St Elizabeth's Hospital and kept him there until 1958, while his new poetry won him the Bollingen Prize and sympathetic literary honours. Then, at the age of seventy-two, when his broadcasts seemed no more than a quaint footnote to the history of the war, the United States government ordered his release. He lived for another fourteen years.

In France, the expression of Fascist or pro-German opinion was no less vexing. Right-wing authors and editors were called to account at the liberation. Some were famous and some obscure but they were not in general men who had turned their coats to profit by the German occupation. On the whole, it was the obscure who were condemned. Robert Brassillach, the young editor of the pro-Vichy *Je Suis Partout*, insisted like William Joyce that he had acted in the best interests of his country. He had undoubtedly been consistent. His views as a journalist had been Fascist before the war. Brassillach had simply not changed them. He died before a firing squad on 6 February 1945 at the fortress of Montrouge with a cry of 'Courage! Vive la France!'

A far greater embarrassment to the new regime were authors of world stature like Louis-Ferdinand Céline, by then in exile at Copenhagen. The execution of such a writer would surely alienate world opinion from the Gaullist regime. Moreover, how could one explain that Communist intellectuals who had turned their coats when Hitler and Stalin concluded the non-aggression pact of August 1939 must now go unpunished for their collaboration?

There was but one answer. As soon as a decent amount of blood had been shed, the matter of treason or collaboration had best be forgotten. No one was going to put Céline before the firing squad at Montrouge if he stayed out of the way until 1950 or 1951.

The treason trials of 1945, so far as they condemned men for the expression of opinion or ideology, now appear as an aberration from that guarantee of freedom of speech which had evolved in England over a century and a half. The offence of treason is so rarely tried that comparisons are difficult. In 1915, when Sir Roger Casement was tried and convicted, it was shown that while in Germany he had tried to dissuade Irish prisoners-of-war from continuing their allegiance to the British crown. The issue might involve freedom of speech but it was at a different level to the expression of opinion in a publicly available book or radio broadcast.

Only the science of broadcasting enabled a man to be a persistent traitor by disseminating propaganda from the enemy in time of war. If Joyce had been merely the author of *Twilight over England*, it is doubtful whether more than a handful of people in Britain would have heard of him, let alone have read his book, by 1945.

Nor would Joyce have been guilty of treason if he had disseminated his views while remaining in England. The *Daily Worker* consistently attacked the war against Germany between 1939 and 1941. In January 1941, it sponsored a 'People's Convention', which demanded both a people's government and a people's peace. When a Communist Congress was held in London that month, the *Worker* dismissed Churchill's war propaganda and reported that these ordinary people 'proclaimed their solidarity with the rest of the world's workers, whether in Berlin, Turin, Paris, or Shanghai'. Since official propaganda held that Berlin was full of Nazis deserving to be bombed and Turin contained Fascists of the same breed, the *Daily Worker*'s philosophy became intolerable. The paper was closed down next day but not a word was spoken to suggest that it had committed treason. Had Joyce remained in England, he would certainly have found himself or his organisation 'closed down' or interned. He would hardly have been tried for his life.

As the post-war years passed, crimes against the state which might have been treason at other times were dealt with instead by non-capital charges under the Official Secrets Act. In the United States, in a case which did a good deal to discredit President Eisenhower, the Rosenbergs were put to death as spies. In England, Klaus Fuchs and Alan Nunn May were tried under the Official Secrets Act and sent to prison for fourteen years.

William Joyce was doubly unfortunate. Soon after his death, treason as the expression of opinion seemed something of an anachronism in the modern world. There were, of course, offences which might be dealt with under a different heading but ideology rather than nationality appeared increasingly to be the higher allegiance. No one, in the early 1950s, would seriously have expected the execution of those British prisoners who broadcast from Pyongyang at their captors' invitation during the Korean War. In the Falklands War of 1982, the BBC devoted a *Panorama* programme to news and views from Argentina. Those who murmured that this was treason were likely to be dismissed as out of touch with the new philosophy of mass communication.

Joyce remains an unlikeable figure, though one for whom it is possible to feel pity. He advocated a political system which brought death and misery to millions. But the law could not hang a man for that. In the story of his downfall there are too many voices hinting at a failure of justice to leave one entirely at ease. It is as if the tenacity of his defender and the fairness of his prosecutor counted for less than some communal and unconscious compulsion of the time.

The execution of Joyce was a greater boost to Fascism than to democracy. It enabled him to show a degree of courage and conviction which won the admiration of those who would have seen him for what he was, had he been serving a sentence of five or

Retribution

ten years as an offender against the Defence Regulations. It gave him a certain political immortality:

> His life will forever remain sacred and holy to us for he unselfishly gave it in the defence of White Christian civilisation. He fought the powers of darkness for he was brave. Today as our White Race seems irreversibly sunk in the pit of dictatorial democracy... the life of William Joyce seems like a flash of lightning illuminating the bleak horizon, giving hope for the survival of our race. Truly, William Joyce represented 'not the last ones of yesterday, but the first ones of tomorrow.'

It would be tempting to suppose that this epitaph was the work of the underground Fascist press in 1946 or of some secret radio station. It actually appeared in 1982, from the Sons of Liberty in Metairie, Louisiana, as an introduction to a new edition of *Twilight over England*.

> As a tribute to Lord Haw-Haw we are proud to present his prophetic book – TWILIGHT OVER ENGLAND. No doubt the same forces of Darkness which Joyce spoke of would like to censor this work and stop its appearance on the American scene – BUT THEY CANNOT! Now after THIRTY FIVE YEARS, once again, Lord Haw-Haw returns.

For this production, the mood of retribution fostered by the press in 1945 and the process which put to death William Joyce can claim a good deal of the credit. He, whose execution was variously described as well-deserved or too good for him, was one more example of a villain made a hero by the hangman's art.

Perhaps the fault lay deeply embedded in the English law, for the crime of treason seemed an archaism, an evocation of the Tudors and the headsman's axe in an age of aeroplanes and radio. Yet it continues to survive in a curious form.

When the Labour government of 1964 abolished capital punishment for murder, it did not abolish capital punishment altogether. There remained the crime of treason, so improbable that it scarcely seemed worth bothering about. Men had died on the rope for murder within the previous couple of years and that was far more to the point.

But the men whose trade it is to make arrangements for death, to weight the sandbags and stretch the ropes, to order straps that the strongest wrists will not break and to find space for another grave by the prison wall, have a stranger immortality than that of Lord Haw-Haw. Their trade is more durable than parliaments and governments. When hanging was abolished for murder, the gallows were dismantled in every prison and, if they survived at all, became museum pieces – except at Wandsworth, where William Joyce had taken that 'last leap in the dark', of which he had spoken in 1940. Even the abolitionist government allowed the beam and the trap to remain there and to be regularly tested from time to time.

Just in case.

SELECT BIBLIOGRAPHY

Leonard Burt, *Commander Burt of Scotland Yard*, Heinemann, London, 1959.

Joseph Chardonnet, *Histoire de Bretagne*, Nouvelles Éditions Latines, Paris, 1965.

William Cole, *Lord Haw-Haw and William Joyce: The Full Story* Faber & Faber, London, 1964.

Julien Cornell, *The Trial of Ezra Pound*, Faber & Faber, London, 1967.

Peter Fleming, *Invasion 1940*, Rupert Hart-Davis, London, 1957.

J. W. Hall (ed.), *The Trial of William Joyce*, William Hodge, Notable British Trials Series, London and Edinburgh, 1946.

Earl Jowitt, *Some Were Spies*, Hodder & Stoughton, London, 1954.

William Joyce, *National Socialism Now*, National Socialist League, London, 1937.

William Joyce, *Twilight over England*, Internationaler Verlag, Berlin, 1940: Sons of Liberty, Metairie, La., 1982.

Nicholas Mosley, *Beyond the Pale: Sir Oswald Mosley and his Family 1933–1980*, Secker & Warburg, London, 1983.

Malcolm Muggeridge, *Chronicles of Wasted Time: The Infernal Grove*, Collins, London, 1973.

C. E. Bechhofer Roberts (ed.), *The Trial of William Joyce*, Jarrolds, Norwich, 1946.

Cecil Roberts, *And So To America*, Hodder & Stoughton, London, 1946.

Ronald Seth, *Jackals of the Reich*, New English Library, London, 1972.

William L. Shirer, *Berlin Diary: The Journal of a Foreign Correspondent 1934–1941*, Hamish Hamilton, London, 1941.

Robert Skidelsky, *Oswald Mosley*, Macmillan, London, 1975.

Jean-Marc Theolleyre, *Procès d'après-guerre*, Éditions La Découverte/Le Monde, Paris, 1985.

Rebecca West, *The Meaning of Treason*, Macmillan, London, 1949.

P. G. Wodehouse, *Performing Flea: A Self-Portrait in Letters*, Herbert Jenkins, London, 1953.

Discover more about our forthcoming books through Penguin's FREE newspaper...

Penguin Quarterly

It's packed with:

- exciting features
- author interviews
- previews & reviews
- books from your favourite films & TV series
- exclusive competitions & much, much more...

Write off for your free copy today to:
Dept JC
Penguin Books Ltd
FREEPOST
West Drayton
Middlesex
UB7 0BR
NO STAMP REQUIRED

READ MORE IN PENGUIN

In every corner of the world, on every subject under the sun, Penguin represents quality and variety – the very best in publishing today.

For complete information about books available from Penguin – including Puffins, Penguin Classics and Arkana – and how to order them, write to us at the appropriate address below. Please note that for copyright reasons the selection of books varies from country to country.

In the United Kingdom: Please write to *Dept. JC, Penguin Books Ltd, FREEPOST, West Drayton, Middlesex UB7 OBR*

If you have any difficulty in obtaining a title, please send your order with the correct money, plus ten per cent for postage and packaging, to *PO Box No. 11, West Drayton, Middlesex UB7 OBR*

In the United States: Please write to *Penguin USA Inc., 375 Hudson Street, New York, NY 10014*

In Canada: Please write to *Penguin Books Canada Ltd, 10 Alcorn Avenue, Suite 300, Toronto, Ontario M4V 3B2*

In Australia: Please write to *Penguin Books Australia Ltd, 487 Maroondah Highway, Ringwood, Victoria 3134*

In New Zealand: Please write to *Penguin Books (NZ) Ltd, 182–190 Wairau Road, Private Bag, Takapuna, Auckland 9*

In India: Please write to *Penguin Books India Pvt Ltd, 706 Eros Apartments, 56 Nehru Place, New Delhi 110 019*

In the Netherlands: Please write to *Penguin Books Netherlands B.V., Keizersgracht 231 NL–1016 DV Amsterdam*

In Germany: Please write to *Penguin Books Deutschland GmbH, Friedrichstrasse 10–12, W–6000 Frankfurt/Main 1*

In Spain: Please write to *Penguin Books S. A., C. San Bernardo 117–6° E–28015 Madrid*

In Italy: Please write to *Penguin Italia s.r.l., Via Felice Casati 20, I–20124 Milano*

In France: Please write to *Penguin France S. A., 17 rue Lejeune, F–31000 Toulouse*

In Japan: Please write to *Penguin Books Japan, Ishikiribashi Building, 2–5–4, Suido, Tokyo 112*

In Greece: Please write to *Penguin Hellas Ltd, Dimocritou 3, GR–106 71 Athens*

In South Africa: Please write to *Longman Penguin Southern Africa (Pty) Ltd, Private Bag X08, Bertsham 2013*

BY THE SAME AUTHOR

Nothing But Revenge
The Case of Bentley and Craig

On a quiet South Croydon Sunday, nineteen-year-old Derek Bentley was watching a music-hall show on television when his young friend Chris Craig called for him. At Craig's prompting they broke into a local warehouse.

But Christopher Craig was carrying a gun that evening, and in the battle that followed their discovery policeman Sidney Miles was shot between the eyes. Bentley was later hanged for the murder.

This fascinating inquiry into one of the most controversial crimes – and sentences – of the fifties weighs up the evidence for and against the death penalty and suggests that, in the words of the hangman, it served 'nothing except revenge'.